LA TAVOLA ITALIANA

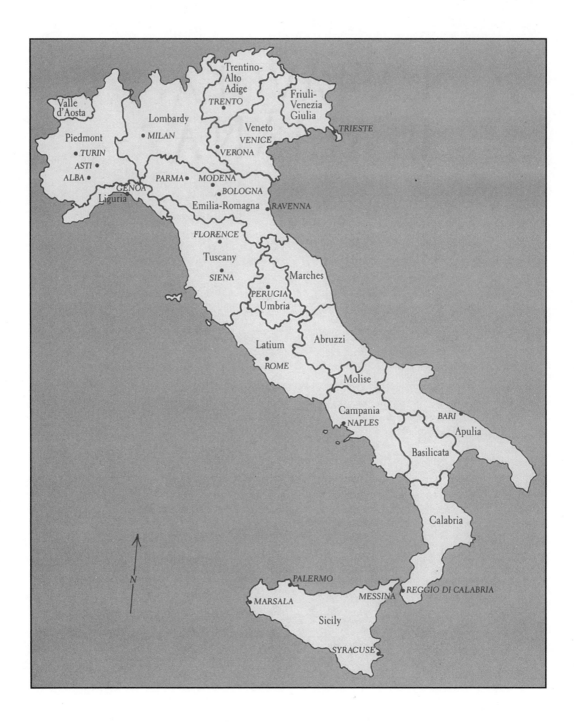

LA TAVOLA ITALIANA

TOM MARESCA
AND
DIANE DARROW

A COMMON READER EDITION
THE AKADINE PRESS

La Tavola Italiana

A COMMON READER EDITION published 1998
by The Akadine Press, Inc., by arrangement with the authors.

We wish to thank the following publications for permission to reprint (in
most cases with variations) recipes that first appeared in their pages:
Attenzione, Bon Appétit, Food & Wine, and *Newsday.* The recipes on pages
143 and 300 (bottom) are reprinted from *Great Meals in Minutes: Brunch
Menus* © 1984 Time-Life Books Inc.; those on pages 67, 87, 190, 224 (top),
and 252 are from *Great Meals in Minutes: Pasta Menus* © 1983 Time-Life
Books Inc., and appear courtesy of Time-Life Books Inc.

A COMMON READER EDITION and fountain colophon are trademarks of
The Akadine Press, Inc.

ISBN 1-888173-39-4

3   5   7   9   10   8   6   4   2

for
Bill Garry and Zack Hanle
who knew before we did

and

in memory of
Frank and Angelina Maresca

PREFACE

Perhaps it's only because I like to eat, but I've spent a lot of time elaborating a metaphysics of the table that seems to me to address most of the knottiest concerns encountered in the conduct of life. Someday we'll have dinner (and a bottle or two of wine) and I can explain it. For the time being, let me note as I introduce this splendid collection of recipes that most of the axioms of my personal philosophy of taste have been inspired by Italy, on the one hand because, being Italian on all four sides of the box of my inheritance, most of the square meals I've eaten are suffused with the character and traditions of that country's cuisine; and on the other hand, because it was while dining in Rome, Venice, and assorted small cities in Umbria that I first understood that, sophisticated as any culinary craft can be, the only genuine gastronomic art begins once preparations are complete and appetites are called to table. Cooking, I had always known, was filled with tasteful satisfactions; eating, I discovered, could be filled with wisdom.

Too many cooks don't understand this wisdom, but the authors of the book you hold in your hands certainly do. They recognize that Italian cooking is but the appetizer to the main course, Italian eating. As Tom Maresca and Diane Darrow so aptly observe:

> *An Italian meal is not just for allaying hunger. Dining in Italy is an affirmation of the preciousness of simple things—of the worth of bread, of oil, of wine, and of ourselves. It's a rite of renewal, a celebration of human triumph over the daily abrasions that wear us down—the heat of the summer, the demands of the job, the indignities of the flu, the indifference of the bureaucracy, the perfidy of inanimate objects. For animals, eating is survival. For humans, eating is a rite of civilization. For Italians, eating is the single great art accessible to us all.*

The ancient, ageless vigor that animates Italian culture is its genius for civilizing, with all the connotations the word carries: the founding and flourishing of cities, the humanizing of nature and of institutions, the integration of craft and fine art into the texture of the common life, the honoring of the graces—courtesy, civility, hospitality—that can dignify the ceaseless round of works and days. The Italian meal strikes me as the perfect emblem of that vigor, for nowhere is civilizing genius so easily, resourcefully, and convivially displayed than at *la tavola Italiana*. In homes or restaurants, in settings or on occasions simple or grand, the casual yet serious attention to the ordering of courses and the balancing of flavors, to the fleeting inspiration of the season and to the natural and artisanal glories of the region, to the dictates of custom and the seductive whispers of immediate need—all mark the meal as an ordinary rite, a nourishing sacrament that, in feeding the soul as well as the body, leavens the weight of the world. The Italian table is set with the knowledge that the great art it so generously makes accessible records, with wit and pleasure, the conversation between nature and culture that defines human existence.

The fragmented business of contemporary life, unfortunately, often makes it impossible for me to turn my appreciation for the art this book celebrates into anything like regular execution. I wish that the exigencies of commutation and modern suburban marketing, of employment and parenting, allowed me to collect my family's meal item by item from discriminating vendors as I made my way home each evening, and that I then had the time (and patience) to turn the groceries into a repast that would salute the day. (I hear my wife, who has been a professional restaurant cook as well as a cooking teacher, muttering, "Go ahead, and while you're at it, don't forget to make the kids macaroni-and-cheese.") Still, the thought of such a happy routine is never far from my mind, and one of the pleasures of Tom Maresca and Diane Darrow's volume is the way it allows me to continually refresh my dreams and to direct my energies on those ideal days I have the wherewithal to pursue them. Their book is a mine of fundamental information and fortunate discoveries about the cuisines of Italy's three major culinary regions and about the dizzying and delectable varieties of wine that complement them. The cumulative effect of the authors' respect for ingredients and their scores of lucid, informed, expertly tested recipes—which cover everything from *antipasti* to *dolci*, pasta to *contorni*, meat to game to fish—is to provide astute students with a genial education in habits of husbandry and appetite that will illuminate a lifetime's eating. Try the *ribollita* or the sautéed rabbit with peppers, the sautéed chicken with basil and tomatoes or the *tagliarini* with sage tomato sauce—to mention just a few dishes that have made their way from *La Tavola*

Italiana to our own. Or pour yourself a glass of wine, open to any page, and wander until you find something that strikes your fancy; it won't take long. *Buon appetito*.

James Mustich, Jr.
Publisher, A Common Reader

ACKNOWLEDGMENTS

We could never have started or finished this book without the help of countless people in the United States and Italy, in the wine trade and the food trade, professional cooks and amateurs, restaurateurs and householders. More people generously and openheartedly shared their knowledge with us than memory or space permits us to thank properly. We are particularly grateful to the following individuals:

Donatella Cinelli and all the Colombini-Cinelli family
Albert R. Cirillo
Frank de Falco and Niki Singer
Annamaria and Vittorio Fini
Teresa Lungarotti and Romano Sartore
Antonio and Walter Mastroberardino
Lorenza dei Medici, Piero Stucchi-Prinetti, and John Meis
Gianluigi Morini
Doreen Schmidt and the staff of the Italian Wine Center
"Zia Nina" Tito
Tom Verdillo

CONTENTS

HOW TO USE THIS BOOK

We've tried in this book to present the authentic flavor of Italy, the timeless food and wine combinations that for generations have typified *la vera cucina italiana*, the kind of meals that Italians themselves think of as home cooking, *cucina casalinga*. To make it easiest for you to re-create those marvelous flavors, we've arranged the book in five main sections: a chapter called "Le Ricette di Base: Staples and Techniques," three separate sections for the cooking of the North, Center, and South of Italy (all with wine recommendations for each recipe), and a concluding chapter on alternative wine and food pairings and how to put together your own cellar of Italian wines.

To get the most out of these recipes, read through the opening section first. That's where you'll find some of the most important fundamental recipes and techniques—making breads, pasta, sausages, etc.—as well as important information about the basic ingredients of Italian cooking. We don't presuppose any great cooking skills on the reader's part; you don't need a *cordon bleu* to make any of our recipes. The great art of Italian cooking *alla contadina* or *alla casalinga* (farmer-style or home-style) is to make much of little. To do so, it works with basics, and so we too start with the very fundamental things: bread and pasta, cheese and tomatoes, sausages, broth, water, and wine.

We talk about wine in this book far more than most food books do. Much of what we say is very simple, for two reasons: because much of Italian wine is still new to many Americans, and because so many of our dishes are rooted in the classic peasant and regional recipes that call for simple, clear pairings of flavors. The choice of not just a good wine but a wine appropriate to the dish contributes much to the harmony of Italian dining. The pleasure of a classic Italian meal depends as much on the wines that go with it as on the dishes that make it up.

No other cuisine we know makes so much of the interactions of food and wine, and especially the interactions of particular foods and particular wines.

Italian dishes that are merely good on their own and Italian wines that are only pleasant by themselves can blossom in each other's company into unforgettable experiences. And why not? These dishes and these wines—some until this century so local they were confined to a single valley or township —have been evolving together for two thousand years. They had nothing else but each other to interact with. The wonder would be if they didn't enhance each other.

To simplify your dealing with the great diversity of Italian wines, we describe the kinds and qualities of wine each region produces, highlighting such unifying factors—a dominant grape variety, or a specialized technique—as will help you get a clear, broad picture of the wine situation in each part of Italy. We've kept a sharp focus on the best wines for matching with our recipes to reproduce some of those wonderful harmonies of wine and food that can make dining in Italy so spectacular. In every case, we've remembered the realities of the American market: Many fine Italian wines simply aren't imported yet, and many that are cannot be found everywhere. Nevertheless, more than enough high-quality Italian wine arrives on these shores to enable the average cook faithfully to re-create the living flavors of Italy.

Italy is a mountainous land, chopped up into segments of odd sizes and shapes by Alps and Appennines and lesser hills. Each of those little lands had centuries to develop its own culinary idiom and its own kind of wine. Each is linked to its nearest neighbors by the produce of hill and field and mountain and ocean, but separated from its nearest neighbors by those very same hills and mountains and seas.

Italian cuisines draw their life not from the great restaurants of the big cities but from the home cooking and the native products of the various regions. That *cucina casalinga* lies at the heart of all the best Italian dishes, which have evolved from the efforts of centuries of family cooks working with the fresh greens and wild mushrooms and local fruits and plump chickens and luscious green olive oil and young wine of their native *paese*, that square mile or so of hillside or plain that is what Italians really mean by their homeland. The recipes in our book attempt to give you the special tastes and textures of that marvelous, uncomplicated, life- and joy-sustaining fare.

The heart of our book lies in the three sections of recipes and wine suggestions. Each section presents one of the three broadly different regional cooking styles of Italy: the North (the provinces of Val d'Aosta, Piedmont, Trentino-Alto Adige, the Veneto, Friuli-Venezia Giulia, Lombardy, Liguria, Emilia-Romagna); the Center (the provinces of Tuscany, Umbria, Lazio, the Marches, the Abruzzi); and the South (Campania, Basilicata, Puglia, Calabria, Sicily).

This three-part division is not one you'll find in either politics or nature. Italian geography, history, and bureaucracy have divided Italy into twenty-two administrative regions, which in turn are subdivided into many regions. "Province" and "region" are precise legal designations. For example, the Veneto is a region and Verona is one of its provinces (as well as being the major city in that province). Italian cookbooks—that is, cookbooks written in Italian—usually follow that pattern and offer twenty-two chapters, one for the cooking of each region. Such elaborate distinctions don't make sense for American cooks and diners, so we have chosen to present a simpler and, we hope, clearer picture of Italy's many cooking styles. Broadly, one could envision the North as winter cooking (but a Mediterranean winter); the Center as the cooking of the seasons; and the South as the cooking of the sun.

Within each of those three sections, our recipes are divided according to their roles in an Italian meal: *antipasto*, *primo*, *secondo*, *contorno*, and *dolce*. Those components don't exactly correspond to our appetizer, main course, and dessert. Italian meals differ in subtle but important ways from American dining patterns, and those ways deserve a word of explanation.

There is a great deal of flexibility about the actual makeup of an Italian meal. Much depends upon the circumstances—the time, the place, the persons, the pomp or informality desired. An Italian meal can consist of anything from one course to eight. An elaborate, formal dinner could include *antipasto* (similar but not identical to an appetizer or hors d'oeuvre course), *primo* of pasta or rice or soup, *secondo* of fish, *secondo* of flesh or fowl, a separate *contorno* (normally a dish served alongside a *secondo* to round it out, usually vegetable), *formaggio* (cheese), and *dolce* (dessert), all accompanied by appropriate wines and concluding with strong espresso (a course in its own right) and brandy or grappa. It is not uncommon to serve multiples of each course —several *antipasti*, a pasta and a *risotto* or two or three different pastas, etc.

Needless to say, this multiplication of dishes and courses is usually reserved for very special occasions and even then is rarely attempted in the home. Day-to-day Italian dining at home is much less elaborate than that. Simplicity, in fact, is one of the characteristics Italians prize most in cooking. An Italian *buona forchetta* will never refuse a white truffle, but he is just as likely to rhapsodize about a slice of fresh country bread topped with a smear of unsalted butter and a tissue-paper-thin slice of *prosciutto crudo*.

A typical everyday meal consists of several courses of roughly equal size and importance. This differs markedly from the French and American custom of a "main" course preceded by an appetizer and followed by a dessert. If anything, it's closer in spirit to the patterns of a Chinese dinner than a French or an American one. It means that any course and/or its wine can be turned into the star or showpiece of the Italian meal. An elaborate *antipasto* accompanied by a fine wine can be followed by a simple pasta, and a *secondo* could be omitted entirely. Or a simple *antipasto* could precede an elaborate *secondo*, with no *primo* anywhere in sight. Everything depends on what ingredients you have to work with and what effect you want to achieve.

Note also that that course Italians call the *secondo* corresponds in position and ingredients but not in size to our main course of fish, flesh, or fowl. As a rule, Italians are not big meat eaters. *Secondo* may often be vegetable rather than meat or fish, and almost always it is the same size or smaller than the *primo*. Because of this, you may sometimes think the quantities indicated in some of our *secondo* recipes are too small for the four people they are supposed to feed. Please remember that those recipes are designed to fit into the context of an Italian meal, and they presume that at least a *primo*, and possibly an *antipasto*, has preceded them.

Desserts in Italy are rarely elaborate. Fresh fruit or *gelato*—that wonderful Italian ice cream, unquestionably the best in the world—or *granita* (water ices, akin to sherbets) occur most frequently, followed in popularity by relatively simple, relatively unsweet fruit tarts. It is not at all uncommon to choose a piece of cheese instead of dessert, especially if there happens to be a bit of red wine left in the bottle.

Many Italians still take their biggest meal at midday and only a light supper in the evening. This is one of the reasons American tourists in Italy looking for a light lunch are so often frustrated or even outraged, as when, despite the conspicuous sign that says "Pizzeria," the waiter insists that *pizza non c'è*. It's only served in the evening, for a simple supper. This habit is, like so many other distinctively Italian behaviors, yielding to modern pressures, and in this book we have treated the recipes as if, in the American manner, the main meal is taken in the evening.

The materials are here, in the recipes in this book, for creating truly spectacular dinners, of as many courses as you please, if your kitchen and your time and energy are up to it. Most Italian recipes are not complex or difficult in themselves; the average home cook can handle them comfortably. For everyday cooking—and that is what most of these recipes aim at, drawn as they are from the traditional dishes and repertoires of generations of home cooks—the Italian style is ease itself, because of its omnipresent emphasis on freshness and simplicity. Some of our recipes may, in fact, look so simple that you can't imagine they will be in any way outstanding. Don't be fooled or put off by that. In cooking as in every other art, "less is more" is a constantly proven rule.

You don't have to worry overmuch about precise measurements either: Most

of our recipes are the result of a choice of the most pleasing-to-us of a whole
range of variations. Certain cooks or towns or valleys prefer a given dish drier
and spicier, and others make it moister and more delicate than the version we
opted for. A bit more or a bit less of a particular ingredient is rarely going to
be the margin between glory and disaster in these recipes. This emphatically
does not mean that they are crude foods: far from it. It means they are versatile,
resilient, adaptable. Once you've learned the techniques, you can put your
own stamp on them. Try them first as ours, then make them your own. That's
the authentically Italian way to work with them.

Unless otherwise noted, all the recipes in this book are calculated to feed
four persons in the context of an Italian meal. If you are excerpting a *primo*
or *secondo* to serve separately as a main course in an American-style meal,
you may want to increase the quantities slightly.

Buon appetito!

LE RICETTE DI BASE

STAPLES AND TECHNIQUES

An Italian meal is not just for allaying hunger. Dining in Italy is an affirmation of the preciousness of simple things—of the worth of bread, of oil, of wine, and of ourselves. It's a ritual of renewal, a celebration of human triumph over all the daily abrasions that wear us down—the heat of the summer, the demands of the job, the indignities of the flu, the indifference of the bureaucracy, the perfidy of inanimate objects. For animals, eating is survival. For humans, eating is a rite of civilization. For Italians, eating is the single great art accessible to us all.

Italian cooking comes from farmers and fishermen and their hard-working wives, butchers and cart drivers and longshoremen, parish priests and whores. It is cooking shaped over centuries by people who work hard and can afford little and still must work cheerfully tomorrow. It is a cuisine of essentials, of simplicity, of an honesty and directness that can be humorous as often as it is serious, frugal as often as generous, casual as easily as sublime.

American travelers, seated for the first time in an Italian *trattoria*, are sometimes struck by what looks like comic ineptitude on the part of Italian waiters. They dash about from table to kitchen, they shout at the cook, they expostulate on all the work they have to do, while the diners—who, in typical Italian fashion, have at 8:31 filled every table in a restaurant that had been totally empty at 8:30—sit unconcernedly with only bread and wine in front of them.

But there it is: Bread and wine are in front of them. Nobody's worried. Survival—and even a fair degree of pleasure—is assured. With bread and wine on the table, you know your evening is intact; and the waiter knows it too, so there is time for a bit of the opera that makes life in Italy more than merely survival. A little drama enhances life, but only after the bread and wine are delivered. First things first.

This book, we hope, will be a little like that: less serious at some times than at others, but always putting first things first.

BREAD

Bread isn't incidental to a meal in Italy. It's a basic nutriment, and it tastes good—which is why so much can be done with it. It's always crusty, though the crumb itself may vary from fine and close-textured to coarse and open. Bread comes with butter only at breakfast, but bread is served at every meal, and even the finest restaurants still add to your bill a *pane e coperto*— a tiny additional charge for bread and cover. This is an item that makes some American tourists (the one who's convinced that all foreigners live only to cheat him) snort with rage, while the waiter rolls his eyes in disbelief.

Bread varies in Italy from region to region. In the Veneto, you are given intricately twisted, glossy rolls, like Siamese-twin croissants joined at the middle, with a crumb so fine that it creates a plastery dust when you break them. In the Piedmont, *grissini* appear; not the neat, pencil-size wands that constitute breadsticks everywhere else, but scaled-down barrel staves, half as long as your arm. Tuscan bread never contains salt, which is a shock at first encounter, until you realize that whatever else you're eating functions as a condiment for the bread. In Campania and Puglia, thick slices are cut from huge domed loaves, two or three feet long, a foot or two wide, always with a thick, dark crust and large, open pores in the crumb. For all the variations, one rule of thumb holds about flavor, though it will win us few friends in the North to say so: By and large, the bread gets better as you go south. (So does the coffee; the wine, however, tends to get better as you go north, so the universe remains in balance.)

In Italy, nobody bakes at home. Bread comes from local bakeries, where it is made fresh every day—usually several times a day. Almost always it is baked on the stone, in very hot ovens, with a lot of steam, or in the traditional *pizza* oven, a large stone beehive affair in which wood burns right on the stones next to the baking bread. A very soft, almost wet dough gives the porous crumb that keeps Italian bread so light. It contains no preservatives, so you buy one day's supply at a time because it stales quickly.

Not that much of it gets a chance to. With a smear of butter and a *caffe latte*, bread is breakfast. Fresh and warm with a slice of *salame* or *prosciutto*, and perhaps a few rounds of a sweet onion, a slice of bread is lunch. Toasted, rubbed with a garlic clove, and drizzled with the best olive oil you can lay your hands on, it's called *bruschetta* and it's either lunch or a fantastic *antipasto*. (Try doing this over a wood fire at your next picnic or barbecue.) Similarly toasted and smeared with a little liver pâté, or topped with a mince of basil and the summer's freshest tomatoes, it makes canapés and snacks and *antipasti* and even light lunches.

And that's only what Italians do with *sliced* bread. Move back in the process, and instead of producing loaves, they will make flat *focaccia*, topped before baking with coarse salt or thin-sliced onions or freshly minced herbs. Or they'll cut the flattened dough into pieces and deep-fry them, plain or stuffed. The apotheosis of bread dough is *pizza*, the ultimate expression of bread as meal in itself.

And that's only fresh bread. Day-old bread constitutes a culinary subcategory of its own in Italy. It goes into salads—the famous Tuscan *panzanella*, for instance—and soups and stuffings. There's a whole class of Italian soups called *zuppe di pane*, all built around day-old bread. If you have no other uses for it, you grate it and save it for stuffings and for breading *costolette*. The last thing you do with stale bread in Italy is throw it out.

What follows are basic recipes for several kinds of bread. All will give you reasonably authentic flavor and texture, given the intrinsic differences between Italian and American flours. Most of the recipes require little real effort, though a fair amount of patience while the bread rises. If you can possibly do so, use a baking stone or baking tiles in making all of these breads, but especially in baking *pizza*. Many large department stores carry baking stones, and most tile outlets or masonry suppliers can sell you oven tiles. They don't cost much and they will last for years. The returns they will give you every time you make bread or *pizza* will be ample reward for any trouble you take to acquire them. Stones or tiles give bread and *pizza* a crustiness that you just can't get with metal pans.

Tuscan Bread Dough

This saltless bread can be made with all white flour, but we enjoy the faint nutty-wheaty flavor that derives from the addition of a small amount of whole wheat flour. Loaves made with this dough (see technique, page 21) are the base on which various savory mixtures are spread to make Tuscan *crostini* (pages 166–167). This bread is also perfect for *bruschetta*.

---

1 ounce fresh yeast, or 2 packages instant dry yeast granules
1¼ cups warm water (125 degrees F)

2¾ cups unbleached white flour
¼ cup whole wheat flour

In a large bowl, dissolve the yeast in the water. Mix the two flours and stir them in to make a soft dough. Knead 10 minutes by hand, or 4 minutes in a heavy-duty mixer with a dough hook.

(continued)

Oil a clean bowl and set the dough in it, cover tightly with plastic wrap, and let rise until double in bulk. (In the traditional warm place, this will take about 2 hours. However, a cooler temperature will do as long as the dough has enough time to rise, including overnight in the refrigerator.) If the dough is ready sooner than it is needed, punch it down and refrigerate it or let it rise slowly again at room temperature until ready to use.

Shape and bake according to the desired recipe.

Olive-Oil Bread Dough

This dough makes a good hearty country loaf all by itself (see technique, page 21). It is also the base recipe for *grissini* (page 66) and *pane con ciccioli* (page 242).

1 ounce fresh yeast, or 2 packages instant dry yeast granules	¾ teaspoon salt
	3 cups unbleached white flour
1¼ cups warm water (125 degrees F)	
2 tablespoons olive oil	

Proceed as for Tuscan bread dough (see preceding recipe), adding the olive oil to the water and the salt along with the flour.

Pizza Dough

With the uncommon addition of milk, this dough is primarily intended for *pizza* (pages 254–256) and *focaccia* (pages 162–163). The milk helps dough made with American flour to develop the baked-on-the-stone crispness that is characteristic of *pizza* made with Italian flour. The dough can also be used to make a simple loaf of bread (see technique, page 21). In a loaf, the milk-based dough produces a softer, denser crumb than those of our other bread recipes.

1 ounce fresh yeast, or 2 packages instant dry yeast granules	½ teaspoon salt
	3 cups unbleached white flour
½ cup milk, at room temperature	
¾ cup warm water (125 degrees F)	

Proceed as for Tuscan bread dough (page 19), dissolving the yeast in a mixture of the water and the milk, and adding the salt along with the flour.

Bread Dough Using a Sponge

Many Italian bakers start their breads with a sponge, which, like a sourdough starter, permits the yeast to develop more fully and creates a richer flavor in the bread. Here's a way to do that with any of the basic dough recipes in this book. It adds a little time to the preparation, but it's well worth doing on a leisurely baking day.

Ingredients for 1 recipe of Tuscan bread dough (page 19), olive-oil bread dough (page 20), or pizza dough (page 20)

Dissolve the yeast in ¼ cup of the water. Put 6 tablespoons of the flour into a small bowl, add the yeast mixture, and work it into a little ball of dough. Cut a deep cross in the top of the ball, return it to the bowl, cover it tightly with plastic wrap, and let it sit in a warm place for 1 hour.

Mix the yeast ball into the remaining ingredients of the recipe to form a soft dough. Proceed as directed in the recipe.

To Bake a Plain Crusty Loaf

This is an all-purpose bread-baking technique, which assumes that you have oven tiles or a baking stone. If you do not, the loaves can be raised on the oiled baking sheet on which you plan to cook them.

Ingredients for Tuscan bread dough (page 19), olive-oil bread dough (page 20), or pizza dough (page 20)

Make the dough as directed in the basic recipe and let it rise once. Rub 2 to 3 tablespoons flour into a lintless dish towel and set the towel on a baking sheet.

When the dough has completed its rising, punch it down, turn it out onto a floured work surface, and flatten it into an oblong about 8 inches wide, 10 inches long, and ¾ inch thick. It will still be very soft, but try to use a minimum of additional flour in handling it.

Roll the dough tight, jelly-roll fashion, into a cylindrical shape. Flatten this to about 1 inch thick and roll it again. (This activates the web of gluten that will keep the loaf from flattening out in the oven.)

(continued)

For a round loaf, tuck both ends of the cylinder under to meet in the center, pinching to seal them. Roll the dough around the work surface under your hands, to shape it into a smooth ball about 5 inches in diameter. For an oblong loaf, roll the dough under your hands into a fat cigar shape, extending it to about 10 inches in length.

Set the loaf on the floured towel and fold the ends of the towel loosely around it. Put the covered loaf, on its baking sheet, in a warm place to rise for 1 hour.

Preheat an oven lined with baking tiles to 400 degrees F. Have a water-filled sprayer handy. Slide your hand under the towel, pick up the loaf, and gently deposit it upside down on the tiles. Spray water into the oven before closing the door, and spray twice more at 2-minute intervals.

After the bread has baked 15 minutes, turn the oven down to 375 degrees. Continue baking about 45 minutes in all, or until a knuckle thumped on the bottom of the loaf produces a hollow sound. Cool the bread on a rack.

PASTA

After bread, the most important nutriment in Italy is pasta; so much so that, for most of the world, pasta is the symbol if not the sum of Italian cooking. Certainly, it provides a grand emblem of the diversity of that cooking, in its myriad shapes and styles and names—fresh-made egg noodles and commercially extruded hard-wheat *spaghetti* and *macaroni*, stuffed pasta and plain, large *lasagne* and *cannelloni*, small *fettucelle* and *penne*, strings and tongues and little stars and butterflies, corkscrews and bridegrooms and quills and wolf's eyes, tubes and hats and shells and snails and ears, and so on through the extraordinary range of sizes and shapes that Italians have squeezed flour and water into. Almost every nation makes some form of pasta, but only Italy has achieved so much with so simple a combination of ingredients.

Don't make the mistake of thinking that all those shapes are interchangeable. Far from it. The same sauce on two different shapes of pasta will not taste the same. Put that to the test yourself if you don't believe it. That's why certain dressings are irrevocably wedded to certain pastas: the double and triple butter of the Alfredo preparation belongs only to *fettuccine*, the fiery bite of an *arrabbiata* sauce to *penne* (or, possibly, *ziti*), a briny *marinara* dressing to *spaghettini* or *capelli d'angelo*.

Subtleties aside, the differences that matter most in pasta are those between pasta made fresh with eggs and the eggless, hard-wheat pasta. This is more than a distinction between moist and dry, soft and hard. These are two different creatures, two different vehicles. For butter or cream-based sauces with luxurious accents like truffle or *funghi porcini*, fresh-made egg pasta, rolled to its airy thinnest, cut and cooked immediately, offers a natural base to which there is no thinkable alternative. The flavors and textures mesh and marry seamlessly. On the other hand, spicy sauces want dry, eggless pasta; they need the firmness of flavor and texture it provides to stand up to their assertiveness. Similarly, fish and seafood sauces—especially those made with tomato—combine peerlessly with thin, thin strands of dry pasta, like the romantically named *capelli d'angelo*, angel's hair.

Not all dry pastas are created equal, by any means. There is a very wide quality gap between commercially made American pasta and Italian, with the import far surpassing the domestic product in texture and in flavor. This is not to say that all Italian brands are alike either, but by and large you will get a superior product, and as a result a superior dish, with an imported Italian pasta.

Each section of Italy has its own characteristic pasta and its own peculiar way of handling it. The specialization is often extreme: Mention Bologna, and an Italian immediately thinks *tortellini*; and everyone knows that Neapolitans dote on *fusilli*. Generally speaking, dry, eggless pasta is the specialty of the South, fresh egg noodles the norm in the North, and the Center divides its allegiances between the two, with a large niche reserved for *gnocchi*.

Northern sauces tend to rely on butter, meats, and mushrooms for their basic flavors. When cheese is used, it's *parmigiano*. Tomato is minimal or absent altogether. In the Center, *parmigiano* begins to share honors with *pecorino romano*, tomato grows in importance, and olive oil fairly consistently replaces butter. The typical sauce base in the central region is a *soffritto* of onion, carrot, and celery, plus maybe garlic, maybe *pancetta* or *prosciutto*. In the South, the cheese will always be *pecorino* or *locatelli* or another of their kin—sharper, more assertive cheeses than the mellow, almost sweet *parmigiano*. Tomatoes are all but ubiquitous in southern sauces, and meat all but disappears from them.

Pasta can be rolled and cut by hand, though thinning the dough with a rolling pin is a tedious process. One of the many kinds of pasta machines now on the market can remove the labor from the process. Our favorite combination for making pasta is to mix and knead the dough in our Hobart KitchenAid heavy-duty mixer—a rock-steady machine that consistently turns out uniform, smooth doughs—and then to thin the pasta and cut it on a manual pasta machine such as the Imperia, a sturdy, made-in-Italy roller/cutter device that seems never to break down. The many brands of electric pasta machines and food processors are other alternatives, of course. We have not given instructions for making pasta in the food processor, on the theory that people who are as devoted to their food processors as we are to our KitchenAid have probably already learned how to adapt every domestic procedure to that astonishingly efficient machine.

———————◆———————

Basic Egg Pasta

This pasta recipe can be turned into all the shape-and-name varieties of flat pasta. It is also perfectly adaptable for pastas that are to be stuffed or filled, though traditional wisdom calls for a little milk instead of water in making pasta for *ravioli, agnolotti,* etc. There is also a rather fierce controversy among Italian cooks concerning the propriety of adding olive oil to the mix. As you will see, we are of the pro-olive oil party. Quantities given here will make about 1 pound of fresh pasta, enough for 4 persons.

———————◆———————

2 cups all-purpose flour   ¾ teaspoon olive oil
⅛ teaspoon salt   1 tablespoon water
3 large eggs

Combine the flour and salt. Add the eggs, olive oil, and water and mix to obtain a firm dough. Knead 10 minutes by hand or 5 minutes by heavy-duty mixer.

Put the ball of pasta into the flour bin, turning it once to cover it with flour, cover the bin, and let it rest there at least 30 minutes.

Set up a pasta machine and flour a work surface. Cut the dough into 4 pieces and run each one through the rollers from the thickest to the thinnest setting. Let each one rest on the floured surface while you prepare the others.

To make fettuccine *(broad noodles) or* tonnarelli *(the square spaghetti-gauge pasta found on most pasta machines):*

Cut each thinned piece of dough into 3 or 4 pieces, for ease of handling, and run them through the selected cutter on the pasta machine. As each piece is cut, catch the strands loosely in your hand and strew them over a floured surface.

If you are going to use the pasta immediately, it can be loosely bunched— just toss it every few minutes to keep the strands from sticking together. If it needs to wait for a few hours, either flour it very heavily (and shake it in a sieve to remove loose flour before cooking), or hang the strands on a suspended broom handle, yardstick, curtain rod, or something similar.

To make ravioli, agnolotti, *or other stuffed pastas:*
As soon as the pieces of dough are thinned, cover them with a dish towel to keep them from drying out. Follow the instructions given in the specific recipe, working with one piece of dough at a time and keeping the rest covered.

To Cook Pasta

Cooking pasta is literally as simple as boiling water—a quart to every quarter pound, plus 1 teaspoon of salt for each quart. The only trick is taking the pasta out of the water soon enough. Italians eat pasta *al dente*, which means firm. As soon as the last trace of uncooked flour leaves the center of the strand, whisk the pasta off the flame, drain it, dress it, and serve it at once. For fresh-made pasta, the cooking time can be as short as bringing the water back to a full boil, if you have rolled and cut your dough very thin. For larger commercially made dry *macaroni*—shapes like *rigatoni*, for instance—the cooking time might be as long as 15 minutes. Test periodically by biting a strand, and if you are in doubt stop cooking at once. The odds are strong that an Italian would already think your pasta overdone. Pasta should never, absolutely never, be mushy.

CHEESE

Italy is a cheese lover's paradise, as anyone who travels there quickly discovers. Here in America, if the USDA could be persuaded to stop protecting us from ourselves, we could easily have many, many more of Italy's luscious cheeses than now reach these shores—soft little goats and old, hard sheep, all the local varieties of young *caprini* and *toma*, aromatic *cacciota* and *groviera*, sweet *mascarpone* . . . As it is, because of U.S. government requirements about pasteurization and aging in the making of cheeses to be imported here, we lose the opportunity to taste an incredible variety of wonderful cheeses.

Nevertheless, we can still get the handful of cheeses that any Italian would rank as the most important: *gorgonzola, parmigiano, pecorino romano, ricotta, mozzarella* (the last two also made quite acceptably in this country).

Italians distinguish between cheeses for eating and cheeses for cooking, though the distinction sometimes comes down to the cheese's age and sometimes to the diner's or cook's preference. Eating cheeses appear often in Italian meals; sometimes *as* the meal, sometimes before or instead of dessert. Most Italian cheeses marry very happily with good red wines, so they will almost always appear if the occasion is a special one and the wine better than the ordinary. In warm weather, bread, cheese, wine, and fruit may well *be* dinner.

Among the eating cheeses, *gorgonzola* stands at the head of the class; it is one of the greatest blue cheeses of the world (never mind that its veins are usually green). It comes in several varieties: an exquisite, creamy young version affectionately called *'zola dolce*, a firmer *stagionata* (aged) with more bite, and the peppery *gorgonzola piccante*. All make marvelous dinner cheeses, and all are imported to the United States.

Taleggio comes from roughly the same section of northern Italy as *gorgonzola*. Meltingly soft and creamy when young, it firms and acquires a bit of a tang as it ages, but never loses its lush velvety texture. It belongs to the class of cheeses known in Italy as *stracchini*; some pretty good ones are made in the United States, but none of the distinction of real *taleggio*.

Also made in both the United States and Italy is *Bel Paese*, a cheese invented at the beginning of this century. Firm and buttery, *Bel Paese* makes (to our mind) a better luncheon or picnic cheese than it does a dinner cheese, but our opinion doesn't stop Italians from eating it anytime they please. Although they are supposedly made according to the same formula, the Italian *Bel Paese* tastes much better than the bland domestic product. (You can distinguish them by their wrappings: the import shows the map of Italy, the other that of the western hemisphere.) Sure proof, if any was needed, that cheeses derive their flavor from what the cows feed on. That's why American-made cheeses are on the whole so utterly uninteresting.

The cheeses Italians use in cooking are fewer in number and fairly consistent over the country. The grating cheeses are primarily two: *parmigiano* in the North and some variety of *pecorino* in the South. These two cheeses actually serve as both cooking and eating cheeses. In their respective areas of production, restaurants keep large wheels of them from which they quarry chunks either for grating or for eating in the hand. Both *parmigiano* and *pecorino* make marvelous eating cheeses when young, and incomparable condiments when older, but beyond that their resemblances stop. *Parmigiano* is made from cow's milk—but not just any cow. The real *parmigiano* bears the name Parmigiano-

Reggiano branded into its side (and often the year it was made as well: it's an aged, vintage cheese), which certifies that all the milk came from cows pastured in the lush lowlands around Parma and Reggio nell' Emilia. (The whey from the cheese making helps feed the area's pigs, which is one of the reasons *prosciutto di Parma* is also so highly prized in Italy.) *Pecorino*, on the other hand, is essentially a sheep's milk cheese (though it may have a percentage of cow's milk in it), and it derives different flavors from the differing pasturages of the flocks. The most prized *pecorini* originate in Tuscany, Lazio, Sardinia, and Sicily.

An aged *parmigiano* is a lovely sight. The fat wheel gleams amber gold, and when you split one open—a task that requires all the tools and muscles of log-splitting—the cheese within jags and glints like fresh-quarried marble. An old, hard *pecorino*, on the other hand, is the very essence of an evil cheese, with its ungainly drumlike shape, its usually black rind, its pale interior, and its strong aroma. Appearances don't lie: Those are the characters of those two wonderful cheeses—*parmigiano* elegant and restrained, *pecorino* homely and assertive. Both should be grated fresh at, or just before, the moment of use to obtain maximum flavor and aroma. Only the imported cheeses are the real items; domestic "parmesan" and "romano" bear no discernible relation to the cheeses they travesty.

The other key cooking cheeses are *ricotta* and *mozzarella*. *Mozzarella* is one of the glories of the South. As you drive down from Rome, you know you are in Campania when you start seeing roadside stands advertising *La Vera Bufala*. The *bufala* is the wife of the *bufalo*, a creature that looks like a dangerously irascible water buffalo, to which it is not-too-distant kin. The *bufala* is an improbable animal; many an Italian child believes it lays eggs, because small ovals of mozzarella are marketed in Italy as *ovalini di bufala*, little buffalo eggs. Besides, that so fierce looking a beast should make so gentle a cheese is unlikely at best.

Unfortunately, the milk yields of *bufale* are small and their space and feed demands high, so real *mozzarella di bufala* is scarce and getting scarcer. Much *mozzarella* these days is made with cow's milk, even in Italy, but if you ever have the opportunity to taste *la vera bufala*, do not hesitate: It is an extraordinary cheese, subtle and rich at the same time. You don't have to cook with it either; it's a treat just as it is, dressed only with extra-virgin olive oil and a crackle of fresh-ground pepper. Alternating *mozzarella* slice for slice with fresh tomatoes, with a squeeze of lemon juice and a drizzle of olive oil, gives you *insalata caprese*, a popular summer dish all over Italy.

Ricotta is made throughout Italy, though Romans seem particularly devoted to it. It belongs to the class of very simple fresh cheeses that are made by a process no more elaborate than curdling milk. So simple is the procedure that it is still often done at home, especially in the countryside. There are several simple cheeses that can be made easily in the home kitchen without any sort of special equipment. Unfortunately, since the only milk normally available in the American home kitchen is homogenized, pasteurized, irradiated, vitamin-enriched, and thereby almost totally denatured, the results we can get here are never so artlessly charming as in Italy, where it is still possible to get milk to which nothing has been done but remove it that same morning from the cow.

We were shown how to make one of those delightful cheeses, *raviggiolo*, by Donatella Cinelli at her family's vineyard, Fattoria dei Barbi. She started it just before we sat down to dinner, and it was ready in time for dessert. Rennet, and the freshest possible milk, are the keys. Donatella used animal rennet, which is derived from an enzyme in the stomachs of cows. Here in the United States, pharmacies or health food stores will sell you vegetable rennet, which also works very well. In fact, a vegetable rennet derived from artichokes is sometimes used in the Tuscan countryside to make this and similar cheeses.

Raviggiolo

This recipe is so easy that once you've tried it, *raviggiolo* may well become a kitchen standard. Although we had it first as a dessert, the fresh curds also make a fine midmorning snack, sprinkled with salt instead of sugar, and the firmed cheese can be used to stuff *ravioli* and other pastas.

---

1 quart milk	**Sugar**
1 tablespoon rennet	

In a glass or enameled saucepan, heat the milk gently to 100 degrees F. (An instant-reading thermometer helps here, but lacking one, the milk should be just about at warm body temperature.) Turn off the heat, stir in the rennet, and take the pot off the stove. Let it sit, partly covered, in a warm place for 20 to 30 minutes, until soft curds have formed.

To serve immediately as a dessert, dip out the curds with a slotted spoon into small bowls, draining off as much of the whey as possible. Sprinkle on sugar to taste. To keep for a day or two, set a sieve lined with dampened

cheesecloth over a bowl and dip out the curds into the sieve. Let them drain
for an hour or more, until they become as firm as you like them. Transfer to
a bowl, cover, and refrigerate.

A final note: Rennets vary in strength. If the *raviggiolo* turns out salty, try
half the amount of rennet next time.

Ricotta

Ricotta is also extremely easy to make at home. Its coagulant is lemon juice,
which produces a flavor and texture different from a rennet cheese. Really
fresh raw milk will almost form ricotta on its own, left to itself on a warm,
dry day. It was in Helen Witty's and Elizabeth Schneider Colchie's excellent
book *Better Than Store Bought* that we first saw this technique for coaxing
American homogenized milk to coagulate properly. Incidentally, the whey
that drains off the curds is a good alternative to water in any bread recipe.

------------◆------------

1 quart milk   **2 tablespoons lemon juice**

Pour the milk into a glass or enameled saucepan, stir in the lemon juice,
and heat the mixture gently to 200 degrees F, or until it is just on the edge
of a simmer. Remove the pot from the heat and let it sit, partly covered, until
the milk coagulates. The curds will take 30 minutes to 2 hours to form,
depending on the temperature of the room.

Set a sieve lined with dampened cheesecloth over a bowl and dip out the
curds into it. Loosely fold the ends of the cheesecloth over the top and let the
ricotta drain for several hours, or overnight in the refrigerator.

------------◆------------

TOMATOES

It's hard to imagine Italian cooking without tomatoes—but then it's hard to
imagine any warm-weather cuisine that doesn't take advantage of the flavor
and versatility of this wonderful fruit. Of all of the New World's gifts to the
Old, tomatoes—*pomodori*, literally, golden apples—may be the best. Happily,
the Old World returns the favor with interest by way of the thousands of uses

it turns tomatoes to. Tomatoes are fundamental to Italian cooking, in salads or sauces, as bases or accents. In many Italian kitchens, tomato is almost like butter or oil: a medium, a seasoning, a foundation. And it is, of course, also a food in itself.

Buying picnic supplies one day in the Neapolitan equivalent of a deli, we watched with watering mouths as the counterman served the customer before us. He split lengthwise a long narrow loaf of bread and lined it with halves of small, firm, half-green tomatoes. He dotted them with pitted black olives and then trickled yellow-green olive oil over everything before closing the bread. It looked like the finest sandwich the world had ever seen. (We were a little hungry.) So, in our then-faltering Italian, we gestured at the departing sandwich and asked the counterman what it was called. He looked at us warily, as if we might be dangerous, and said, very slowly and carefully, "po-mo-do-ri." First things first, even when dealing with idiots.

Italians have the good sense to grow tomatoes for flavor, rather than for packing quality or perfect roundness. You'll see many kinds in the average Italian market: huge half-greens for eating, all creased and involuted and luscious, though they look ugly and half-finished; tiny, tiny egg- and pear-shaped tomatoes for sauce, bright fire-engine red, with thin skins and very low acidity; and the king of the sauce tomatoes, the fabulous San Marzano, a largish plum tomato of simply incomparable flavor. San Marzanos rightly dominate southern Italian cooking.

Throughout Italy, the most ubiquitous use for the tomato is in sauce—but that one word covers myriad recipes, simple to complex, long-cooked and intricately prepared to not cooked at all. Most are sauces for pasta or *gnocchi* (and sometimes for *risotto* or *polenta*), though Italians also make some tomato-based sauces for meats that are appetizingly distant kin to our homely ketchup. As with almost everything in Italy, each province—virtually each town—has its own version of tomato sauce, but three basic kinds predominate: a long-cooked, meat-flavored sauce in the North; a long cooked, vegetable-flavored sauce in the Center; and a briefly cooked, almost-totally-tomato sauce in the South. In each area, these sauces not only serve in their own right as dressings for pasta but also provide the bases for further elaboration by the addition of other ingredients or by combination with other sauces (for example, the northern *ragù* and *besciamiglia*, or *béchamel*, combine in the Emilian version of *lasagne*).

We offer recipes for the three basic regional sauces, plus one tomato-based sauce for boiled, roasted, or grilled meats. In preparing them, you'll get the tastiest results by using fresh, locally grown, plum tomatoes. If you can't find fresh plum tomatoes with some flavor, use canned tomatoes—preferably imported Italian. Most domestic canned tomatoes are much too acid to give really good results, but even they are preferable to the wan cotton balls sold as fresh tomatoes in most markets. The conversion formula for adapting our recipes is simple: 1 pound fresh tomatoes equals 1 cup drained canned tomatoes.

You can do one other thing to fight tasteless tomatoes. When the summer crop of tomatoes is at its best and most abundant, freeze some. If you have a large freezer, you can even freeze them whole. Slip the skins off (10 seconds in boiling water and they peel very easily), lay them out, whole or halved, on trays until they solidify, then wrap them in freezer bags or foil and use them as needed.

If you need to be more economical of space, you can coarsely chop fresh tomatoes, cook them gently for about 15 minutes in a heavy-bottomed pot (stir them frequently so they don't scorch) with, if you wish, some fresh basil leaves. At the end of that time, put them through the coarse blade of a food mill (which will remove the skins) and freeze them in pint or quart containers. Either way, you will have fresh, height-of-the-summer tomato flavor available all winter.

Basic Southern Tomato Sauce

This lovely, fresh-tasting sauce is one of a battery of light, vibrant tomato sauces that are used everywhere throughout the South. They vary slightly with the seasons and with individual preferences. In summer, for example, it is always made with fresh San Marzano tomatoes. It takes no more than 20 minutes from start to finish and yields about 2½ cups.

3 cups drained canned plum tomatoes (one 35-ounce can)
1 garlic clove
3 tablespoons olive oil

1 tablespoon chopped parsley
Salt

Coarsely chop the tomatoes on a plate, saving the liquid they release. Halve the garlic clove.

Heat the olive oil in a broad sauté pan and simmer the garlic in it until lightly golden, then press the pieces against the pan and remove them. Raise heat to medium-high and add the chopped tomatoes and their juices from the plate. Simmer, stirring occasionally, for 10 minutes, until the sauce is lightly thickened. Add the chopped parsley and ¼ teaspoon salt, stir all together once, then remove the sauce from the heat.

Basic Central Tomato Sauce

A nubbly-textured, smooth-tasting sauce for all uses. This is the sort of sauce that Italian home cooks start making up in large quantities in the early autumn. Carefully bottled, it will last them through the winter until the next season's fresh produce becomes available, when they will begin making it again as they need it to dress pasta or flavor soups and *risotti* or to enrich other dishes. Total preparation time for this sauce, which freezes well, is about 2½ hours. It yields about 3 cups.

1 carrot	⅓ cup olive oil
1 celery stalk	3 cups drained canned plum toma-
1 onion, about ¼ pound	toes (one 35-ounce can)
1 tablespoon chopped parsley	½ teaspoon salt
4 to 5 basil leaves	Freshly ground black pepper

Finely chop together the carrot, celery, onion, parsley, and basil, or pulse them in a food processor.

Warm the olive oil in a large skillet. Sauté the chopped vegetables for 10 minutes, stirring often. Purée the tomatoes through a food mill into the pan. Add the salt and several grindings of pepper. Bring to a simmer and cook, partly covered, over very low heat, for 2 hours.

Pass the finished sauce through the medium blade of the food mill.

Basic Northern Tomato Sauce
[RAGÙ ALLA BOLOGNESE]

This is perhaps the most famous of all pasta sauces. The Bolognese are renowned throughout Italy as *buone forchette* (literally, good forks, meaning they love to eat well), and their version of the standard northern Italian meat sauce reflects the richness and suavity they prize. Ours is a very authentic, not to say old-fashioned, version. It requires a lot of time to make—about 2 hours —and should even be allowed to have further time to ripen before using. Since it is so fine a sauce on so many pastas, and since it freezes very well, we give you a recipe to make a good amount of it—about 5½ cups in all, which is enough to dress pasta for 10 to 12 persons. If you are making it up in advance, do not add the cream as directed below, but stop after the 40 minutes' simmering, let the sauce cool, and package it in pint- or quart-sized freezer containers.

½ ounce dried *porcini*
½ pound lean veal shoulder
½ pound lean beef round or shin
2½ ounces *pancetta* or blanched
    bacon
4 ounces large yellow onion
1 large carrot
1 large celery stalk
5 tablespoons butter

3 tablespoons olive oil
1 tablespoon salt
¼ teaspoon freshly ground black
    pepper
½ cup dry red wine
2½ cups drained canned plum
    tomatoes
½ cup heavy cream
Freshly grated *parmigiano*
Freshly ground pepper

Put the *porcini* in a small bowl. Pour boiling water over them and let them sit for 30 minutes. Drain them, rinse carefully, chop coarsely, and rinse carefully again.

With a food processor or meat grinder, finely chop first the veal and beef, then the *pancetta*, onion, carrot, and celery. Sauté the *pancetta* and minced vegetables in the butter and oil in a heavy-bottomed casserole for 2 minutes over medium heat. Then turn heat to very low, cover, and continue cooking 30 minutes, stirring occasionally.

Uncover the pot and raise heat to medium-high. Add the beef, veal, mushrooms, salt, and pepper. Cook, stirring constantly, until the meats just begin to lose their raw red color. Then pour on the wine and cook until it is entirely evaporated. Set a food mill with the medium blade over the pot and mill in the tomatoes. Stir everything together and simmer, covered, for 40 minutes.

If possible, complete preparations to this point several hours in advance, or even the night before you plan to use the sauce. Take it off the stove and let it cool. Refrigerate if weather requires it. The sauce may also be made to this point and frozen.

Shortly before serving time, bring the sauce slowly to a simmer. Simmer 5 minutes. Stir in the heavy cream and serve immediately over freshly cooked pasta, passing *parmigiano* and a pepper mill.

To serve *ragù* in smaller quantities, heat about ½ cup of sauce per person and stir in 1½ to 2 tablespoons cream per serving.

Tomato Sauce for Meats

A little dab of this thick, concentrated sauce is delicious on grilled steaks and chops (and, even though it's not very authentically Italian, on hamburgers, too); it also goes well on vegetables like deep-fried eggplant. It takes about an hour and a half to make, yields 1½ cups, and freezes well.

3 cups drained canned plum tomatoes (one 35-ounce can), juice reserved
2 tablespoons minced onion or
scallions
1 bay leaf
¼ teaspoon dried thyme

¼ teaspoon dried rosemary
2 tablespoons olive oil
2 ounces *prosciutto*
½ teaspoon flour
½ teaspoon sugar
Freshly ground black pepper
Salt

Pulse the tomatoes briefly in a food processor or put them through the coarse blade of a food mill.

Finely chop together the onion, bay leaf, thyme, and rosemary. Warm the olive oil in a skillet and sauté the chopped onion and herbs over low heat for 2 to 3 minutes. Finely chop the *prosciutto* and add it to the pan. Sauté 2 to 3 minutes, then stir in the flour and cook for another minute.

Add the tomatoes, sugar, and several grindings of pepper. Bring to a simmer and cook over low heat, uncovered, for about 1 hour, stirring occasionally. If the sauce appears to be drying out toward the end, add a few spoonfuls of the tomato liquid. When done, it should be very thick and nubbly. Taste for salt: If the *prosciutto* was very salty, none may be needed.

SAUSAGES

If you had to name the Italian national meat dish to stand alongside the American burger and fries, it would almost certainly be grilled sausages and something: sausages and *polenta* in the North, sausages and *fagioli* in the Center, sausages and *peperoni* in the South.

In one form or another, pork is the commonest variety of meat in Italy. Every cut of it appears somewhere: loin in Tuscan *arista*, the whole animal (a suckling pig) in Roman *porchetta*, hams in northern *prosciutti*, shoulders in southern *capicolla*, and everything else in the hundreds of local varieties of *salame*, the most ubiquitous form of sausage. Pork livers and a bay leaf are wrapped in caul fat and grilled over a wood fire to make one of the best innards dishes known to humanity. Pork skins enrich bean dishes and soups and go into a whole range of sausages as well.

Animal Farm got the principle right: All pigs are equal, except some pigs are more equal than others. Even in Italy, some pork products are more sublime than others. Many *salami* are excellent meats, but mere commoners compared to the aristocratic *prosciutti* of Parma and of San Daniele and the deep-flavored wild-boar *prosciutto* they make around Caserta in Campania and in the high hills of Calabria. It seems perversity on the part of the U.S. government to hold up the importation of Italian *prosciutto* out of fear of African swine fever or some such fairy tale.

For the same reason, we cannot buy the exquisite *mortadella* of Bologna —though, in honesty, there are some pretty fair domestic versions of that particular sausage on the market. None, however, that match the grandeur of a five-foot-long, foot-and-a-half-wide cylinder of *mortadella gigante*, such as is the pride of Italian makers like Fini of Modena. Seeing one of these cannon on a restaurant's *antipasto* table can send shivers of pleasure along a sausage lover's spine and tremors of appetite through his frame—so much so that we have considered seriously the possibility of smuggling one past American customs by putting it in a wheelchair, draping a slouch hat and sport jacket over it, and lamenting loudly about poor Cousin Jack's collapse. It might work.

Moist and dry, hot and mild, seasoned and simple, made this morning and one-year aged, tiny two-inch links and arm-long beams and every length in between, in logs and links and balls and coils, stuffed into pig's trotters and pig's bellies as well as more ordinary casings—the profusion of types of sausages offered by a neighborhood *salumeria* in Italy exhausts an American's ability to distinguish one from another, even though the regular customers can tell which is which in the flick of an eye. We here at home have to make do, for the most part, with what the supermarket offers as Italian sausage; if we're lucky, we get a choice of hot or sweet (which, by the way, is not a distinction an Italian would recognize).

You can do much better by simply making your own sausage at home if you've got a heavy-duty electric mixer with meat-grinding and sausage-stuffing attachments. For that matter, you can do much better at home if you have only a stuffing horn. You can make quite good sausage without even that rudimentary piece of equipment if you can persuade a butcher to sell you some caul fat. This is the thin, lacy membrane that lines a pig's belly. You can cut it to whatever size you need and simply wrap your seasoned sausage meat in it. You may have to buy a lot of it in order to get any at all, but it keeps almost indefinitely in the freezer. You just thaw it in a bowl of cold water when you need it. Wholesale butchers should have ready supplies of caul fat if your local shop fails you. The same is true of ordinary sausage casings, which are the small intestines of the pig, scrubbed and cleaned and (usually) packed in salt. They, too, should be briefly soaked in cold water before using.

We offer recipes for a few of the more standard kinds of Italian sausage. Except for the *cotechino*, they are all good simply grilled or pan-fried, and all can be used in sauces as well. A word of warning, however: The secret of making succulent sausages is simply to include what seems an inordinate amount of fat. No matter how appalling you find the fat-to-meat proportions in these recipes, *don't* attempt to "decalorize" sausages. You'll get heavy, dry, fibrous, and unappetizing lumps of meat. Much of the fat in a good sausage liquefies and runs off in the cooking, leaving the meat with a pleasing, light texture and a toothsome juiciness.

Plain Sausage

Supermarket-grade pork, though often disappointingly fatty and stringy as a straight piece of meat, is fine for sausages. Shoulder is the handiest cut. You may have some trouble finding pork fat in quantity, but a special request to the butcher should produce it. (Every pig comes with an ample supply.) If all else fails, you can use salt pork, first thoroughly blanching it; but the texture is not quite the same. This recipe makes 1 dozen 4-inch sausages, enough to serve 4 in an Italian-size meal.

6 to 8 feet of sausage casing, packed in salt
1½ pounds boneless pork
½ pound fresh pork fat
1 tablespoon salt

½ teaspoon freshly ground black pepper
2 teaspoons fennel seeds, lightly crushed
2 tablespoons dry red wine

Scrape the loose salt off the sausage casing and set it in a bowl of cold water to soften for at least 30 minutes. (You will need only about 4 feet of casing for this amount of meat, but it's useful to have extra in case of ruptures.)

Cut the pork and fat into pieces that will go through your meat grinder and grind them, using the coarse blade. Mix the salt, pepper, and fennel seeds thoroughly into the ground meat. (Hands are the best implement.) Then mix in the wine.

Drain the casing, open one end gently with your fingers, and run a stream of cold water into it, to flush any remaining salt out of the interior. Thread the casing onto the stuffing horn and fit the horn over the meat grinder. Feed the sausage meat through the horn, supporting the emerging tube of sausage with your hands to prevent rips. (Actually, sausage making is much more conveniently done with two people.)

When all the sausage meat is in the casing, lay the filled tube on the work surface and pinch it at 4-inch intervals to produce individual sausage links. At the same time, fill and firm any air pockets in the casing. Tie off the links with kitchen string. Coil the sausages onto a plate and set it, uncovered, in the refrigerator to season for 48 hours. Turn the sausages over once or twice during that time.

Spicy Sausage

These piquant nuggets of meat are to the typical American supermarket's "Italian hot sausage" as Hyperion to a satyr. If your Shakespeare is rusty, suffice it to say that there's no comparison.

6 to 8 feet of sausage casing, packed in salt
1½ pounds boneless pork
½ pound fresh pork fat
1 tablespoon salt

1 to 1½ teaspoons freshly ground black pepper
6 *peperoncini rossi*, crushed (about 1 teaspoon)
½ teaspoon fennel seeds, lightly crushed
2 tablespoons dry red wine

Follow the instructions for making plain sausage (see preceding recipe), adding the *peperoncini* along with the other spices.

Parsley and Cheese Sausage

Under the name *luganega* or *lucanica*, this is one of the most ubiquitous flavored sausages in Italy. Presumably, it originated in the South (in Lucania, from the name), but now you find it throughout Italy and even quite commonly in the United States. Properly speaking, it should be stuffed into small-gauge casings, about half the diameter of the usual casing, and coiled in a continuous ring, not separated into individual sausages. Even in our broader-gauge version, however, this is a lovely sausage.

6 to 8 feet of sausage casing, packed in salt	½ teaspoon freshly ground black pepper
1½ pounds boneless pork	½ cup minced parsley
½ pound fresh pork fat	½ cup freshly grated *pecorino romano*
1 tablespoon salt	2 tablespoons dry white wine

Follow the directions for making plain sausages (page 36), adding the parsley and cheese to the ground pork along with the other spices.

Cotechino

Cotechino is a pig of a different color. Its uses are far more limited than the other sausages we've been talking about, but its flavor is so distinctive and satisfying that it remains one of the most popular sausages throughout Italy. A boiling sausage, it is close kin to the famous *zampone*, which is essentially the same mix of meat, ground-up pork skin, and spices forced into a boned-out pig's trotter. Both sausages are classic components of *bollito misto* (page 123) and both are born soul mates of lentils, with which they are traditionally served as a New Year's Day dinner. (The idea is that lentils look like coins, and the more of them you eat on the first day of the year, the more money you'll have that year. It doesn't work.) Tradition also demands that *cotechino* always be made as a large, fat sausage, so it is not suited to regular casings. Use a large sheet of caul fat instead (page 35), or even cheesecloth dipped in melted cooled fat. Once you've made a *cotechino*, you'll never again regard pigskin as suited only to gloves and footballs.

¼ pound pork caul fat	1 tablespoon freshly ground black pepper
1 pound boneless pork	1½ teaspoons dried thyme
¼ pound fresh pork fat	½ teaspoon freshly grated nutmeg
¾ pound pork skin	¼ teaspoon ground cloves
2 teaspoons salt	2 tablespoons dry white wine

Soak the caul fat in a bowl of cold water while you prepare the meat mixture. Cut the meat and fat into pieces that will go through your meat grinder. Cut the pork skin into thin strips with poultry shears or a heavy knife. (If the pork skin is at all dry and hard, blanch it briefly in boiling water before cutting it up.) Grind the meat, fat, and skin together, using the coarse blade. Thoroughly mix in all the seasonings.

Drain the caul fat and spread it out on a work surface. Position the meat mixture close to one edge of the caul fat and shape it into a firmly packed cylinder about 8 inches long and 3 inches in diameter. Roll up the meat in the caul fat, making several layers of covering and folding in the ends as you go to make a neat package.

Set the *cotechino* on a plate and leave it uncovered in the refrigerator for 3 days. Turn it over two or three times during that time. Then wrap and freeze it, or cook as directed below.

On the day you wish to cook the *cotechino*, set it in its cooking pot, cover with cold water, and let it soak for 6–8 hours. Drain and cover it again with cold water. Set the pot on medium heat, cover and bring it to a boil. Lower heat to maintain a steady simmer and cook for 2 hours. Turn the sausage over once or twice during the cooking, but don't pierce it with a fork. (This is to keep the juices in, which is even more important if your *cotechino* is in a sausage casing rather than cheesecloth.)

———————— • ————————

CONDIMENTI

The Italian kitchen relies on a few staple condiments—olive oil, wine vinegar, garlic, red pepper, dried mushrooms, anchovies, *prosciutto*, and *pancetta*. Each is capable of standing alone or dominating a dish, but each is also linked to the others in time-honored combinations in countless recipes. Italian cooking also glories in fresh herbs, both those grown in kitchen gardens and—for special pungency—those gathered in the wild. (For some years, we've believed that the frequent, apparently random closings of the Italian *autostrade* are designed to allow the country folk to gather salads along the verges and medians.) Parsley, basil, oregano, rosemary, and fennel are the essential Italian kitchen herbs, all fortunately abundant in American gardens and markets. Leaving aside those green growing things, the following paragraphs discuss the Italian cook's basic tool kit.

Olive Oil

Olive oil is omnipresent in Italy. Even in the North, where it shares honors in cooking with butter and sometimes even with lard, no one would dream of dressing a salad with anything else. Further south, olive oil becomes the universal cooking medium, condiment, and even cure-all (a little warm olive oil poured in the ear for earache, a little taken on a spoon for a sore throat, and so on). There are three grades of it to know about: extra-virgin, from the first and lightest pressing of the olives, virgin, and simple olive oil. In Italy, simple olive oil is a servant of a thousand household uses, from salad dressing to frying to wiping the grill. Extra-virgin is the richest, thickest, darkest, and most intense of the three. It is only rarely used in cooking, in part because it is often unfiltered and contains olive solids that will easily burn, in part because it is too expensive. But anywhere that the direct, clear taste of olive oil is wanted, extra-virgin oil stars—on salads, on *bruschetta*, on grilled meats and fish, as the final lacing on a *ribollita*. All olive oils are monounsaturated fats, hence don't contribute to the buildup of cholesterol in the human body. In fact, it has finally been proved that olive oil inhibits cholesterol formation, which brings medical science back in line with ancient Mediterranean folk wisdom.

Balsamic Vinegar

Balsamic vinegar is a strange substance, more an elixir than a foodstuff. Modena is the center of production of *aceto balsamico*, and it is made there on every scale from artisan to industrial. Fini is the biggest and the best of the large-scale producers. Ordinary vinegar results from a fermentation of wine, cider, or any alcoholic liquid. A vinegar mother (a kind of colonial organism that looks a bit like a jellyfish) converts the alcohol into acetic acid. Balsamic vinegar starts from wine, but no vinegar mother is involved. Instead, the wine is passed gradually through a series of barrels made of different varieties of wood (up to a dozen may be involved) over a course of years. The wine oxidizes, undergoes a very slow bacterial action, and slowly evaporates and concentrates. The result, in five to fifty years, is a dark, smooth, deeply flavored liquid that bears very little relation to commonplace vinegar. Balsamic vinegar is costly, and its price goes up with its age. Small casks of it are ceremonially presented as wedding gifts. A few intense drops of it are used to dress not only salads, but soups, meat, fish, and vegetables. In recipes that specifically require *balsamico*, no other vinegar can be substituted. Otherwise, the vinegar normally used in Italian recipes is good-quality red wine vinegar.

Garlic

Garlic has had a bad press. Properly used, garlic is gentle, fragrant, and definitely nonthreatening. One of the richest, most comforting dishes in the Italian repertory is, in fact, *spaghetti aglio e olio*—*spaghetti* bathed in olive oil in which large amounts of minced garlic (and maybe a single *peperoncino rosso*) have been warmed and softened. If you've had dishes with a heavy, acrid garlic taste, you have in all probability been subjected either to garlic salt (or an equivalent ersatz substance) or to garlic that has been burnt. To avoid that bad taste in your own cooking, first you must start with fresh, firm, clean cloves, pure white or ivory in color—not spotted or sprouting or brown or soft or wrinkled or rocklike. Second, never cook garlic long enough for it to turn brown, even if a recipe says something like "brown the garlic in the oil." Brown is too close to black. Sauté garlic only until it is a light golden color, then either remove it or proceed with the next step in the recipe. Faithful observance of this rule will tame garlic and release its perfume without danger of overpowering other elements in the dish.

Peperoncino Rosso

Hot red pepper is not, as you might think, just a southern taste: Tuscans and Ligurians and Venetians, too, enjoy *diavolillo* (the little devil), as it is sometimes called. This is not a cherry pepper, but a member of the chile family. It is rarely more than an inch long and fire-engine red; firm and lightly wrinkled when dried; long and tapered; straight, not curved like a cayenne. A little *peperoncino* goes a long way, but if reasonably fresh (dried peppers shouldn't be kept around for years, no more than any other spice or herb) its flavor doesn't build into a fire or go beyond the point of pleasant, revivifying warmth. You can control the effect *peperoncino rosso* has on a dish by the length of time you leave it in—the longer, the hotter. The crushed red pepper sold by large spice firms is not a good substitute: Even when not stale, it can't be retrieved and discarded when it's done as much to the dish as you want it to. If you can't get authentic *peperoncino rosso* at a specialty food store, try experimenting carefully with pequin chiles.

Mushrooms

Italians are confirmed mushroom lovers, and they enjoy many wild varieties in addition to ordinary cultivated mushrooms. The principal mushroom used as a condiment is the *porcino* (known to the French as *cepe* and the Germans as *Steinpilz*). *Funghi porcini*, in their dried form, are often called for in recipes to add an earthy pungency to dishes, or to deepen the flavor of cultivated mushrooms. In that same form they are, happily, widely available in the United States. They aren't cheap, but a tiny quantity does a lot of work. You can get extra mileage out of dried mushrooms by filtering the water in which you soak them (to reconstitute them) and using it as part of the liquid called for in your recipe. Fresh *porcini*, with caps up to eight inches in diameter and weighing half a pound apiece, are not a condiment but a magnificent food in themselves. They rarely appear in American markets, and when they do, usually cost their weight in diamonds. A reasonable substitute can be found in *cremosini* (also called *cremini*). These look like a large, dusky-capped, dark-gilled version of domestic mushrooms, but they have a richer flavor and are more fleshy, almost meaty in the manner of *porcini*. You can also try substituting oriental *shiitake* for fresh *porcini*: The texture is different, but the flavor comes close.

Anchovies

Italian delicatessens and specialty food stores should be able to supply you with imported, salt-packed anchovies, which are far superior in taste (and despite being packed in salt, not salty tasting) to most canned, oil-packed anchovies. They are not, however, so neatly cleaned. You have to scrape their skin off —most of it, anyway—which you can do very simply with a knife blade under running water. Then you work the point of the knife down the body to separate the two fillets, discarding the fragile skeleton, the small fins and tail, and any guts that may be attached. The salt tends to partly liquefy the entrails, but that doesn't mean there's anything wrong with the fish. If you can buy salt-packed anchovies only in large quantities, don't worry: Just cover them over with more salt and tuck them away in the refrigerator. They'll keep for quite a long while. If you can't find dry-packed anchovies, try soaking ordinary canned ones for 10 minutes or so in a generous amount of water: that at least will draw off some of their unpleasant "fishiness."

Prosciutto

The word *prosciutto* means simply ham, but 99 percent of the time when Italians say *prosciutto* they mean *prosciutto crudo*, the lightly salted, uncooked, air-cured whole hams that, sliced paper thin, constitute the country's most popular *antipasto*. More thickly cut, *prosciutto crudo* is also used in cooking. At this writing, Italian *prosciutti* are still awaiting U.S. government permission to enter the country, but acceptable domestic versions are available from firms

like Citterio and Volpe and even Hormel. If you can't get those, try substituting
Black Forest ham or—this is trickier, because it can be very salty—Smithfield
ham. *Prosciutto* fat, diced and rendered, is a superb cooking medium for the
battuto of finely chopped vegetables that is the foundation of many Italian
sauces and sautés. There is also a *prosciutto cotto*—our boiled or baked
ham—which is used in Italy primarily as a cooking ingredient.

Pancetta

Pancetta is another one of those ingenious pork products that proliferate all
over Italy. It's made from the same cut of meat we use for bacon, but it isn't
smoked. Instead it is air-cured, sometimes packed with crushed black peppercorns, sometimes not. If not, it is cut and sold from the slab, just like bacon.
If it is cured with pepper, it is usually wrapped around a similarly cured piece
of pork loin, and the whole assemblage is then packed as a thick tube, from
which the amount you want is sliced. In either version, *pancetta* tastes sweeter
and meatier than bacon. It is often used in cooking, particularly to add substance to a sauce. Italians also sometimes use it raw as an *antipasto* meat or
on sandwiches. In almost any recipe that calls for *pancetta*, you can substitute
blanched bacon if necessary, but the flavor will not be quite the same.

———————◆———————

BROTH

We're really back to basics now. Broth is, after all, just flavored water—
but it's the nature of the flavor that counts. Broth is not the same thing
as stock. Stock is heavy and concentrated; broth is lighter in color and flavor.
Stock is usually a means to an end, one ingredient in the building up of a
complex sauce. Broth often can be an end in itself; much pasta is served very
simply *in brodo*. Or broth can be a major component in a dish, as it is in
stracciatella, which is a bowl of broth enriched and clarified just before serving
with a mixture of parsley, *parmigiano*, and eggs beaten together and drizzled
into the boiling broth—Italian egg drop soup, if you will.

Italians also use broth to flavor other dishes, but with a light hand. Often,

Italian cooks will use just a small quantity of broth and, after that is exhausted, add only water to the dish, rather than render it too heavy. Even more important—and this is a fundamental Italian cooking technique—they rarely introduce a lot of liquid at one time and then reduce it. Rather, they keep adding a little bit of broth at a time, so the dish is never more moist than it is supposed to be when finished. The cooking process therefore concentrates the flavors in the solid ingredients rather than dissipating them in the liquid. That, in brief, is the difference between an Italian *risotto* and the rice pilaf technique of other cuisines.

In Italian cooking, it hardly matters if the broth is made with meat or chicken. There are at least as many recipes for broth as there are Italian cooks, and only a few of those are strictly adhered to. Making broth is more art than science, more whim of the cook and luck of the season than either. Try our recipe once, and then feel free to alter ingredients or proportions or cooking times to suit your own palate.

Your butcher can provide you with some of the bones needed, but they will usually be pretty meatless. It is a useful habit to keep a scrap bag in your freezer, in which you collect chicken trimmings (necks, backs, wing tips, gizzards, even cooked chicken carcasses) and meat bones and scraps. Your broth may never turn out exactly the same twice, but these odds and ends will keep it very tasty.

For lighter broths, increase the quantity of celery, carrot, and onion, or add other scraps from your refrigerator—wilted lettuce leaves, celery greens, wrinkled mushrooms, a little parsnip, some limp green beans, or zucchini. Such vegetables may not be handsome, but they've probably still got a bit of flavor that they can contribute to your broth. Making broth is an all-day process, but it requires very little attention, and it provides a wonderfully warming and aromatic background for the activities of a chilly day.

One last word, about fish broths. A very tasty fish broth can be made in much the same way as the following meat broth. Save, or ask your fish man for, a few fish heads, frames, and trimmings. Add a few sliced vegetables— onion, carrot, celery, and a bay leaf—and simmer for 30 to 45 minutes. Strain the liquid carefully before using.

———————◆———————

2 large celery stalks
2 carrots
1 cup coarsely chopped onion (or leek, or scallion)
5 to 6 pounds mixed bones (beef, veal, chicken), preferably with a little meat left on

1 to 2 tomatoes, canned or fresh (about ½ cup)
Fresh herbs, if available (a few sprigs of thyme or oregano, a handful of parsley, or—best of all—parsley root)
1 tablespoon salt
Freshly ground black pepper

Preheat the oven to 375 degrees F. Cut the celery and carrots into large pieces and put them, the onion, and all the bones into a large roasting pan. Bake for at least 1 hour, but not more than 2, until the bones and vegetables are browned (a little char is no problem).

Transfer the bones to a large (3-gallon) pot. Flush the roasting pan and scrape up any loose bits by heating water in it. Pour the water over the bones and cover them by at least 4 inches (approximately 7 quarts of water in all). Add the tomatoes and herbs, the salt, and several grindings of pepper. Bring to the boil and simmer steadily for 4 to 6 hours, covered, until the larger bones are falling apart.

At the end of that time, discard the bones, press the vegetables and meat pieces to extract their liquids, strain the broth, and discard all the solids. Defat the broth if you wish (if you've had a lot of good marrow bones in your mix, you may not want to). Taste for seasoning; in all likelihood, you will want to add more salt. But essentially your broth is ready; it may be used immediately or frozen until needed. Refrigerated, it will keep about a week. This recipe yields about 5 quarts of broth.

WATER

Water is so basic that we never even think about it. Here in the United States, it takes a calamity of nature, like a drought, or a very fundamental kitchen chore, like making broth, to remind us just how important water is. Diners in Italy aren't ever allowed to forget that. The second question you are asked in every restaurant (the first is *rosso o bianco?* and it concerns the wine) is *gasata o non gasata?* Meaning, do you want your mineral water sparkling or still?

Italians automatically assume that you want mineral water; what else would you drink? It's good for your liver, your heartbeat, your kidneys, all the mysterious processes that go on in the healthy human body. If you don't believe that, just read the label of a mineral water bottle and see the catalog of its valuable components and health-giving properties and the certificates of its purity that are stuck all around the bottle.

The strange thing is that it appears to be so. We were once mineral-water skeptics; now we are mineral-water addicts. For us, an Italian meal—any sort of meal, really—is as unthinkable without our bottle of *acqua minerale gasata* as it would be without wine. Mineral water seems to keep the body lubricated and the palate limber. There's probably a scientific explanation for it, but all we know is that we enjoy a meal more with mineral water than without it, that we feel better afterward, and that—maybe this is the real point—we really like the taste of mineral water.

You don't have to be a world traveler to know that some waters taste better than others. Italy is blessed with a few natural sources that are almost matchless in flavor and purity—for instance, the famous Acqua Vergine that aqueducts have been bringing to Rome for two thousand years now, and that accounts for the nationally confessed excellence of the coffee at Bar Tazza d'Oro and Caffè Sant' Eustachio. The United States has several good natural waters of its own, and a few Italian imports (notably Ferrarelle and San Pellegrino, both excellent) are fairly readily available here.

———•———

WINE

So we've come full circle, to the question of wine, the other half of the eucharist-under-two-species that is an Italian meal. Italy produces many more kinds of wine than it does cheese—and that means a lot of wine: more than two thousand kinds, at last (unofficial) count. The vast majority of those wines never see the shores of the United States. Indeed, the vast majority of them never see the banks of the next river or the inside of a bottle. They are consumed within a few miles of where they are made, sold in bulk or in small barrels or in demijohns, or by the liter from the barrel—*vino sfuso*—into whatever jugs and carriers the purchaser brings. A few of those are memorable, as-yet "undiscovered" wines. Many of them are charming—pleasant, delicate, unshippable because of their fragility. Most are merely drinkable, and some are no doubt quite awful. It makes little difference: Almost all will be consumed, usually before the next harvest comes round to fill the barrels again.

Most Italians, except for a small percentage of sophisticates, drink the wines of their region, whatever they are, all their lives, without ever worrying about other possibilities. Wine for them is a food, a necessary beverage. A meal without it is unthinkable, and it is just as unthinkable to devote any thought to wine. You eat the food and wine you grew up with, the food and wine that have grown up together over the centuries, and you don't question the goodness of either.

For us, on this side of the Atlantic, it's not that simple. We didn't grow up with these foods. The combinations aren't bred in our bones—and even if they were, we still wouldn't have access to all the wines to make them work. The tiniest fraction of Italy's hundreds of wines appears in our markets. Fortunately for us, that tiny fraction is overweighted on the side of quality. We may not get all of Italy's wines, but we get a nice percentage of Italy's best wines—a fact that both simplifies our shopping and increases our pleasure. And even though only a fraction of the wines made in Italy are available here, that fraction is still enough to provide a willing American palate with as much, perhaps more, knowledge of Italian wines than all but a handful of Italian oenophiles possess. As the Piedmontese winemaker and historian Renato Ratti so wryly puts it, "The Italian discovery of wine is quite recent."

Italian sophisticates may be only recently discovering the wonderful wines of their own country, but most of those wines have been in place for centuries. This is particularly true of red wines, whose varieties and qualities still follow lines and traditions set generations ago. Since World War II, as new wine-making technologies have emerged, Italian winemakers have made major changes, particularly in the way they handle white wines. California has led the way in this development, and Italian winemakers have happily apprenticed themselves to the New World's techniques. As a consequence, they now produce large quantities of fresh, light, and delightful white wine that makes pleasant drinking on almost any occasion.

The flip side of that coin is that only a handful of white wines in all Italy rise to the levels of greatness that many Italian red wines achieve. But all in all there is an ample choice of wines, both red and white, still and sparkling, dry and sweet, to meet the needs of any dinner occasion.

THE NORTH

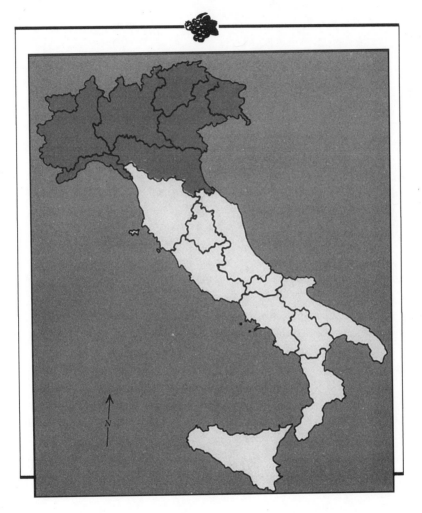

THE NORTHERN ITALIAN MENU

ANTIPASTI

Piedmontese Breadsticks
Grilled Zucchini with Balsamic Vinegar
Sliced Tomatoes with Tuna Sauce
Stuffed Bresaola Rolls • Venetian Liver Pâté • Veal Tartare
Miniature Green Omelets • Miniature Onion Omelets
Rice and Spinach Tart
Roasted Peppers with Ham and Fontina
Baked Artichokes Stuffed with Chicken, Ham, and Mushrooms
Broiled Mushroom Caps Filled with Veal and Pesto

PRIMI

Poached Egg in Broth
Rice and Rape Soup • Chick-Pea and Rape Soup
Friulian Bean and Sauerkraut Soup • Beef Tripe and Vegetable Soup
Venetian-Style Pasta with Beans
Tagliarini with Sage Tomato Sauce • Trenette with Pesto
Pappardelle with Sausage and Cream
Tortellini
Tortellini in Broth • Tortellini with Cream
Tortellini with Bolognese Meat Sauce
Agnolotti Filled with Sweet Potato • Giant Ravioli with Whole Egg Yolks
Gratinéed Crepes with Cheese and Basil
Gnocchi with Prunes • Ofelle
Venetian Rice and Zucchini • Risotto with Sausage
Polenta

SECONDI

Fresh Sardines with Fennel • Broiled Tuna Steaks with Fennel
Grilled Tuna Steaks • Grilled Monkfish
Venetian-Style Braised Cuttlefish

Ligurian Fish Stew • Chicken with Morels
Sauté of Chicken with Salami, Mushrooms, and Chicken Livers
Sautéed Rabbit with Peppers
Herbed Baked Rabbit with Piquant Anchovy Sauce
Duck Braised in Barolo
Guinea Hen with Cabbage and Mushrooms
Sautéed Breaded Veal Chops • Rolled Pan Roast of Veal
Braised Veal Shanks • Lamb with Fresh Horseradish
Lamb Shanks with Beans • Calf's Tongue in Red Wine
Calf's Liver with Sautéed Onions • Oxtails
Roast Loin of Venison • Bollito Misto
La Finanziera • Calf's Liver Sausage Rolls
Baked Eggplant Parma Style

CONTORNI

Asparagus with Hard-Boiled Egg Yolk Mayonnaise
Cabbage in Casserole • Deep-Fried Fennel • Stewed Lentils
Grilled Mushrooms • Venetian Pan-Fried Potatoes
Ligurian Potato-Cheese Pie • Grilled Radicchio di Treviso
Salad with Pancetta and Balsamic Vinegar

DOLCI

Baked Stuffed Peaches
Raspberries, Blueberries, and Strawberries in Grappa
Lario Lemon Cream • Monte Bianco • Bonet
Ladyfingers • Barolo Chocolate Cookies
Miascia • Paradell • Sage-Scented Tea Bread
La Gubana • Almond Torte

It was America's discovery of northern Italian cooking, starting in the mid-seventies, that shattered the long-held American stereotype of Italian cooking as heavy, red, and greasy immigrant fare. There's more than a little irony in the new stereotype of northern Italian cooking itself as lean and elegant. Fact is, northern Italians are probably the heaviest eaters in the peninsula. Certainly they are the largest meat eaters—perhaps because those nearby Alps and their foothills demand that the human furnace be generously stoked, perhaps because the rich pastures of those mountain slopes simply provide more meat on the hoof. For instance, the *antipasti misti* for which Piedmontese restaurants are famous throughout Italy—notorious, if you are a light eater—consist of a procession of dishes that may number up to twenty. Alongside the irresistible *carne cruda all'Albese*, they include such very un-light concoctions as marinated eels or sausages and beans.

Perhaps it's the prominence of meat that has given the cooking of northern Italy such wide acceptance in America: It is in many respects a cuisine at least roughly similar to our own. Of all the Italian regions, dining habits in the North come closest to the northern European and American norm, where a good-size chunk of meat is usually the star attraction of the meal. Ironically, it's in that very respect that the northern culinary style differs most widely from the styles of Italy's other regions.

Generally speaking, the inland or upland cooking of the Italian North is hearty, honest, copious, and tasty, reflecting directly the freshness and quality of its ingredients. The northern hills—Alps, Dolomites, and their foothills—produce lamb and veal, game and wild mushrooms and wonderful white truffles, and big red wines to accompany them. Typical meat dishes run from the well-known, like *costolette alla milanese* or *osso buco*, to the rarer and more intricate, like the exquisite mélange called *la finanziera*, which shows the region's best wines to their best advantage.

Risotto and fresh egg noodles often grace the northern table, but what is ubiquitous, especially when the weather grows chilly, is the region's beloved *polenta*. To call *polenta* simply cornmeal mush is like describing Michelangelo as a well-known Florentine: It's true, but that's not even half the story. *Polenta* is an institution. It's served by itself with grated cheese and freshly ground pepper as a *primo*. As it cooks, cubes of *gorgonzola* or *fontina* may be stirred into it. It's sauced with tomato and sometimes with béchamel. It's combined with meats or vegetables in sauce as a one-dish meal. Cold slabs of *polenta* are buttered and fried or grilled to serve as a *contorno* with a meat or fish, or smeared with the livers of game birds and served as a bed for the roasted birds, their warm juices moistening and flavoring the earthy simplicity of the *polenta*. Accompanied by ample supplies of the area's young red wines or judicious amounts of its greatest reds, *uccelli con polenta* are one of autumn's finest treats.

Polenta typifies the style of cookery that reflects those hard upland winters, a *cucina invernale* that emphasizes substance and authority. Northern Italian dishes stick to the ribs and keep out the chill. They build on basic, earthy flavors—things like rice with sausages, or grilled mushrooms, especially wild ones that taste deeply of the woods. If such cooking seems lean and elegant to American palates, it is because it is honest cooking; the true flavors of the ingredients are allowed to shine through, unobscured by heavy sauces or fussy preparations—and that is a virtue the North shares with all the other Italian cuisines.

When you wander out of the hills and down to the coast, you find the foods you are served in much closer touch with the rest of Italy. The seaside or coastal cooking of the North shares a great deal in style and substance with other parts of the country. The milder coastal climate produces throughout Italy a cooking that is more uniform in techniques and ingredients than what has developed over the centuries in the more isolated inland areas. Coastal cooking, in the North as in the Center and the South, is lighter than the upland style. The marine species available for eating—and all that are available are eaten, without qualm at their ugliness or remorse at their beauty—vary from region to region, as do the spices and herbs that flavor them and the dishes that accompany them. But the basic approach to seafood is much the same throughout Italy: Cook it fresh, cook it fast, and interfere as little as possible with its own flavor.

In northern coastal cooking, *polenta* yields pride of place to rice, just as game gives way to fish. Adriatic fish, from the lagoon of Venice around to the gulf of Trieste, are particularly tasty, and especially prized are the smallest of them: tiny shrimp and squid (*calamaretti* only an inch or two long); soft-shell crabs (*molleche*) the size of the fiddler crabs you see running from the tide; clams no bigger than a bean; baby soles (the same variety as the prized Dover sole) of three or four inches; whitebait; sea sparrows; sea dates; sea truffles; and small razor clams. The profusion of species is seemingly far more numerous than what the much larger Atlantic and Pacific oceans offer our fish markets.

Especially in Venice, the favorite way to handle those tiny finfish and mollusks is to deep-fry them, and the clams and their kin are most usually steamed very simply with a little olive oil and perhaps a touch of white wine, perhaps a clove of garlic, but always plenty of fresh parsley and freshly ground pepper. Everything turns on the bright, just-out-of-the-sea flavor of the fish. Happily, some ocean fish available here do correspond to Mediterranean kinds and allow for very authentic approximations of the flavors of the Italian originals, and those are the seafood recipes we have concentrated on in this book.

You will not find a lot of tomato in any of these northern dishes, nor much garlic—just a whiff of either for an accent or an aroma is the usual rule. The typical flavors of northern dishes run to the assertive; everything from the heady scent of white truffle and the woodsy pungency of *funghi porcini* to the vivacity of a classic *pesto genovese*.

Northern dishes can be complex and elegant, but they are rarely delicate; not spicy, but bold and forthright. Sauces tend to be highly concentrated rather than abundant; meats and fishes are never awash with their dressings but modestly garnished. Pasta sauces too follow this practice. What Americans are likely at first to think a skimpy amount of sauce is in fact the norm throughout Italy, and the pasta tastes the better for it.

One final thought to aid your appreciation of the dishes of the Italian North. As elsewhere in Italy, every northern province speaks its own dialect, and depending on where you are, you will detect modifications of the basic Italian by French or German or Serbian or Croat. The same infusions have enriched the cuisines of the region. Cooking reflects geography not just through terrain but also through politics, and the North is where Italy joins the rest of Europe. France, Switzerland, Austria, and Yugoslavia all touch Italy here, and all have touched northern Italian cooking, so don't be surprised to find authentically Italian dishes that evoke memories of French sauces or German dumplings. Cooking has always been an international affair, and just as Italy gave the rest of the world forks, so it has helped itself to whatever it could assimilate to its own style and taste.

———————◆———————

THE WINES OF NORTHERN ITALY

Northern Italy is a paradise for the wine lover. It produces an abundance of wines of an amazingly high level of quality—everything from light, aperitif-style whites like Pinot grigio to hefty, long-aging reds like Barolo and Barbaresco, with significant stops in between at serious white wines like Gavi and Tocai and youthful, pleasant reds like Barbera and Dolcetto. On top of that, the North is grappa country; every wine zone, almost every township, distills its own special kind from its own peculiar *vinaccie* (the solid residues left after grapes have fermented into wine: what the French call *marc*, the English pomace). So we have grappa from Piedmont and Trento and Friuli and the Veneto, grappa from Nebbiolo grapes and from Picolit, from Sauvignon, from Amarone, and even from single vineyards, like Brunate in the Barolo zone.

The best wine-growing terrains of northern Italy share pretty much the same general qualities, even though climates and soil compositions can vary tremendously. Technically, it's all subalpine, and the grapes are cultivated just about everywhere a suitably sunny slope at sufficiently hospitable altitude offers itself. The principal wine-producing zones from the point of view of the American market are:

- The Piedmont, especially around the towns of Asti (where the famous Spumante, one of the world's greatest dessert wines, comes from) and Alba (home of incomparable white truffles and some of Italy's finest red wines)
- The valley of the Adige river in the region of Trentino-Alto Adige (a source of some red and much fine white wine)
- The area of the Veneto lying around the town of Verona and running west to Lake Garda (pleasant, light reds and whites and one memorable big red wine)
- The easternmost hills of Friuli, just north of Trieste and right against the Yugoslavian border (some red but primarily fine white wines)
- The Veneto around Treviso (some nice inexpensive sparkling wines and a good production of still red and white wines)
- A section of Lombardy midway between Milano and Brescia (lovely sparkling wines, perhaps Italy's best dry sparklers, made according to the exacting champagne method).

For those familiar with American wine, it helps in understanding the extremely varied output of these many large areas to think of it as dominated by the production of varietal wines, that is, wines made entirely (or almost so) from the juices of a single kind of grape. Indeed, many of the grape varieties cultivated here are familiar international favorites: Cabernet sauvignon, Merlot, and Pinot noir (Pinot nero locally) among the reds, and Chardonnay, Pinot blanc and Pinot gris (Pinot bianco and grigio, respectively), Riesling (Riesling renano), Gewurztraminer (sometimes Traminer aromatico), and Sauvignon blanc among the whites. But there are many other, locally famous white grape varieties (for instance, Tocai, or Verduzzo), and the most important red grape of the area is one not much cultivated outside Italy, the Nebbiolo.

The Nebbiolo grape makes a wonderful range of full-bodied red wines. A few are suitable for drinking fairly young, at three to five years of age, but the noblest of them are much better laid down for aging. The least of the Nebbiolo wines (usually called simply by the grape's name, Nebbiolo) are round and full, with deep flavors of fruit and earth. The best of them—Barolo and Barbaresco—rank with any wines from anywhere in the world: They are big wines with big bouquets, smelling richly of truffles and tobacco and pepper and even tar; deep, intense scents that reflect the depth and intensity of their flavors. These are wines to serve in places of honor, with great roasts of meat or game, with richly sauced dishes, or with strong cheeses.

The Nebbiolo production zone includes several subzones and many different appellations. It centers on the Piedmont, with three separate and very different districts there: loosely, Carema in the west, Alba in the center, and Novara in the east. Nebbiolo has also established large buttresses farther east in a distinctive area of northern Lombardy, the Valtellina, and to the west in the half-French province of Val d'Aosta, where the wine is called Donnaz. Oenologically, the Nebbiolo wine classification includes a few well-known appellations and many less famous ones, most of whose labels don't even mention the word Nebbiolo. Barolo and Barbaresco, Gattinara and Spanna, Boca and Ghemme and Fara, Sassella and Inferno and Grumello—all are wines made either exclusively or predominantly from the Nebbiolo grape, as is also, of course, Nebbiolo. Most often, the wines made from Nebbiolo grapes take the names of the regions or towns that are or were the centers of their production:

- Donnaz in the region of Val d'Aosta
- Carema in the extreme western Piedmont
- Barolo and Barbaresco in the middle of Piedmont
- Gattinara, Ghemme, Bramaterra, Lessona, Sizzano, Fara, and Boca in northeastern Piedmont
- Grumello, Inferno, Sassella, and Valgella farther east, in the Valtellina, the Nebbiolo-growing section of Lombardy.

In the central Piedmont growing zone, around the small city of Alba, the grape is called Nebbiolo, and in addition to Barolo and Barbaresco the zone also produces a lesser but by no means insignificant wine, grown on lower slopes of the hills and called Nebbiolo d'Alba. Farther east in Piedmont near Novara, the grape is called Spanna, and much good wine used to be bottled simply under that name. Some still is, though the township appellations now predominate. In Lombardy, the grape is known as Chiavennasca, but we have never encountered a bottled wine of that name either here or in Italy. What you will occasionally encounter from this area, in addition to the four local names (Sassella, Inferno, Grumello, Valgella), is Sfurzat, a Nebbiolo-based wine vinified somewhat in the manner of Amarone (discussed below) to reach higher alcohol levels and greater intensity of flavor.

Most experts agree that the Nebbiolo grape reaches its greatest heights around Alba, and that Barolo and Barbaresco constitute its supreme achievements. Both are very big wines, often hard and tannic in their youth and needing many years of cellaring before they show their true worth. Both are emphatically wines to buy young and relatively inexpensively, since fully mature bottles are always scarce and costly.

Barolo is already three years old when it comes on the market, because it must be aged minimally two years in barrel and one in bottle before sale. Barbaresco's regulations call for a year less barrel age, but makers of both wines often substantially exceed those minimal requirements: They pride themselves on making wines that are built not merely to last, but to improve with age. Nebbiolo d'Alba, from this same area, is usually lighter bodied and faster maturing than Barolo or Barbaresco. It can be best enjoyed when it is between five and eight years old, whereas Barolos and Barbarescos from good harvests start hitting their stride only at ten to twelve or more years of age.

Many excellent makers of all three send wines to the American market: Ceretto, Conterno, Cordero, Fontanafredda, Gaja, Marchese de Gresy, Moresco, Pio Cesare, Produttori di Barbaresco, Prunotto, Renato Ratti, Vietti—those are some of the many good labels to look for. And look especially for their *cru* bottlings, wines made from the grapes of a single prized vineyard, like Brunate, Cannubbi, or Rocche in Barolo; or Asili, Martinenga, or Montestefano in Barbaresco. Wines like these will not be cheap by any absolute standard, but by the relative scale of value-for-dollar that prevails among the great wines of the world, the quality they deliver for the price you pay often makes them bargains indeed.

Spanna, Gattinara, and the wines of the other Novara townships rarely have the heft of the three Alba wines, though they frequently show more suppleness. While by no means small wines, they create a primary impression of grace and elegance. Antoniolo, Dessilani, Monsecco, and Vallana are the key makers to look for. Several of them offer single-vineyard bottlings; especially fine are those from Antoniolo and Vallana. The prices of these wines, which are still pretty much neglected outside Italy, tend to be both absolutely and relatively much lower than those of the Alba wines, which are already in the process of being "discovered" by international connoisseurs.

The Valtellina (Lombardy) Nebbiolo wines—Sassella, Inferno, Grumello, and Valgella—usually feel softer on the palate than those of Piedmont. They tend to have huge aromas, but less follow-through in flavor than their cousins to the west. However, they have what is often the advantage of maturing sooner and what is always the advantage of costing less. Depending on vintage conditions, they will reach their peak at anywhere from five to ten years old, at which age they make marvelous partners for strongly flavored meats and cheeses. We think of them as superb holiday-dinner wines, forceful enough to make their presence felt amid the merriment, but not so powerful as to overwhelm the table. The best makers to look for here are Negri and Rainoldi.

Northern Italy's other great red wine, Amarone, is one that breaks most of the rules. It is not a single-varietal wine, but one blended from a number of different grapes. It is an enormous, slow-aging wine from a region that otherwise produces only light wines intended to be drunk young. And on top of that, it is not fermented from freshly picked grapes but rather from selected, top-quality bunches that have been allowed to dry and become slightly raisiny before crushing.

Amarone comes from the Veneto, where the several varieties of grapes that compose it grow on picture-book hillsides around Verona. It is—surprisingly—vinified from exactly the same mix of grapes that produces the popular and very light red wine, Valpolicella. Despite that, Amarone possesses exceptional robustness and depth and, when properly mature, very great elegance. Because its grapes are partly dried before they are fermented, Amarone has an incredibly rich but totally dry fruitiness, combined with a high level of alcohol: 14 percent is the legal minimum, and most Amarones easily exceed that. That concentration of flavor and intensity makes for a real powerhouse of a wine—so much so that many of its devotees prefer it after dinner, with a rich cheese (a creamy *gorgonzola dolce*, say, or a fine nutty *parmigiano*), rather than as an accompaniment to dinner.

Like Barolo and Barbaresco, Amarone is a fine wine to buy young and lay away for a few years or decades. There have been many good recent vintages: 1983, 1982, 1979, 1978, and especially 1977. Good older vintages include 1974, 1970, 1969, 1964, and 1962. Recommendable larger makers include Allegrini (luscious fruit, velvety wine), Bertani (matures splendidly over ten or fifteen years), Bolla (a good introduction to Amarone: more restrained than many others), Masi (wines somewhat more accessible younger), and Tommasi (excellent fruitiness, early accessibility). Among the smallest producers, Le Ragose and Quintarelli are the names to look for.

A shopping tip about Amarone. The full name of the wine is Recioto della Valpolicella Amarone. Amarone is the key term that indicates a fully dry dinner wine. If the label simply says Recioto della Valpolicella, the bottle contains a sweet red dessert wine—often quite wonderful, but not exactly what you want with your venison steaks or your roast goose.

Northern Italy also abounds in lighter red wines, suitable for everyday drinking and less grand dinners than Amarone and the big Nebbiolo wines seem to require. From the same area as Amarone come the well-known Valpolicella and Bardolino, two very light red wines marked by similar freshness and acidity. They are partnered by two similarly styled white wines, the well-known Soave and its kin, Bianco di Custoza. All four of these are versatile, pleasing wines, meant to be drunk with simple foods and as young as possible. Because of their acidity, even the reds can stand a bit of chilling, a fact that makes them all very useful picnic, party, and aperitif wines.

From the area around Alba we get Barbera (the name is both the wine and the grape it's made from, and is emphatically not to be confused with Barbaresco) and Dolcetto, both medium-bodied, fully dry red wines that make good partners to dishes that range from meat or cheese *antipasti* to substantial *secondi*. Barbera is the lighter-bodied of the two, and usually slightly more acidic, with a pleasing little bitter tang. Dolcetto is fuller and fruitier and often a bit softer. Either wine would easily be an improvement on Beaujolais in the sort of non-Italian dining circumstances that call for a young, fruity, and not-overpowering red wine.

Although predominantly red wine country, the Piedmont also turns out two important whites: the still Gavi and the sparkling Asti. Gavi is made from the Cortese grape, and you may see bottles labeled variously as simply Gavi, or Gavi di Gavi (from the heart of the growing zone), or Cortese di Gavi, or simply Cortese. At its best, Gavi can be a full-bodied and sapid wine, round in the mouth and capable of matching well with rich fish courses or fowl or white-fleshed meats. Good, reliable producers include La Scolca, Villa Banfi (Principessa), Bersano, Contratto, Granduca, La Giustiniana, and Pio Cesare.

Everybody knows—or thinks he knows—Asti Spumante. It may be Italy's most famous wine, and most people think of it as cloyingly sweet. Once that was true, but things have changed in Asti (that, by the way, is the name of the town where the wine is made; *spumante* simply means sparkling, and outside of Asti is applied to dry wines as well as sweet). Modern fermentation techniques now allow vintners to extract maximum flavor from the wonderfully aromatic Moscato grape (the only grape from which Asti Spumante is made) while controlling sugar levels and retaining a nice bright acidity to balance them. The result is that Asti Spumante stands almost unrivaled among sparkling dessert wines. The best producers include Bersano, Calissano, Cinzano, Contratto, Fontanafredda, Gancia, and Martini & Rossi. A small amount of still, sweet Moscato is also produced, and it too can make a lovely dessert: Look particularly for bottles from Ceretto, Valentino (Podere Rocche dei Manzoni), or Vietti.

Outside the Piedmont, northern Italy produces an amazing profusion of dry white dinner and aperitif wines, most of them emanating from two major areas, the valley of the Adige river in the region of Trentino-Alto Adige and the easternmost hills of Friuli-Venezia Giulia. Both regions specialize in varietal wines, turning out relatively light-bodied, fruity, and bright versions of internationally popular white grapes: Chardonnay, Sauvignon blanc, Pinot bianco, Pinot grigio, Gewurztraminer, and Riesling renano. Pinot grigio in particular, with its light fruitiness and bright, dry acidity, makes a wonderful aperitif wine as well as a reliable everyday white.

Here is a list of some of the more widely available, reliable-to-superb producers of white wines (but don't entirely ignore their reds) from these two regions:

- Trentino-Alto Adige: Bollini, Cavit, Gaierhoff, Istituto Agrario di San Michelle all'Adige, Kettmeir, Alois Lageder, Pojer & Sandri, Santa Margherita
- Friuli-Venezia Giulia: Borgo Conventi, Collavini, EnoFriulia, Livio Felluga, Gradnik, Gravner, Jermann, Plozner, Pradio, Russiz Superiore (Marco Felluga), Tenuta Santa Anna.

Italians for the most part treat Chardonnay in a distinctive style that departs widely from French and California handling of the grape. With very few exceptions (Gaja in the North, Frescobaldi and Lungarotti in the Center), Italian Chardonnays are light-bodied (medium-bodied at very most), markedly fruity, and brightened by high acidity—wines to drink as young as possible with a wide variety of foods. Sauvignon blanc, too, is often treated in this style, though some vintners (Borgo Conventi, Russiz Superiore, Jermann, Gradnik) seem interested in experimenting with this variety to develop a deeper, more resonant wine—a more important wine, in effect.

Friuli also possesses a native grape of great charm, the Tocai (pronounced to rhyme with high, and not to be confused with the sweet Hungarian dessert wine, Tokay, pronounced to rhyme with hay). Natives of the region savor the spice-and-nut overtones of this medium-bodied white wine, and they drink it on nearly every occasion and with nearly every sort of food (even some that would seem to demand red wine), which is an accurate indication of its versatility and pleasingness. Livio Felluga's Tocai is generally reckoned to be a benchmark. Another local grape, the Verduzzo, also makes a pleasing and distinctive white wine of the same name. Small quantities of it appear in the United States at, unfortunately, irregular intervals.

The Treviso area turns out many of the same sort of varietal wines as Trentino and Friuli, but it adds to that list some pleasant dry sparkling wines—Prosecco and Cartizze—and a handful of very interesting blended reds. These last are wines consciously in the Bordeaux style, mixing Cabernet (both sauvignon and franc) and Merlot grapes to achieve a balanced, subtle wine capable of maturing well in bottles. In Treviso and in Friuli these grapes are usually made into eponymous varietal wines of medium body, great charm, and some small aging ability. While those varietal reds are very pleasant to drink, the Bordeaux-style blends offer a lot more interest and depth and promise much more for the future of the area. Right now, the hands-down best maker of these sorts of wines is Conte Loredan Gasparini: His labels bear the name Venegazzù.

Finally, the Franciacorta zone in Lombardy produces both Bordelais-type blends like the last described (Ca' del Bosco is the best of these) and some absolutely top quality champagnes, though by Common Market law they can't be called that. Look for names like Bellavista, Berlucchi, and Ca' del Bosco. Other fine Italian champagne makers (not situated in this zone) include Cinzano, Contratto, Equipe 5, Ferrari, Gancia, Martini & Rossi, and Riccadonna.

Part of the Italian culinary philosophy holds that you should waste nothing. Winemakers operate by that principle too, and in line with it, even the solids left after fermenting the grapes are routinely turned to account. All through the North, they are soaked and refermented, and the weak wine that results is distilled into grappa, a brandy that varies from town to town and province to province as greatly as the grapes they grow and the wines they make from them. That great variety of flavors and aromas constitutes one of the greatest pleasures of grappa for those who have acquired the taste—and it usually requires just one exposure to the northern idea of hospitality to acquire it, since grappa's other greatest virtue is that it is one of the world's most efficient digestives.

Grappas can bear either brand names (usually those from large distilleries, like Stock's Grappa Julia, the largest selling grappa in Italy), or regional names (Grappa di Barolo, Grappa di Barbaresco), or the name of the grape they're made from (Grappa di Nebbiolo, Grappa di Sauvignon, etc.). They come in two basic styles: unaged, clear as they run from the still (these are usually served well chilled, which seems to free their heady aromas and rein in their youthful fire); or aged for one or more years in one or more kinds of wood. The latter may be any color from a faint straw (probably only briefly aged in wood) to almost coffee-black, with aromas and flavors as complex and intriguing as any Cognac. Aged grappas should never be served chilled. Rather, treat them like Cognac, and pour them into large snifter glasses, the better to enjoy their wonderful bouquet.

A final international note. Popular as grappa is all through the Italian North, way out east near Trieste the Yugoslavian plum brandy slivovitz vies with it for the place of honor after dinner.

The lists that follow present a brief guide to the northern Italian wines that, at this writing, are widely available in the United States.

RED WINES

NAME	PLACE OF ORIGIN	CHARACTERISTICS	SERVE WITH/AS
Amarone	Veneto	big, full-bodied, long-aging	roasts, game, strong cheese
Barbera	Piedmont	light, dry	antipasti, primi, light secondi
Barbaresco	Piedmont	full-bodied, tannic, long-aging	roasts, game, strong cheese
Bardolino	Veneto	light, fruity, acidic, dry	antipasti, primi, light secondi
Barolo	Piedmont	full-bodied, tannic, long-aging	roasts, game, strong cheese
Cabernet	Lombardy, Trentino, Friuli	medium-bodied, soft, fruity, dry	meat antipasti, primi, simple secondi
Dolcetto	Piedmont	medium-bodied, soft, fruity, dry	meat antipasti, primi, simple secondi
Merlot	Trentino, Friuli, Veneto	medium-bodied, soft, fruity, dry	meat antipasti, primi, simple secondi
Valpolicella	Veneto	light, fruity, acidic, dry	antipasti, primi, light secondi

Carema, Gattinara, Ghemme, Grumello, Inferno, Nebbiolo, Sassella, Spanna, Valgella, and Valtellina are all similar to Barbaresco, though slightly lighter-bodied

WHITE WINES

NAME	PLACE OF ORIGIN	CHARACTERISTICS	SERVE WITH/AS
Asti Spumante	Piedmont	sparkling, fruity, sweet	dessert
Bianco di Custoza	Veneto	light, clean, acidic	as aperitif; with antipasti, primi, light secondi
Chardonnay	Friuli, Trentino	medium-bodied, aromatic, full-flavored	antipasti, primi, fish, white meats
Cortese, Gavi, Cortese di Gavi	Piedmont	medium-bodied, pleasantly tart	fish, fowl, simple veal dishes, primi, antipasti
Moscato	Piedmont	sweet, fruity	dessert
Pinot bianco	Friuli, Trentino	medium-bodied, aromatic, full-flavored	antipasti, primi, fish, white meats
Pinot grigio	Trentino, Friuli	light- to medium-body, bright, dry, and fruity	as aperitif; with antipasti, primi, light secondi
Prosecco	Veneto	bright, clean, fruity; both still and sparkling	as aperitif; with antipasti, primi, light secondi
Riesling	Friuli, Trentino	medium-bodied, very aromatic, delicate flavor	as aperitif; with antipasti, primi, fish, white meats
Sauvignon	Friuli, Trentino	bright, herbal, acidic	as aperitif; with antipasti, primi, light secondi
Soave	Veneto	light, clean, acidic	as aperitif; with antipasti, primi, light secondi
Tocai	Friuli	medium-bodied, nutty aroma and flavor	as aperitif; with primi and simple secondi

ANTIPASTI

For everyday dining in the Italian home, *antipasti* can be quite minimal—a few thin slices of *prosciutto* or a local *salame*, some olives, or even just a few crisp stalks of celery or fennel. During the months when the figs come ripe, the most frequently served *antipasto* all over Italy has to be *prosciutto* and figs: paper-thin slices of pink, moist ham surrounded by meltingly ripe green-skinned globes of sweet, soft fruit. Right behind that in popularity come *prosciutto* and melon, especially the succulent, small variety of cantaloupe one finds all through the Mediterranean countries. Both combinations are ambrosial in their utter simplicity.

That, however, is just about as elaborate as an *antipasto* ever gets at home. After a large midday dinner, in fact, the evening family meal may omit an *antipasto* entirely. But in a restaurant or for a special occasion at home, the story is very different. In the North especially, *antipasto* takes on a life of its own and may very well become the star of the feast.

We discovered this fact many years ago, on our first visit to the Piedmont, when we accepted a restaurateur's suggestion that we try his *antipasto misto*. Restaurants all over Italy offer mixed *antipasto*, and we assumed that this one would consist of a single plate of assorted items—probably, like most *antipasti misti*, a sampling of the various items listed on the menu under *antipasti*. Our error was soon revealed, as dish succeeded dish and the antipasto seemed destined to go on forever. *Bresaola* and *salame* and sausages cooked with beans, fresh anchovy fillets and marinated eel, *frittatine* of onions and of zucchini, salads of mushroom and of *nervetti* (a substance derived from some unfindable and probably unspeakable place in a young steer): fifteen dishes in all, after which we were expected—the local people do it all the time—to go on to *primi* and *secondi*, and at least to consider cheese and dessert. We were lucky we had enough strength left to order the grappa we needed to tamp all that food down. It was wonderful, but . . . So a word to the wise, if you're traveling in the North of Italy: Whenever you hear the word *misto* attached to any dish or course—but especially *antipasto*—don't say yes until you ask how many.

———————◆———————

Piedmontese Breadsticks

[GRISSINI]

These are a scaled-down version of the giant free-form breadsticks that are laid directly on your tablecloth in Piedmontese restaurants. They're good alone, or with a slice of *prosciutto* wrapped around them, or a smear of mixed butter-and-truffle paste and then the *prosciutto.* They'll keep crisp for several days in the kind of earthenware cylinder designed for cooling white wine. Quantities given make about 2 dozen.

———————◆———————

½ recipe olive-oil bread dough (page 20)

Make the dough as directed, letting it rise once. Preheat an oven lined with baking tiles to 425 degrees F.

On a floured work surface, roll the dough out to a rectangle about 12 inches by 14 inches, and ¼ inch thick. (It's important to have the dough an even thickness; otherwise the *grissini* will burn on the thin end.) With a pizza wheel, cut the dough into ½-inch-wide strips along the 14-inch side. Place them on a lightly floured board, for easier transport to the oven.

Lay out the strips of dough on the hot oven tiles, leaving an inch or so of space between. (If they won't all fit, leave them on the board, covered with a towel, for a second batch.) Bake 12 minutes, or until the *grissini* are a light golden brown. Transfer them to a rack to cool.

Grilled Zucchini with Balsamic Vinegar

[ZUCCHINI AL BALSAMICO]

This deceptively simple dish offers a wonderful richness of flavor. The fresh zucchini take on real sophistication from the balsamic vinegar. Like many other dishes that are based on grilled vegetables, this one tastes even better if you cook the zucchini over a wood or charcoal fire. The whole process requires about 15 minutes for cutting and cooking and about 1 hour for the flavors to ripen.

———————◆———————

4 medium zucchini (1¼ pounds)   Salt
4 to 6 sprigs fresh thyme   1 tablespoon balsamic vinegar
½ cup olive oil

Preheat a broiler with the rack on its highest setting. Scrub the zucchini and cut them, unpeeled, crosswise on the diagonal into ¼-inch-thick slices. Wash the thyme and strip the leaflets from the branches.

Brush the zucchini slices on both sides with olive oil and place them on the broiler pan. Broil 3 minutes to a side, until they are soft and turning golden.

Lay out the zucchini slices in a single layer on a plate, salt them lightly, and sprinkle 3 to 4 drops of balsamic vinegar on each one. Then sprinkle on the fresh thyme. Cover the dish with plastic wrap or aluminum foil and let it sit at room temperature for at least an hour before serving.

WINE SUGGESTION
A good dry white wine matches well here: Pinot grigio if you prefer a lighter, more acidic taste, Pinot bianco for a fuller, rounder style.

Sliced Tomatoes with Tuna Sauce
[POMODORO TONNATO]

This clever adaptation of a much more elaborate dish, *vitello tonnato*, is a fine way to highlight summer's ripest, top-of-the-season tomatoes.

FOR THE SAUCE

1 egg	1 can (7 ounces) Italian tuna packed
1 teaspoon Dijon mustard	in olive oil
⅛ teaspoon salt	1 anchovy fillet
2 tablespoons lemon juice	2 tablespoons capers
1 cup olive oil	

1½ pounds ripe tomatoes	8 oil-cured black olives
1 lemon, quartered	

Make the tuna sauce:
Process the egg, mustard, salt, and 1 tablespoon of the lemon juice in a blender or food processor for 1 minute. Gradually add the olive oil in a thin stream of droplets, to make a mayonnaise. Add the tuna and all its oil, the anchovy, capers, and remaining 1 tablespoon lemon juice. Process until smooth.

Assemble the dish:
Cut the tomatoes into ¼-inch slices. Spread a large serving platter with a
(continued)

thin layer of the tuna sauce. Lay out the tomato slices in an overlapping pattern on the platter. Mask them with the remaining sauce.

The dish can be refrigerated at this point for an hour or two. When ready to serve, garnish with lemon quarters and olives.

WINE SUGGESTION

Almost any dry white wine will taste just fine with this, and even Verona's two quaffing reds—the light, acid Bardolino and Valpolicella—will accompany it very nicely, especially when served lightly chilled, as they almost always are in the North in the heat of the summer.

Stuffed Bresaola Rolls

[INVOLTINI DI BRESAOLA]

Bresaola is a lean, dense cut of beef that has been air-dried in the manner of the best *prosciutto*. Like *prosciutto*, it is often served as an *antipasto* by itself, sliced paper-thin. *Bresaola* is sometimes sold in the United States under the name *bundnerfleisch*, which is what the Swiss right across the northern Italian border call it. *Speck*, a sort of Tyrolean version of *prosciutto* (lightly smoked in addition to being air-dried), can also be used for these recipes, though the result tends to be more unctuous and rich that way. *Speck*, too, is often sliced very thin and served alone as an *antipasto* throughout the Italian Alps and Dolomites. Very good *speck* is now being made in this country. Making the two fillings in this recipe is the essence of simplicity, but the results are anything but negligible.

———————◆———————

24 slices bresaola (about ¼ pound)

FOR FILLING #1

1½ ounces *gorgonzola dolce*   **1½ ounces unsalted butter**

FOR FILLING #2

¼ pound soft young Italian goat cheese (e.g., *caprini*)   **¼ teaspoon freshly ground black pepper**
1½ teaspoons olive oil

Bring the cheeses and the butter to room temperature. In one small bowl, mash the butter and *gorgonzola* together into a smooth paste. In another, make a paste of the goat cheese, olive oil, and pepper.

Spread about 1 teaspoon of a filling on a slice of *bresaola* and roll it into a tube. Make 12 rolls with each filling and arrange them attractively on a platter. Chill the *involtini* briefly before serving.

WINE SUGGESTION
Excellent with a crisp white wine like Pinot grigio, a dry Spumante (even an Italian champagne-method sparkler), or a relatively full-bodied white wine such as one of the Cortese-based wines.

Venetian Liver Pâté
[PÂTÉ DI FEGATO ALLA VENEZIANA]

This simple, delicious pâté was designed as a way of using leftover *fegato alla veneziana*, Venice's hallmark dish of palest pink calf's liver and mild, sweet onions. Since we've found that there are rarely any leftovers, this recipe starts the pâté from scratch. The treatment of the liver differs a little from our main-course recipe (page 120); essentially, the preparation can be a little less delicate when the liver is not to be served fresh. It's an elegant spread for toast triangles, and it also goes nicely on plain crackers. Quantities given will make about 2½ cups. Total preparation time is under an hour, plus time to chill and firm the pâté. It keeps well, refrigerated, for up to a week.

¾ pound calf's liver, sliced very thin
½ pound plus 2 tablespoons butter
3 tablespoons olive oil
2 cups thin-sliced large yellow (Bermuda) onion

¼ cup minced parsley
¼ cup broth
Salt
Freshly ground black pepper

Rinse the liver slices and trim any bits of tube or tough membrane. Remove the skin only if it will come away easily, without tearing the delicate meat. Pat the slices dry.

Melt the 2 tablespoons of butter with the olive oil in a very large skillet over medium heat. When the foam subsides, add the onions and parsley. Stir well, cover the pan, and reduce heat to very low. Stew the onions gently for 30 minutes, or until very soft, stirring occasionally.

Uncover the pan, raise heat to medium, and add the liver. Brown the pieces quickly on both sides, then add the broth and cook, stirring occasionally, about 5 minutes. The liver should still be moist.

Remove the pan from the heat and let the contents cool to room temperature.

(continued)

Meanwhile, cut the ½ pound of butter into 12 to 16 small pieces and leave them unrefrigerated.

Scrape the entire contents of the sauté pan into the bowl of a blender or food processor and purée until smooth. With the motor still running, drop in the pieces of butter one at a time. Continue blending until the mixture is again smooth. Transfer the pâté to a serving bowl and chill it thoroughly.

WINE SUGGESTION

This dish loves wine of all sorts, so choose your wine according to what you're serving around it. A soft red, like Merlot or Cabernet (from Friuli or the Veneto or Trentino), would be excellent, and a simple dry Spumante (Prosecco or Cartizze, for instance) would be even better.

Veal Tartare

[CARNE CRUDA ALL'ALBESE]

This elegant *antipasto* could also be served as the main course in a luncheon or light supper. Its goodness depends entirely on the quality of the ingredients. The palest pink veal, the best extra-virgin olive oil, and well-aged imported *parmigiano* are what keep the dish from being just another *steak tartare*. In this dish's native city of Alba (white truffle capital of the world), in season, truffles replace the mushrooms. But fine firm white mushrooms are preferable to canned truffles. The veal can be ground and the minced mushrooms prepared an hour or so in advance, but the remaining preparation should be done only when ready to serve.

1 pound lean veal shoulder	⅓ cup olive oil
⅔ pound small firm white mushrooms	2 teaspoons salt
	Freshly ground black pepper
2 large garlic cloves	A large chunk of *parmigiano*
3 tablespoons freshly grated *parmigiano*	2 lemons, quartered

Trim all fat and sinew off the veal. Grind the veal fine in a meat grinder or food processor and put it into a large bowl.

Reserve 8 small, attractive mushrooms. Mince the rest. Place a few tablespoons of minced mushroom in the corner of a lintless dish towel, close over the towel, and wring it over the sink to press out all the juices in the mushrooms. Separate the fragments and add them to the veal. Repeat with the remaining minced mushrooms.

Shortly before serving time, put the garlic cloves through a press and add them to the veal, along with the grated cheese, olive oil, salt, and freshly ground pepper to taste. Mix well, then form into an attractive mound on a serving platter.

Slice the reserved mushroom caps very thin and strew them over and around the veal. With a vegetable peeler, shave about ⅓ cup of slivers of *parmigiano* off the chunk, and strew these over and around the veal. Garnish with lemon quarters.

Serve at once. Each diner should squeeze lemon juice over the meat just before eating (any earlier, and the acid in the juice would "cook" the meat).

WINE SUGGESTION

This great dish deserves a serious red wine and will match well with all but the heaviest and most robust of them. In and around Alba, its traditional partners are top-quality Dolcetto (Prunotto or Vietti, for example) or Nebbiolo d'Alba (Ceretto, Gaja, Prunotto, Vietti, etc.). If you wish, you can instead serve a substantial white wine: Gavi di Gavi, Gaja's Chardonnay, or Jermann's Vintage Tunina.

Miniature Green Omelets

[FRITTATINE ALLE ERBE]

Frittatine are savory little vegetable pancakes. They should be firmer and drier than a French-style omelet, though still moist and supple. The amounts given here make 8 *frittatine*: Serve 2 per person if this is the only *antipasto*. This dish also works well for a light lunch. The vegetables for the filling may be prepared up to a day in advance.

½ pound spinach
½ pound Swiss chard
1 small leek
4 to 6 ounces large yellow (Bermuda) onion
⅔ cup olive oil

6 to 8 basil leaves, coarsely chopped
6 to 8 sage leaves, coarsely chopped
Salt
Freshly ground black pepper
8 eggs

Wash the spinach and chard, trimming off stems. Trim the leek, slice it lengthwise, cut it into ½-inch slices, and wash the pieces carefully. Cut the onion into ¼-inch slices. Put all the vegetables into a large pot.

Bring a kettle of water to the boil. Pour boiling water over the vegetables to cover them generously. Cover the pot and simmer for 10 minutes, then drain and let sit until cool enough to handle. Lightly squeeze them and coarsely chop them.

Heat 4 tablespoons of the olive oil in a frying pan; add the vegetables, basil, sage, ½ teaspoon salt, and ⅛ teaspoon pepper and toss over moderate heat for 2 to 3 minutes.

For each *frittatina*, beat 1 egg in a small bowl with a little salt and pepper. Stir in 3 tablespoons of the vegetable mixture. Heat 2 teaspoons of the olive oil in a 6-inch, heavy-bottomed, well-seasoned, cast-iron skillet or crepe pan. Put the egg mixture into the pan, smoothing it into a neat pancake. Cook over medium heat about 3 minutes on each side, turning only once.

Keep the finished *frittatine* warm while making the rest. Serve warm or at room temperature.

WINE SUGGESTION
Tocai from Friuli (preferably from the Collio or Colli Orientali zones) or Pinot bianco from Trentino-Alto Adige.

Miniature Onion Omelets
[FRITTATINE ALLE CIPOLLE]

In contrast to the green vegetable *frittatine* of the preceding recipe, these onion *frittatine* are softer, richer, and a warm golden color. One of each type for each diner makes a very nicely counterpointed *antipasto*. If you are serving only this one, the recipe makes 2 *frittatine* apiece for 4 persons. Because our domestic onions tend to be sharper and more acrid than their Italian counterparts, we like to use the very large yellow globe onions called Bermudas in all Italian recipes where the onion flavor is prominent. The onions may be cooked in advance and reserved for several hours before the final assembly.

1¼ pounds large yellow (Bermuda) onions	Freshly ground black pepper
3 tablespoons plus 8 teaspoons olive oil	8 eggs
	Nutmeg
Salt	1 cup freshly grated *parmigiano*

Slice the onions ⅛ inch thick. Warm 3 tablespoons of the olive oil in a large frying pan. Add the onions and let them cook very gently, stirring often, until they are translucent and completely wilted but not colored—10 to 20 minutes, depending on the size of the pan. Off heat, sprinkle lightly with salt and pepper.

For each *frittatina*, beat 1 egg in a small bowl with ¼ teaspoon salt, several grindings of pepper, a few gratings of fresh nutmeg, and 2 tablespoons of the *parmigiano*. Add 2 to 3 tablespoons of the onions, mixing thoroughly.

Heat 2 teaspoons of the olive oil in a 6-inch, heavy-bottomed, well-seasoned, cast-iron skillet or crepe pan. Put the egg mixture into the pan, smoothing it into a neat pancake. Cook over medium heat about 3 minutes on each side, turning only once.

Keep the finished *frittatine* warm while making the rest. Serve warm or at room temperature.

WINE SUGGESTION

If serving these onion frittatine *alone, accompany them with an acid, fruity, dry white wine such as Pinot grigio (Cavit or Bollini are excellent brands), Sauvignon blanc (Jermann, Russiz Superiore, Borgo Conventi, many others), or even a good Soave.*

Rice and Spinach Tart
[TORTA VERDE]

Thin wedges of this delicious, crustless vegetable tart are served at room temperature as an *antipasto*. Larger portions make an excellent light lunch. Although simple to make, the dish is time-consuming; however, you can do everything up to the final mixing and baking a day in advance.

———————

¼ cup chopped onion
2 ounces *pancetta* (or blanched bacon), chopped
1 large garlic clove, chopped
3 tablespoons olive oil
5 tablespoons butter
1 quart broth (page 45)
1 cup arborio rice
2 packages frozen spinach, defrosted and drained

½ teaspoon salt
Fine dry bread crumbs
4 eggs
½ cup freshly grated *parmigiano*
1 teaspoon dried marjoram
½ teaspoon freshly grated nutmeg
½ teaspoon freshly ground black pepper

In a broad, deep pan, sauté the onion, *pancetta*, and garlic in the oil and 3 tablespoons of the butter over low heat for 10 minutes, until the vegetables are soft and the *pancetta* rendered but not browned. Meanwhile, bring the broth to a simmer.

Add the rice to the sauté pan, raise the heat slightly, and cook, stirring, 2 minutes. Stir in the drained spinach, add the salt, and bring the dish back to the simmer. Start adding the broth, ½ cup at a time, stirring regularly. Add more as the liquid is absorbed. The whole process should take about 25 minutes.

Taste a grain of rice. When it is nearly done but still hard at the center, remove the pan from the heat and let the mixture cool to room temperature. Everything up to this point can be done a day in advance and left covered in a cool place overnight.

When ready to proceed, preheat oven to 350 degrees F. Generously butter a 9-inch pie dish with 1 tablespoon of the butter. Sprinkle in several tablespoons of bread crumbs, tilt and shake the pan until all the butter is covered with crumbs, then gently tap out the excess.

In a small bowl, beat together the eggs, *parmigiano*, marjoram, nutmeg, and pepper. Stir this into the spinach-rice mixture and fill the pie pan with it. Sprinkle more bread crumbs over the top and dot with the remaining tablespoon of butter.

Bake 45 minutes to an hour, until the *torta verde* is firm but not too dry. Run briefly under a hot broiler to brown the top, if you like. Let cool completely, slice, and serve.

WINE SUGGESTION

A dry white wine with good fruit and medium body will make the best accompaniment to this dish. Try a Friulian Tocai (Livio Felluga's, if possible) or a Pinot bianco from Trentino-Alto Adige.

Roasted Peppers with Ham and Fontina
[PEPERONI ALLA CASTELLANA]

A standard *antipasto* that you'll find all over Italy consists of roasted bell peppers, simply topped with anchovy fillets. Tasty as that is, this elaboration of the roasted-pepper theme is even better—and much prettier. It's important that the *fontina* be from Italy; the Nordic and American cheeses that bear that name fall far short of the real thing.

2 large red bell peppers	3 ounces imported Italian *fontina* in
Salt	4 slices
Pepper	2 tablespoons olive oil
1½ ounces cooked ham in 2 slices	

Preheat the oven to 400 degrees F.

Turn two front burners of the stove to high. Set a pepper directly onto each grate. Watch them closely, and as the skin blackens in the flame, turn the peppers with tongs until the entire surface is black. As each pepper is finished, put it into a brown paper bag and close the mouth of the bag.

Under a thin stream of running water, scrape away all the blackened skin of each pepper with a paring knife. Then cut the peppers in half, remove all seeds and membrane, rinse briefly, and blot dry with paper towels.

Lay the pepper halves out on a board, skinned side down. Lightly salt and pepper the insides. Put half a slice of ham and a slice of *fontina* on each pepper. Fold in half and secure with a toothpick.

Oil a shallow baking dish with ½ tablespoon of the olive oil. Set the peppers in the dish and drizzle on the rest of the oil. Put them in the preheated oven and bake until the *fontina* melts, about 10 minutes (longer if the peppers were very thick-walled). Let cool briefly and remove toothpicks before serving.

WINE SUGGESTION

An excellent wine with these peppers is Sauvignon blanc, from Friuli or Trentino-Alto Adige.

Baked Artichokes Stuffed with Chicken, Ham, and Mushrooms

[CARCIOFI RIPIENI ALLA TORINESE]

A special-occasion dish, and an elegant, sophisticated way to present artichokes. While it involves many steps, the work can be spread out over 2 or more days. Final assembly and cooking require less than 1 hour.

3 lemons	1½ ounces boiled ham
4 large artichokes	2 tablespoons chopped parsley
1 chicken leg, or 4 ounces boneless breast of chicken	Salt
4 ounces mushrooms	Freshly ground black pepper
2 tablespoons butter	¼ cup dry white wine
1 tablespoon olive oil	4 thin slices *pancetta* or blanched bacon

Prepare the artichokes:

Quarter 1 of the lemons. Holding an artichoke with the top facing you, and starting at the bottom, bend each leaf backward until it snaps off close to the base. Continue until you reach the soft inner core of leaves. Slice these off close to the base (the cut should expose the inner layers of spiky leaves covering the choke). Slice off the stem at base. With a vegetable peeler, pare away all the green exterior of the artichoke bottom, leaving white flesh. Rub the cut parts all over with a piece of lemon, to prevent darkening. Drop each finished artichoke bottom into a bowl of acidulated water while preparing the rest.

Bring a large pot of water to a boil. Squeeze the remaining juice from the quartered lemon into the water, and drop in the lemon pieces. Add the artichoke bottoms and boil slowly, uncovered, for 30 minutes, or until bottoms are just tender when pierced with a fork. Drain and cool them.

If desired, this preparation can be done well in advance. Artichokes can then be refrigerated or frozen. If frozen, defrost and drain them upside down on paper towels. Let artichokes come up to room temperature before proceeding.

Prepare the stuffing:

Poach the chicken leg in simmering water for 25 to 30 minutes, or until its juices run clear when pierced with a fork. Drain, cool, skin, and bone it.

Chop the mushrooms and sauté them in the butter and olive oil, over fairly high heat, for 5 minutes, stirring.

Put the chicken, ham, mushrooms, and parsley through a meat grinder, or pulse them briefly in a food processor to obtain a paste. Season generously with salt and pepper. This filling can be made up a day in advance and refrigerated if necessary, but do not freeze. Return it to room temperature before proceeding.

Assemble and bake:

Preheat the oven to 400 degrees F. Slice each artichoke bottom in half vertically, being careful not to tear the leaf bases. Remove the chokes and spiky inner leaves, preserving a thin shell of leaf bases around the perimeter. Generously salt and pepper the interiors and fill them with the stuffing. Arrange the filled halves snugly in a buttered baking dish. Bathe each one with 1 tablespoon of wine and top with ½ slice *pancetta*. Cover and bake 20 minutes.

At this point the dish can be uncovered, cooled, and set aside at room temperature for several hours, loosely covered.

Final steps:

Run the baking dish under a low broiler for 5 minutes to heat the artichokes through and crisp the *pancetta*. Either serve directly from the baking dish or arrange attractively on a platter. A moment before serving, squeeze a quarter of a lemon over each half artichoke. (Don't forget this step; it makes an astonishing difference to the finished dish.) The artichokes can be eaten hot, warm, or at room temperature.

WINE SUGGESTION

> *Artichokes make problems for all wines, though the flavorful filling of this recipe makes them more accommodating than most. Still, your best bet is a simple, fruity white with lots of acid—Pinot grigio is ideal—or a dry, high-acid Spumante, such as a Prosecco.*

Broiled Mushroom Caps Filled with Veal and Pesto
[FUNGHI RIPIENI ALLA GENOVESE]

Another dish that can serve as a light lunch as well as a dinner *antipasto*. Though perfectly good when made with ordinary cultivated white mushrooms, it is particularly striking and savory if the brown-capped Italian *cremosini* mushrooms are available. If the *pesto* is already made, this recipe will require only about 20 minutes to prepare.

12 large firm mushrooms (caps 3 inches across)	Salt
½ cup olive oil	Freshly ground black pepper
½ pound lean ground veal	¼ cup *pesto* (page 86)
	Freshly grated *parmigiano*

Clean the mushrooms. Carefully remove their stems, keeping the caps intact. Mince the stems and heap them on a linen towel. Close the towel around them and wring it firmly over the sink until no more moisture emerges.

In a large skillet, heat ⅓ cup of the olive oil and sauté the minced stems for 2 minutes, stirring frequently. Add the ground veal and continue sautéing and stirring until the meat loses its rosy color. Salt and pepper the mixture moderately.

Transfer the veal-mushroom mixture to a bowl and stir in the *pesto*. If not ready to serve, this can be set aside for several hours, refrigerated or at room temperature.

Preheat the broiler. Lightly salt the insides of the mushroom caps. Brush their tops with the remaining olive oil and broil them, oiled side up, for 1 minute. Turn the caps upside down, quickly fill them with the *pesto* stuffing, and top with a thin layer of *parmigiano*. Return them to the broiler for another minute or two, until the stuffing is browned and sizzling.

Serve hot, warm, or at room temperature.

WINE SUGGESTION

Accompany these mushrooms with either a light, fruity red wine (Merlot or Cabernet, Dolcetto or Barbera) or a reasonably full white (Pinot bianco, Tocai).

PRIMI

Northern Italians divide their allegiance among many sorts of *primi*. Winter brings out an array of rich, often thick soups as well as *polenta*, in both its fresh, moist form and reincarnated as firmer slabs for eating cold or grilled. *Risotto* is served all year round—in fact, *risotto* is a surefire way to turn a few leftovers and odds and ends of vegetables or meats or fish into a satisfying and nutritious dish. Pasta also appears often, always as fresh egg pasta, and almost always with a rich sauce. If the sauce is a simple one, it will contain staggering amounts of butter and/or cream. If it is a complex sauce, it will almost certainly be reinforced with meat flavors. The one *primo* you almost never see in the North is commercial dry pasta.

Because of their richness, many northern *primi* make a very satisfactory dinner accompanied only by an *antipasto* or a salad; if you are planning to use them this way, however, you might slightly increase the quantities per person. Certainly many of these dishes serve very happily as centerpieces of a not-too-elaborate dinner with good wine; northern *antipasto*, *primo*, cheese, and dessert provide a very pleasurable sequence of courses that will not send anyone away from the table either overstuffed or undernourished.

Poached Egg in Broth
[ZUPPA PAVESE]

It's hard to imagine a simpler elegant soup than this. With the economy of ingredients here, everything should be of the highest quality: the broth home-made, the eggs very fresh, the bread an honest country loaf.

4 slices day-old bread	Salt
4 tablespoons butter	Freshly ground black pepper
1 tablespoon oil	4 eggs
3 cups meat broth (page 45)	4 tablespoons grated *parmigiano*

Trim the crusts off the bread. Fry the slices in the butter and oil until lightly golden. Bring the broth to a boil. Taste for seasoning, and slightly undersalt it.

(continued)

Lay a slice of bread in the bottom of each soup bowl. Break an egg on top of each—carefully, so as not to break the yolk. Sprinkle 1 tablespoon of grated cheese on each egg. Again carefully, add 2 ladlefuls of very hot broth to each bowl. Either serve at once, or let the egg poach briefly in the hot broth before serving.

WINE SUGGESTION

This is one of the few times that wine is a distraction. At most, serve a glass of a simple, light white alongside the soup.

Rice and Rape Soup

[ZUPPA DI RAPE]

This is one of those deceptively simple country soups where the whole is far more than the sum of the parts. Rape, or broccoli rape, or broccoli rabe, as it is variously known, is a bitter green that looks like leafy side shoots of broccoli. Its intensity and pleasing bite make it well worth searching out, though it is becoming more common in markets everywhere.

½ to ¾ pound broccoli rape	1½ tablespoons butter
3 ounces lean salt pork	5 cups broth (page 45)
2 garlic cloves	Salt
1 tablespoon parsley	½ cup long-grain rice

Trim all the hard stems off the broccoli rape. You need about 6 ounces of leaves, flowers, and tender stems. Wash, drain, and roughly chop them.

Either chop together the salt pork, garlic, and parsley, or pulse them in a food processor to obtain an even-textured mash. Melt the butter in a 4- to 5-quart heavy-bottomed casserole, add the chopped mixture, and sauté 4 to 5 minutes.

Add the broth, the broccoli rape, and 2 teaspoons salt. Bring to a boil, reduce to a simmer, and cook, covered, until the rape is tender, about 20 minutes.

Stir in the rice and cook gently 10 to 15 minutes longer. Taste for seasoning; depending on your salt pork, the soup may or may not need more salt.

WINE SUGGESTION

Zuppa di rape *will go quietly with almost any wine but a sweet one. Best* options are to serve either an undemanding white (such as Soave or Bianco di Custoza) or the same wine you are planning to serve with your secondo.

81

Primi

Chick-Pea and Rape Soup

[CISRÀ ALLA PIEMONTESE]

A nice variant on the rape-and-salt-pork theme. The chick-peas add an interesting new flavor and texture element. Cooking time is 2 to 2½ hours, after the overnight soak for the chick-peas.

1 cup dried chick-peas
½ pound broccoli rape, leaves and
    thin stems only
2 ounces salt pork, chopped
2 tablespoons olive oil
⅓ cup chopped onion
⅓ cup chopped carrot

1 celery stalk, chopped
1 garlic clove, minced
Freshly ground black pepper
Salt
4 slices country bread, toasted in the
    oven

The night before serving, pick over the chick-peas and soak them in cold water to cover.

Next day, drain them, put them into a large soup pot with 6 cups water and 1 teaspoon salt. Bring to a boil, reduce to a simmer, and cook for 1½ hours.

Wash, drain, and shred the rape. Add it to the pot when the 1½ hours are up and continue cooking 30 minutes longer.

Sauté the salt pork in the olive oil over low heat for about 5 minutes, then add the chopped onion, carrot, celery, garlic, and a generous quantity of pepper. Sauté for 10 more minutes, stirring occasionally, then add the contents of the pan to the soup pot. Cover and cook 5 more minutes. Taste for salt.

Serve with a slice of bread in the bottom of each bowl.

WINE SUGGESTION
Same as for the preceding soup.

Friulian Bean and Sauerkraut Soup

[LA JOTA]

This soup is virtually a dinner in itself. In Friuli, they like it very tangy, so they use well-cured sauerkraut and sometimes stir in the sauerkraut juice at the end of the cooking. This is a milder version, and for a milder one still you can soak the kraut for an hour or two before adding it to the pot. *La jota* is fairly time-consuming to make, and since it tastes even better the second day, you may as well make a lot of it. Quantities given here will serve 8 as a *primo*.

¾ pound dried pinto or Great Northern beans

6 ounces *pancetta,* with its rind, or well-blanched lean salt pork with rind

2 ounces fatty salt pork

4 ounces sliced bacon

2 tablespoons olive oil

1 tablespoon flour

¼ cup chopped onion

6 fresh sage leaves, or 1 teaspoon dried leaves

1 large garlic clove

3 tablespoons minced parsley

2 tablespoons cornmeal

1 pound fresh sauerkraut

Salt

The night before you plan to serve the soup, pick over the beans and leave them to soak in abundant cold water.

Next day, chop the *pancetta,* mince the salt pork, and cut the bacon into 1-inch pieces. Keep the meats separate. Warm the olive oil in a large pot and stir in the flour. Stir over low heat until this roux turns a warm nut-brown. Add the drained beans, the diced *pancetta,* and 1½ quarts fresh cold water. Cover and bring to a boil. Reduce heat to maintain a brisk simmer and cook, covered, for 30 minutes.

Put the minced salt pork, onion, sage, garlic, and parsley into a food processor or blender. Process to a paste. Sauté this gently in a skillet for 5 minutes, then slowly sprinkle on the cornmeal, stirring it in to distribute it well. Add this mixture to the beans and continue cooking, covered, for another 30 minutes, or until the beans are just tender, stirring occasionally. Scoop out ½ cup of beans and purée them through a food mill back into the pot.

Rinse, drain, and squeeze the sauerkraut. Render the bacon pieces in the skillet. Sauté the sauerkraut in the bacon for 5 minutes, stirring to coat all the shreds well with bacon fat. Add the contents of the skillet to the bean soup, cover, and simmer 10 minutes. Stir often to prevent sticking. Off heat, test the soup carefully for salt (it will depend on how salty the bacon and salt pork were).

Beef Tripe and Vegetable Soup

[MINESTRA DI TRIPPA]

This is a hearty country soup, good stick-to-the-ribs, cold-weather fare. Even people who think they don't like tripe usually love this. Half of them don't even realize it's tripe they're eating, because the vegetables really give the dish its savor; the tripe provides succulence and body. This soup requires a little more than 2 hours' total cooking time.

¾ pound tripe
Vegetables for boiling with the tripe:
  1 small carrot, 1 celery stalk, 1 scallion or small onion
1 tablespoon salt
2 small zucchini
1 potato
4 large outside leaves of a savoy cabbage

1½ tablespoons lard
½ cup minced onion
½ cup coarsely chopped carrot
½ cup coarsely chopped celery
2 sage leaves
4 slices country bread, toasted in the
  oven
Freshly grated *parmigiano*, optional

Wash the tripe, drain it, and cut it into strips approximately ¼ inch by 1 inch. Quarter the carrot, celery, and onion. Put the tripe and vegetables in a large pot with 2 quarts of water and the salt. Bring to a boil, reduce to a simmer, and cook, covered, for 1 hour. Remove the tripe, discard the vegetables, and reserve the cooking liquid.

Wash the zucchini, potato, and cabbage. Cut them into bite-size pieces.

Melt the lard in a large, deep, heavy-bottomed casserole. Add the minced onion and cook until it is translucent. Add all the remaining vegetables and the sage leaves. Stir together and cook for a few minutes. Add the tripe, stir well, and cook for 3 minutes. Strain in the reserved tripe-cooking liquid and simmer for 1 hour. Taste for salt and pepper.

Serve with a slice of bread in the bottom of each bowl. Pass *parmigiano* at the table (not everyone feels the cheese is necessary).

WINE SUGGESTION
  Serve a simple, robust red wine with this soup: Dolcetto or Barbera would be excellent choices.

Venetian-Style Pasta with Beans

[PASTA E FASOI]

This is the first of three regional versions of this dish we're going to give you in this book. *Pasta e fagioli*—macs and beans, pastafazool, to give it its American names—is as close as you get to Italian soul food, and just about every square kilometer of Italy has its own rendition of the dish. In Venice, where this recipe originates, it is often prepared with rice rather than pasta (though it's usually still called *pasta e fasoi* in Venetian dialect). You can, if you wish, substitute rice in the following recipe. You can also omit puréeing any beans at all or you can purée all of them. In texture, this *primo* can be anything from a very moistly sauced pasta dish to a thick soup, as you like it. It tastes just fine either way.

½ pound dried pinto beans
1 pork shoulder bone
1 carrot, chopped
1 celery stalk, chopped
¾ cup chopped onion

Salt
½ recipe basic egg pasta (page 24)
Extra-virgin olive oil
Freshly grated *parmigiano*
Freshly ground black pepper

The night before serving, pick over the beans and soak them in a large quantity of cold water.

Next day, drain them and put them in a large pot with the pork bone and the chopped vegetables. Add 10 cups cold water and 2 teaspoons salt and bring to a boil. Reduce heat and simmer, partly covered, for 1 hour, or until the beans are tender and nearly cooked. Skim the surface several times during the cooking, if necessary.

Taste for salt before proceeding. The beans should be slightly oversalted before the pasta cooks in them. Remove the bone, and if the broth is very thin, purée about a cup of the beans through a food mill and back into the pot.

Roll the fresh pasta to the next-to-last setting on the pasta machine. Cut it into 2-inch lengths and feed them through the *fettuccine* cutters. Add the pasta to the bean pot and cook at a rapid boil, uncovered, about 3 minutes, or until pasta is *al dente*. Turn off heat, cover the pan, and let it sit another 3 to 5 minutes before serving.

After filling individual bowls with the *pasta e fasoi*, pour a tablespoon of extra-virgin olive oil over each one, and add grated *parmigiano* to taste. Black pepper is nice, too.

Simple red wines work best with this: A Cabernet from Friuli or the Veneto or Trentino-Alto Adige is a good choice, and so is a Merlot from the same regions.

Tagliarini with Sage Tomato Sauce
[TAJARIN]

Tajarin is Piedmontese dialect for *tagliarini*, also known as *tonnarelli*. Whatever you call them, you can get them by running fresh pasta dough through the thin cutters of the pasta machine, as described on page 23. This version of *tajarin* has a very distinctive sauce, vibrant with the flavor of fresh sage. It is also unusual for a northern sauce in that tomato plays so important a role in it. Try it on people who think they're tired of pasta with tomato sauce.

⅓ cup olive oil
¼ cup finely chopped carrot
⅓ cup finely chopped onion
1 large garlic clove, minced
3 pounds fresh ripe plum tomatoes
   (or 3 cups canned, with their juice)

¾ teaspoon salt
40 fresh sage leaves, tied in two bundles
2 to 3 tablespoons butter
Freshly ground black pepper
1 recipe fresh *tagliarini* (page 24)

In a pan large enough to hold the pasta and the sauce, heat the olive oil and sauté the carrot, onion, and garlic very gently until soft—5 to 10 minutes.

Roughly chop the tomatoes and add them to the pan along with the salt and bundles of sage leaves. Simmer, covered, for 20 minutes. Then remove and reserve the sage bundles.

Pass the sauce through the medium blade of the food mill and return it to the pot along with the sage. Simmer about 5 more minutes. (The sauce should just hold its shape in a spoon, but not be too thick; when the pasta is finished in it, the pasta will absorb some of the liquid.) Discard the sage bundles. The sauce can be made to this point up to an hour in advance.

At serving time, bring the sauce back to a simmer and stir in the butter and a generous quantity of black pepper. Bring 4 to 5 quarts of water to a boil and add 1 tablespoon of salt. Add the *tagliarini* and cook until about three-quarters done—which may take as little as 30 seconds if they are really freshly made. Drain the pasta thoroughly, transfer it to the saucepan, and toss with the sauce over low heat for about 2 minutes. Serve at once.

(continued)

WINE SUGGESTION

A richly fruity red wine like Dolcetto makes the perfect accompaniment to this sauce. For a different effect, you could try a bright, acid white like Pinot grigio or even Sauvignon blanc.

Trenette with Pesto

[TRENETTE AL PESTO]

Trenette is the name used in Genoa for the medium-width egg noodles elsewhere known as *fettucelle*. *Pesto*—a wonderful sauce, capturing the essence of summer in its velvety green depths—is also a Genoese specialty. It is extremely easy to make and—when fresh basil is abundant—extremely inexpensive. The base sauce freezes very well, so our recipe makes a lot. Freeze it in small containers (or even ice-cube trays, popping the cubes out and storing them in plastic bags). To dress individual portions of pasta, use 2 tablespoons *pesto* base and 1 tablespoon grated *parmigiano* on each.

FOR THE PESTO BASE (MAKES ABOUT 1½ CUPS)

3 packed cups fresh basil leaves	¾ cup olive oil
3 garlic cloves	1½ teaspoons salt
3 tablespoons *pignoli*	4 tablespoons softened butter

½ cup grated *parmigiano*	1 recipe basic egg pasta (page 24)

Make the pesto *base:*

Wash and dry the basil leaves. Purée all the ingredients in a food processor or blender. Freeze any *pesto* base that is not to be used at once.

Finish the dish:

Mix 1 cup of the *pesto* base with the grated *parmigiano*. Roll and cut the pasta dough into *trenette*, using the medium-width (*fettuccine*) cutters of the pasta machine. Bring 4 to 5 quarts water to the boil and add 1 tablespoon salt. Drop in the *trenette* and cook until *al dente*, probably less than a minute. Drain and turn the pasta into a warmed serving bowl. Stir in the *pesto* and serve immediately.

WINE SUGGESTION

Any and all dry white wines love pesto, *and it loves them. The best match for our palates is either Chardonnay or Pinot bianco.*

Pappardelle with Sausage and Cream
[PAPPARDELLE ALLA CONTADINA]

Northern cream sauces for pasta can sometimes be a bit bland. Not this hearty farm-style dish that adds sausage meat, mushrooms, and onions to the cream and butter base. You can serve the sauce over ordinary *fettuccine* or flat noodles, but we like to roll the dough a little thicker than that and cut broad, stubby *pappardelle* (about 6 inches by ½ inch) by hand, using a fluted pastry wheel to add textural interest to the pasta.

——————————◆——————————

½ **pound firm white mushrooms**	¾ **cup minced onions**
2 **links of homemade spicy sausage**	¾ **cup heavy cream**
(page 37), or ⅓ pound commer-	**Salt**
cially made Italian-style hot sau-	**Freshly ground black pepper**
sage	1 **recipe basic egg pasta (page 24), cut**
4 **tablespoons butter**	**into *pappardelle***
2 **tablespoons olive oil**	**Freshly grated *parmigiano***

Wash or wipe clean the mushrooms. Slice them very thin (e.g., using the 3-millimeter blade on the food processor). Strip the sausages out of their casings and roughly chop the meat.

In a large enameled sauté pan or casserole, melt 1 tablespoon of the butter in the olive oil. Add the sausage meat and onions and sauté over medium heat, stirring often and breaking up the chunks of sausage, for about 5 minutes, or until onions are translucent and sausage has lost its raw red color. Turn heat to medium-high. Add the mushrooms and continue to sauté, stirring often, another 5 minutes.

Melt the remaining 3 tablespoons butter in half the cream. When the cream is just at the simmer, turn off heat and set aside.

When mushrooms have cooked for 5 minutes, lower heat, salt moderately and pepper generously, and add the remaining cream. Cook gently, uncovered, until liquid thickens somewhat, about 5 minutes. Set aside, covered, until ready to use.

Bring 4 to 5 quarts of water to a boil and add 1 tablespoon salt. Put in the *pappardelle* and cook until *al dente*. Drain them and transfer them to a warmed serving bowl. Toss with the cream-butter mixture, then with the sausage sauce. Serve at once. Pass *parmigiano* and the pepper mill at the table.

WINE SUGGESTION
A robust red wine is called for here. Try Nebbiolo d'Alba, or one of the Lombardy reds—Grumello, Sassella, Valgella, or Inferno.

Tortellini

Tortellini ought to be declared an endangered species before they're destroyed by their own popularity. These tiny purses of pasta, which used to be compared in shape to Venus's navel, also used to be made painstakingly by hand and filled with only the best-quality ingredients. All the charm of these dime-size nuggets disappears when they are made huge, soft, and flaccid, as many mass-produced American *tortellini* are. Even in Italy these days you encounter a lot of middling-to-abysmal machine-made *tortellini*. Done lovingly by hand, however, *tortellini* are *da morire* (to die for). Try this recipe on people you really care for and see if it isn't worth the labor. Quantities given make about 8 dozen; fewer than that is hardly worth going to the trouble for, and anyway *tortellini* freeze very well.

FOR THE FILLING

2 chicken thighs, or 5 ounces boneless chicken breast
½ fresh sweetbread, about ⅓ pound
2 tablespoons butter
1½ ounces *prosciutto*, diced
2 tablespoons Madeira or Marsala

4 tablespoons freshly grated *parmigiano*
1 egg yolk
1 teaspoon salt
¼ teaspoon freshly ground black pepper
¼ teaspoon freshly grated nutmeg

1½ recipes basic egg pasta (page 24)

Make the filling:

Skin and bone the chicken thighs. Cut them and the sweetbread into 1-inch chunks.

Melt the butter in a sauté pan, add the sweetbread, chicken, and *prosciutto*. Sauté, turning often, for 15 minutes. Scrape the meats into the bowl of a food processor. Add the Madeira or Marsala to the sauté pan and simmer 1 minute, loosening any browned bits.

Scrape the contents of the pan into the food processor bowl and process until well minced. Add the grated *parmigiano*, egg yolk, salt, pepper, and nutmeg; process briefly to blend. Set aside, refrigerated, until ready to use.

Form the tortellini:

Flour a large pastry board. Divide the pasta dough into 6 or 8 pieces and work with one at a time, leaving the others under a cloth to prevent their drying out.

Roll the dough to the next-to-last setting on the pasta machine and lay it out on the floured board. Cut it into rounds with a 2-inch cutter. Place a scant ¼ teaspoon of filling on each round.

Take one round of dough and fold it in half over the filling, pressing edges tightly with fingertips to seal. Pick the semicircle up with one hand, holding it lightly between thumb and little finger, curved side up.

Using your other hand, bend the ends around your little finger, pressing them together against the fingernail to seal them together. Gently slide the *tortellino* off your finger and onto the floured board.

Continue with the remainder of the dough, arranging the finished *tortellini* on the floured board so they do not touch each other. Move them about occasionally to prevent sticking.

If *tortellini* are not to be used the same day, freeze them. Spread them on cookie sheets in the freezer at first to prevent their sticking together. When frozen solid, transfer them to plastic bags.

Cook the tortellini:

Do not defrost *tortellini* if frozen. Bring a large pot of salted water to a boil and drop them in. Reduce heat to a simmer and poach them very gently until done. Start checking after 5 minutes. They are done when a fork easily pierces the unstuffed, sealed ends of the dough. Be careful not to overcook them. Drain them into a heated serving bowl, add sauce of your choice, toss, and serve immediately.

Tortellini in Broth

[TORTELLINI IN BRODO]

This is the simplest way to serve *tortellini*. Bolognesi probably eat more of them this way than all the rest of the world consumes.

8 cups broth (page 45)　　　　　　Freshly grated *parmigiano*
4 dozen *tortellini* (see preceding　　Freshly ground black pepper
　recipe)

Bring the broth to a simmer. Cook the *tortellini* according to the directions above. Into each diner's bowl, ladle 12 *tortellini* and 2 cups of broth. Pass *parmigiano* and pepper at table.

(continued)

WINE SUGGESTION

*Almost any wine will accompany this dish, but a Pinot bianco is partic-
ularly enjoyable.*

Tortellini with Cream
[TORTELLINI ALLA PANNA]

Even by Bolognese standards, this is a luxurious dish: the city's favorite pasta, its favorite cheese, its favorite dressings. The cream and *parmigiano* together create a delicious, velvet cloak for each pasta morsel. Very few ingredients, but they add up to extraordinary flavor.

4 tablespoons butter
1 cup heavy cream
4 dozen *tortellini* (page 88)

1 cup freshly grated *parmigiano*
Freshly ground black pepper

Melt the butter in a medium-size saucepan; add the heavy cream and heat through.

Cook the *tortellini* according to the directions on page 89, then drain them and place them in a heated serving bowl. Pour the cream-butter mixture over them and toss thoroughly so that some of the cream is absorbed. Add ½ cup grated *parmigiano* and a generous quantity of pepper, and toss again. Pass additional cheese at table.

WINE SUGGESTION

A fine, full-bodied white wine is called for here: Gaja Chardonnay, Gavi di Gavi, Jermann's Vintage Tunina would all be fine.

Tortellini with Bolognese Meat Sauce
[TORTELLINI AL RAGÙ]

This third mode of serving *tortellini* is the great Bolognese extravaganza, but to our taste it can easily be overkill, because the complexity of the sauce can fight the complexity of the *tortellini* filling. The trick is to sauce the pasta sparingly: *Tortellini* need only about half as much *ragù* as unstuffed pasta, though of course exact proportions are a matter of taste. By the *ragù* called for below, we mean the sauce as described on page 32 *before* the addition of cream—which you'll stir in to finish the sauce only at the moment before serving.

4 dozen tortellini (page 88)	3 to 4 tablespoons cream
½ cup basic northern tomato sauce (page 32)	Freshly grated *parmigiano*
	Freshly ground black pepper

Bring the cream to room temperature. Warm 4 individual soup bowls. Bring about 4 quarts of salted water to the boil. Reheat the *ragù* in a small pot and simmer, covered, 5 minutes. Drop the *tortellini* into the boiling water; cook and drain them as directed on page 89. Divide the *tortellini* among the soup bowls. Stir the cream into the *ragù*, spoon it over the *tortellini*, and serve at once. Pass *parmigiano* and a pepper mill.

WINE SUGGESTION

Tortellini al ragù *will match well with a number of dry, fruity red wines; Merlot, Cabernet, Dolcetto, Barbera, even young Nebbiolo are all good choices.*

Agnolotti Filled with Sweet Potato

[AGNOLOTTI DI ZUCCA]

These half-moon-shaped *ravioli* are the pride of their native region, around Ferrara and Modena. The zucca is a large squash, allied to our butternut, but with a distinctive flavor that's hard to match in the United States. The closest we've come to the flavor of the real thing—very close, in our estimation—results from using yellow sweet potato (it's really yam, but the lighter-skinned, yellow-fleshed variety, not the lurid orange one) with a little *ricotta* and nutmeg. The rich sweetness of the filling usually comes as a bit of a surprise, but even more of a surprise is the delicacy of a dish made with such a heavy-seeming main ingredient.

FOR THE FILLING

⅔ cup mashed baked sweet potato	Freshly ground black pepper
⅓ cup *ricotta*	Few gratings of fresh nutmeg
⅛ teaspoon salt	

½ recipe basic egg pasta (page 24)	8 to 12 fresh sage leaves
4 tablespoons butter	

(continued)

Put the filling ingredients in a bowl and stir to combine.

Roll the pasta to the thinnest setting on the pasta machine and cut it into twenty-four 2½-inch rounds (see technique, page 24). Put about 2 teaspoons of the filling on one side of each round, fold them over, and seal them firmly, moistening the edge with a fingertip dipped in water if necessary.

Melt the butter in a small pan with the sage leaves, then turn off heat and set aside.

Bring 4 quarts of salted water to the boil. Slide the *agnolotti* into the water and let them cook, maintaining a slow boil. Start testing after 5 minutes. As soon as the *agnolotti* are done, drain them and divide them among 4 bowls. Quickly reheat the butter-sage sauce and pour it over the pasta. Serve at once.

WINE SUGGESTION

A chilled bottle of Riesling or Gewurztraminer (Traminer aromatico) from Trentino-Alto Adige makes a great match with this pasta, as does a Friulian Tocai.

Giant Ravioli with Whole Egg Yolks
["IL" RAVIOLO DI SAN DOMENICO]

This recipe is based on an extraordinary dish we were served at the Ristorante San Domenico, in the town of Imola, thirty-five kilometers southeast of Bologna. A serving is one piece—*un singolo raviolo*—per person. When you break into your giant *raviolo* with a fork, you find a golden sunburst of perfectly poached egg yolk nestled within a spinach-and-ricotta filling. It's not as difficult to achieve as it looks, though you do have to be a deft separator of eggs. (We always have extras on hand in case of accidents.) Although the filling can be made up in advance, the *ravioli* must be cooked immediately after assembling them.

½ **pound spinach**	1 **tablespoon grated** *parmigiano*
½ **pound** *ricotta* **(1 cup)**	5 **eggs**
⅛ **teaspoon salt**	½ **recipe basic egg pasta (page 24)**
Few grindings of pepper	4 **tablespoons butter**
Scrape of nutmeg	8 **to 12 fresh sage leaves**

Make the filling:

Wash and trim the spinach. Cook for 5 minutes in a large pot with only the water adhering to the leaves. Drain, cool, squeeze hard, and chop. Mix the spinach, *ricotta*, salt, pepper, nutmeg, *parmigiano*, and 1 egg yolk.

Start the water heating:

Bring 4 quarts of water and 1 tablespoon salt to a boil; keep it simmering so that the *ravioli* can be cooked as soon as they are made.

Make the ravioli:

Roll the pasta out to the next-to-last thickness on the pasta machine. Cut 4 rounds 4 inches in diameter and 4 rounds 4½ inches in diameter, and let them sit on a floured board, covered with a towel, except for the one you are working with.

On one of the smaller rounds of pasta, spread 1 tablespoon of the spinach-*ricotta* filling, leaving a border of ½ inch all around. Make the filling thinner in the center and higher at the edges.

Separate an egg, being careful to keep the yolk whole. Nestle the yolk in the center of the *raviolo* and carefully enclose the yolk completely with 1 more tablespoon of the filling. Take a larger round of pasta, moisten the edges with water, and place it over the filling, making a tight seal.

Make 3 more *ravioli* in the same way. Leave them on the floured board, covered with a towel, while you bring the water back to a full boil. Melt the butter in a small heavy-bottomed pan together with the sage leaves and keep warm until ready to serve.

When the water is back to a boil, slide in the *ravioli*. Maintain the water at a rolling boil and cook the *ravioli* for 3 minutes. (Any longer than that, the egg yolk will begin to hard-boil. The yolk should be as soft as the yolk of a perfectly poached egg; for that reason the pasta has to be fresh and soft enough to cook in the 3-minute span.)

Drain and serve, 1 to a person, with the butter and sage spooned over the top. Pass grated *parmigiano* at the table. When each diner breaks into the pasta, the egg yolk combines with the sage butter and *parmigiano* to create a marvelous fresh and rich fluid that is at the same time sauce and substance.

WINE SUGGESTION

A full-bodied white or a light, elegant red wine will partner well with this tour-de-force of a dish. For the red, a Venegazzù from the Veneto (if you can find one) or a Barbera (from Gaja or Granduca, perhaps) would be fine. For the white, try a Pinot bianco or a Riesling from Trentino-Alto Adige.

Gratinéed Crepes with Cheese and Basil
[CRESPELLE ALLA MANDRIERA]

For this dish we've adapted the prizewinning recipe of Mario Suban, proprietor of the Antica Trattoria Suban in Trieste, a must stop on any gastronomical tour of the North. The cheeses and herbs in the filling make a sophisticated and not easily identifiable blend of flavors, and the finishing technique gives the dish even more distinction. The *crespelle* can be made up well in advance (and, like all crepes, they can be stored in the freezer after cooking) but the final assembly and baking of the dish does require about 45 minutes of the cook's attention.

FOR THE *CRESPELLE*

5 tablespoons butter
⅞ cup flour
1 cup milk

1 whole egg plus 2 yolks
Pinch of salt

FOR THE FILLING

6 ounces *Bel Paese* cheese, grated
4 ounces *parmigiano*, grated
3 garlic cloves, roughly chopped
¼ cup loosely packed basil leaves

⅛ teaspoon freshly grated nutmeg
⅛ teaspoon freshly ground black
 pepper
8 to 9 tablespoons olive oil

FOR FINAL PREPARATIONS

5 to 6 tablespoons butter
6 tablespoons heavy cream

3 tablespoons broth
2 tablespoons grated *parmigiano*

Make the crespelle:

Melt 1 tablespoon of the butter. Put it into a blender or food processor with the flour, milk, whole egg, extra yolks, and the salt and process to obtain a smooth batter. Let it rest 30 minutes.

Heat a well-seasoned 7-inch crepe or omelet pan. Melt 1 teaspoon butter in it, then pour in about ¼ cup of the batter. Tilt the pan to cover it evenly with the batter and cook until the *crespella* is lightly browned on the bottom, about 2 minutes. Turn and cook the other side, then remove to a dish.

Cook 11 more *crespelle* in the same way, using the remaining butter as necessary. They can be made in advance and refrigerated or frozen until needed.

Make the filling:

Put all ingredients except the olive oil into a blender or food processor and process into a crumbly meal. With machine still running, pour in olive oil 2 tablespoons at a time, until the mixture becomes a soft, spreadable paste.

Assemble and cook the dish:

Preheat oven to 375 degrees F. Spread each *crespella* with 2 tablespoons of the filling and fold it in half. Lay them out on a platter while preparing their gratin dishes.

Prepare one portion at a time. Set an individual gratin dish over direct heat and melt 1½ tablespoons of the butter in it. When foam subsides, lay in 3 folded *crespelle* and cook over medium-high heat for 30 seconds on each side, then turn off heat. Pour on 1½ tablespoons of the cream and 2 teaspoons of the broth. Sprinkle on 1½ teaspoons grated *parmigiano*.

Prepare remaining servings the same way. Then put the four dishes into the preheated oven and bake 8 minutes, or until the *crespelle* are brown and lightly puffed, the sauce creamy and bubbly. Serve at once.

WINE SUGGESTION

Pinot bianco matches well with these, as does Vintage Tunina. Soave and Bianco di Custoza are considerably less expensive and almost as satisfying with this dish.

Gnocchi with Prunes
[GNOCCHI ALLE PRUGNE]

In Friuli, in the extreme northeastern corner of Italy, the cooking traditions of Italy, Austria, and Yugoslavia merge. The results are often surprising and unusual, as in this recipe. This unlikely combination of prunes and a potato-based dough makes a lively and refreshing dish, a real palate-awakener.

8 small pitted prunes	1 egg
2 teaspoons brown sugar	¾ teaspoon salt
1 pound baking potatoes	4 tablespoons butter
1¼ cups flour	1½ tablespoons fine fresh bread
3 tablespoons milk	crumbs

Soften the prunes by soaking them briefly in hot water if they are stiff. Put ¼ teaspoon of brown sugar into the cavity where each one's pit was.

Boil the potatoes in their jackets in salted water until done, about 45 minutes. Drain, peel, and pass them through the coarse blade of a food mill.

(continued)

To the potatoes add 1 cup of the flour and the milk, egg, and salt. Mix and work until it makes a homogeneous paste, adding the remaining flour if the dough is very sticky.

Flour your hands, pick up approximately ¼ cup of dough, and enclose a prune with it, making a smooth round ball about the size of a small handball. Place the *gnocchi* on a floured surface and cover with a cloth until ready to cook.

Bring 5 to 6 quarts of water to the boil and add 1 tablespoon of salt. Slide the *gnocchi* into the water and let them cook at a simmer about 5 minutes. As they cook, they'll rise to the surface and roll themselves over. They are done after about 1 minute at the surface.

While the *gnocchi* are cooking, bring the butter to a sizzle in a small, heavy-bottomed pan. Stir in the fresh bread crumbs and sauté, stirring, until they are a deep golden brown. (This will take only a minute or two.)

Remove the *gnocchi* from the water with a slotted spoon, drain well, and put two on each of four plates. Distribute the bread crumbs and butter over the tops and serve at once.

WINE SUGGESTION
Tocai is great with these gnocchi; *next best is Sauvignon.*

Ofelle

An untranslatable name, though the flavors involved are readily understandable. A Friulian specialty, *ofelle* are in effect *ravioli* made with a *gnocchi* paste rather than pasta dough, and filled with a savory mixture of spinach, veal, and sausage. To a cook accustomed to making normal *ravioli*, the very soft *gnocchi* dough will seem strange at first, but once you get the feel of it, it handles well.

FOR THE DOUGH

14 ounces baking potatoes
½ cup flour
½ egg

1 tablespoon baking powder
¼ teaspoon salt

FOR THE FILLING

10 ounces fresh spinach
3 ounces lean veal
1–2 links homemade plain sausage (page 36) or 3 ounces commercially made Italian-style sweet sausage
½ tablespoon butter

¼ cup minced onion
Salt
Freshly ground black pepper
Freshly grated nutmeg

4 tablespoons butter   **Freshly grated *parmigiano***

Make the dough:

Scrub the potatoes and boil them unpeeled in lightly salted water until tender. Peel and put them through a food mill. Mix in the flour, egg, baking powder, and salt, to make a smooth dough. Let rest for half an hour.

Make the filling:

Wash the spinach well. Put it in a pot with a tight cover and cook in the water that clings to it for 5 to 8 minutes, until completely limp and tender. Set aside to cool.

Grind the veal and sausage coarsely in a food processor. Gently squeeze excess water from the spinach and add the spinach to the meats. Process until well mixed but still nubbly in texture.

Heat the butter and soften the minced onion in it, then add the meat mixture and cook gently until the meat loses all its raw red color, about 5 minutes. Season lightly with salt, pepper, and nutmeg.

Form the ofelle:

On a well-floured work surface, roll the dough with a rolling pin to a thickness of 1/8 inch. Cut a straight edge along one side. Dot half-teaspoonfuls of filling about 2½ inches apart along its length, about 2 inches from the edge. Fold the edge over the dots of filling to enclose them and press the dough gently to seal it. Cut the *ofelle* into individual squares and set them on a floured surface while you continue working. Briefly knead together the excess dough, roll it out again, and continue forming *ofelle* until you have used up the filling. The longer you work with the dough, the more flour it will want; try to keep the additional flour to a minimum.

Melt the butter in a small saucepan and keep it hot. Bring 4 to 5 quarts of water to a boil, add 1 tablespoon of salt, and quickly drop in the *ofelle*, one at a time to prevent sticking together. Maintain the water at a brisk simmer and cook about 5 minutes, until the *ofelle* rise to the surface and swell gently. Drain them and distribute them in individual serving bowls. Pour the melted butter over them and top each portion with about 1 tablespoon grated *parmigiano*. Pass additional *parmigiano* at the table.

WINE SUGGESTION

In Friuli they drink Tocai with this, but then they drink Tocai with everything. If you'd prefer a red wine, try a Friulian Merlot or Cabernet.

Venetian Rice and Zucchini

[RISO E ZUCCHINI ALLA VENEZIANA]

Italian rice is different from American—short-grained, nutty-flavored, and more glutinous. It behaves differently in cooking, too. It becomes creamy and unctuous without dissolving into mush. Two types of Italian rice are available in the United States: arborio, which is the kind most commonly used for risotto, and ambra, a lovely golden-tinged rice that has an even more pronounced nutty flavor. This typically Venetian combination of zucchini and rice produces a dish at once rich and mild—especially comforting on a chilly autumn night.

———————◆———————

¾ pound small zucchini	1 tablespoon chopped parsley
6 cups broth (page 45)	½ teaspoon salt
5 tablespoons butter	1½ cups arborio rice
¾ cup coarsely chopped onion	½ cup grated *parmigiano*

Scrub and trim the zucchini and slice them into ⅜-inch rounds. Bring the broth to a simmer.

In a heavy-bottomed pot, melt half the butter and sauté the onion for 3 minutes. Stir in the parsley, then the zucchini and the salt. Raise heat, turn everything once or twice, and then add the rice. Sauté, stirring, for about 30 seconds.

Pour on 2 cups of the simmering broth (or enough to cover the rice). Simmer over medium heat, stirring often and adding a ladleful of broth as the rice dries out, for about 30 minutes, or until the rice is *al dente*.

Mix in the remaining butter and the grated *parmigiano*. Serve at once, with additional *parmigiano* and a pepper mill.

WINE SUGGESTION

Try a full-flavored white wine with this dish: Pinot bianco or, for a more prickly attack, Sauvignon blanc (from Gradnik or Borgo Conventi, if possible).

Risotto with Sausage

[RISOTTO CON LA LUGANEGA]

The basic Italian *risotto* technique can be adapted to an infinite number of variants, with meats, fish, cheeses, or vegetables. The key to bringing arborio rice to its plumpest perfection is to add liquid a little at a time, only as fast as the rice absorbs it. This means you really can't walk away from the stove for very long while a *risotto* is cooking, but it also means you never have to worry—as with the closed-pot pilaf technique—whether your rice might have required more or less liquid than the standard amount. Tasting and adjusting as you go, you'll never end up with either scorched or soupy results.

---

3 links parsley and cheese sausage (page 37), or ½ pound commercially made *luganega*
1 quart meat broth (page 45)
⅓ cup finely chopped onion
3 tablespoons butter

2 tablespoons dry white wine
1½ cups arborio rice
¾ cup grated *parmigiano*
Salt
Freshly ground black pepper

Remove the casing from the sausage and crumble it. Bring the broth to a simmer.

In a casserole, soften the chopped onion in half the butter. Add the sausage meat and brown it. Raise heat, sprinkle on the wine, and let it evaporate.

Add the rice, stirring to coat all the grains with the fat. Sauté 1 to 2 minutes. Reduce heat to medium-low and start adding broth, a ladleful at a time. Stir often and add more broth only as the rice begins to dry out. Cook for 35 to 45 minutes, or until the rice is *al dente* and has absorbed almost all its liquid. (If you run out of broth before then, use boiling water.)

Stir in the remaining butter and all the grated cheese. Taste for salt and pepper. Serve at once.

WINE SUGGESTION
The best accompaniment for this risotto *would be an unassertive red wine, such as a Barbera or a Merlot.*

Polenta

If you grew up with *polenta*, you can't begin to imagine life without it. If you didn't, it takes a while to figure out what all the fuss is about. For northern Italians, *polenta* is a staple, an indispensable. They use it as if it were bread, as if it were rice, as if it were pasta, as if it were potatoes. They eat it hot and cold, dry and moist, plain and seasoned, soft and hard, and they can't imagine anyone doing otherwise. Soft and fresh from the pot, it's eaten as is, or has cheese stirred into it, or becomes an edible container for sausages in tomato sauce. Cold and hard, it's sliced and brushed with butter, or sliced and grilled and served hot alongside steaks or chops or under game birds. What follows is the basic recipe for a sturdy thick *polenta*, either to be eaten as is or adaptable for other dishes. If you like it thinner, use only 1½ cups cornmeal.

————•————

5 cups water   1⅔ cups cornmeal
2 teaspoons salt

In a large, heavy-bottomed pan, bring the water and salt to a boil. Have the cornmeal ready in a bowl nearby.

Take a handful of cornmeal and let it shower gradually through your fingers into the water, stirring constantly. Continue with the remaining cornmeal, a handful at a time, regulating heat as necessary to avoid eruptions as the *polenta* thickens. This showering-in process should take 5 to 10 minutes. If splotches of dry cornmeal remain on the surface for more than a few seconds, stop adding cornmeal until they are stirred in, and then proceed slowly.

Continue cooking and stirring the *polenta* for 30 minutes. (Contrary to what many traditional recipes tell you, you do not have to stir *constantly* once all the cornmeal is in; but don't let more than 30 seconds go by without giving the mixture a good thorough stir.)

To serve plain as a primo:

Spread the *polenta* out on a marble or lightly oiled surface to a thickness of about ½ inch, let it cool, and cut it into strips or diamonds. Brush it with melted butter and broil it until the top is crisp.

To serve as an accompaniment to a sauced meat dish:

Spread the freshly made *polenta* out on a platter, making a slight depression in the center, and pour the meat and its sauce into the well. For other serving suggestions, see the discussion of *polenta* on pages 53–54.

WINE SUGGESTION

If your polenta *is being served as a* contorno, *let the* secondo *determine your choice of wine. If it's being served very simply as a* primo, *drink whatever pleases you—there's no right wine, and there's no wrong one either, though most people will find that a soft red wine like a Dolcetto or Cabernet or Merlot will taste best with it. If the* polenta *is being served with a cheese or a sauce or other ingredients, they should provide the clues to the wine you want.*

————•————

SECONDI

Fish

The only real secret of Italian fish cookery, in any part of Italy, is freshness, and when Italians describe a fish as fresh they mean caught that morning, not yesterday. So fanatical are they about this that a national law—one of the more strictly observed in a generally scofflaw society—requires restaurants to identify on the menu any fish that has been frozen. Woe betide the cost-cutting restaurateur who tries to pass off a frozen fish as a fresh one to the world's most knowing audience.

Buy your fish as fresh as possible and use it quickly, while it still has the richest flavor. Look for fishes with clear eyes, bright, clean gills, firm flesh, and no disagreeable odors (in fact, very little odor of any sort, save a clean, oceanic scent). The best rule to keep in mind about shopping for fish is to take what the market offers, which is most likely to be the freshest catch, rather than marching determinedly from shop to shop seeking one particular kind of fish, which may very well no longer be fresh.

Fowl and Rabbit

Poultry covers a broader range in Italy than in the United States. In addition to distinguishing between four or five kinds of chicken by age and sex, Italian butcher shops routinely offer—and Italian families routinely prepare—quail, guinea hen, and rabbit. All these animals have usually been allowed to walk around and scratch for their food, with the result that each not only has some flavor, but also tastes different from the others. American breeders seem to have used all the wonders of modern science to produce a race of chickens that tastes like cardboard, so seek out the best and most flavorful birds you can find in order to get the best out of these recipes.

Any recipe we offer for chicken can be prepared in exactly the same way for rabbit, and vice versa.

Flesh

Once more, there are important differences between ingredients that bear the same names. Young lamb in Italy is much younger than ours, and veal comes from an animal of half the age and weight of those that supply our veal. Consequently, those meats are tenderer and more delicate there than they are here. Beef is not all that common anywhere in Italy, and steaks and large roasts are rare indeed. The same is true of large cuts of pork. The whole hams and loins are often dedicated to curing—to produce succulent *prosciutti, coppa,* and the like. Fresh pork, most often served in the form of chops or cutlets or rolled stuffed fillets, makes more frequent appearances on central and southern tables than in the North.

———————◆———————

Fresh Sardines with Fennel
[ACCIUGHE FRESCHE AL FINOCCHIO]

This simple preparation works very well with most small fresh fish, even smelts, though it reaches its height with sardines. In cleaning the sardines, don't forget to scale them. (The scales are so tiny your eyes might not notice them—but your tongue will.) A light scraping from tail to head with an ordinary kitchen knife does the job easily. It's your choice whether to leave on or remove the little heads: In Italy, fish of any size is invariably served as intact as possible, but many Americans are squeamish about that. We prefer the heads still on; it makes the fish easier to handle and is a more attractive serving presentation.

———————◆———————

16 small fresh sardines or anchovies
  (about 1½ pounds)
2 garlic cloves
½ teaspoon fennel seeds

3 tablespoons olive oil
Salt
4 large slices country bread, toasted
  in the oven

Clean and dry the sardines. Peel and cut the garlic cloves into 3 or 4 slices each. Grind the fennel seeds to a powder in a mortar.

Heat the oil in a large sauté pan. Add the garlic and sardines. Cook 1 minute on each side over moderate heat, then sprinkle with salt and the powdered fennel. Reduce heat, cover, and cook very gently for 5 to 10 minutes, depending on the size of the fish, until the flesh flakes easily.

For each portion, lay 4 fish on each slice of toasted bread and pour the pan juices over the top.

WINE SUGGESTION

A very dry, very crisp white wine matches perfectly with this dish; Pinot grigio, Chardonnay, a still Prosecco, or an excellent Soave are all possibilities.

Broiled Tuna Steaks with Fennel

[TONNO AI FERRI]

This remarkably simple preparation takes full advantage of tuna's own satisfying flavor. One of the better things that Americans seem to have learned from the Japanese is what a wonderful fish uncanned tuna is, and consequently fresh tuna is now widely available in United States markets, and not only in sushi bars. As you may gather from this and the preceding recipe, Italians thoroughly enjoy combining the flavors of the freshest possible fish with fennel.

2 teaspoons fennel seeds
4 fresh tuna steaks, 1 inch thick (about 1½ pounds)

Salt
Olive oil

Grind the fennel seeds to a powder in a mortar. Preheat the broiler.

Sprinkle one side of each tuna steak with salt and a little powdered fennel. Add a few drops of olive oil and spread it over the surface. Place the steaks on the broiler, seasoned side down, and season the upper side in the same way. Broil for 6 minutes.

Sprinkle a little more powdered fennel on the upper sides, turn the steaks, and broil the other sides for 4 to 6 minutes, or until juices run clear when the fish is pierced with the point of a knife.

WINE SUGGESTION
With this dish try a Trentino Chardonnay or Pinot bianco.

Grilled Tuna Steaks

[TONNO SULLA GRATICOLA]

Even greater simplicity rules here than in the preceding recipe; only a delicate marinade intensifies the tuna's own flavor. This classic marinade can be used for any fish steaks or fillets, whether they are to be broiled, pan-fried, or oven-roasted.

3 tablespoons finely chopped onion
1 bay leaf
2 teaspoons minced parsley
2½ tablespoons lemon juice
2½ tablespoons olive oil

Salt
Freshly ground black pepper
4 fresh tuna steaks, 1 inch thick (about 1½ pounds)

(continued)

Mix all the ingredients except the tuna in a large flat dish. Pat the tuna steaks dry and turn them in the mixture to coat both sides. Let them sit for 1 hour, turning once or twice.

Broil in a hot broiler, about 6 minutes on the first side and 4 to 6 minutes on the remaining side, or until juices run clear when the fish is pierced with the point of a knife.

WINE SUGGESTION
Same choices as for the preceding recipe.

Grilled Monkfish
[CODA DI ROSPO ALLA GRIGLIA]

Monkfish are amazingly ugly to look at and amazingly good to eat. They have a dense, firm flesh and a flavor akin to scallops or lobster. Grilling them almost without adornment, as in this recipe, brings out the best in them. The very light flouring and subsequent brushing with the oil and lemon juice seals in the fish's natural moisture and also gives it a delightfully crisp surface. This technique works wonders with any scaled, whole fish the size of these monkfish tails or smaller. Another advantage of this technique is that, when you combine it with rubbing the broiler rack with lemon, it prevents your fish from sticking.

2 monkfish tails, each about 1 pound	Freshly ground black pepper
1 lemon	3 to 4 tablespoons olive oil
¼ teaspoon salt	Flour for dredging

Rinse and pat dry the monkfish tails. Squeeze the lemon into a small bowl and beat in the salt, pepper, and 2 tablespoons of the oil.

Preheat the broiler to very hot, with the pan 4 to 6 inches from the heat source. Just before cooking the fish, rub the broiler rack with the cut sides of the squeezed lemon halves.

Rub the monkfish tails with olive oil and toss them in a small bag with the flour, then tap them to knock off all but the lightest coating. Lay them on the broiler rack and brush their tops with the lemon and oil mixture. Grill a total of 18 to 20 minutes, turning them once after 10 minutes and brushing each side with the lemon and oil mixture when you turn. The fish is done when a sharp knife inserted into the center of the fish releases only clear juices. The exterior of the fish should be crisp and firm, the flesh uniformly opaque. Serve at once, with lemon wedges.

Monkfish's richness responds well to either the complement of a round, full-bodied wine (Pinot bianco, Gavi) or the contrast of a bright, acidic one (Pinot grigio, Sauvignon blanc).

Venetian-Style Braised Cuttlefish
[SEPPIE ALLA VENEZIANA]

This dish is one of the glories of Venetian cooking, and to taste it in its full dimensions you must use true cuttlefish, not squid. Cuttlefish or inkfish are more squat than squid; their mantle is bell- or dome-shaped and thicker-fleshed. They are also much richer than squid, and we say this as fans of squid in all its forms. Cuttlefish are not easily come by: The fresh item is a great rarity. But they freeze very well—we've tested this recipe with frozen cuttlefish and it tasted just fine—and the frozen ones do occasionally appear in the market. So whenever you see them, seize the opportunity to try this wonderful braise. All the labor lies in obtaining and cleaning the cuttlefish; the actual cooking is a snap.

2 pounds cuttlefish	¼ cup white wine
1 garlic clove, minced	1 tablespoon tomato paste
3 tablespoons chopped onion	½ cup broth
¼ cup olive oil	Salt
3 tablespoons chopped parsley	

Clean the cuttlefish:

Lay a cuttlefish out on a chopping board, the side with the spatulate spine-bone up. Slit the skin at the bottom end of the mantle and pull out the bone, in the direction of the tentacles. Loosen the membrane around the bone with your fingers if necessary. Then slit the body cavity all the way up to the tip.

Insert your thumbs between the smooth white flesh on the bottom and the intestines on the surface, and working upward, separate off the innards. (Take care not to squeeze the intestines, or they'll burst.) Discard them.

Cut off the tentacles, just underneath the eyes, and remove the hard, cartilaginous beak. Drop the flat body piece into a bowl of cold water for a few minutes (to loosen the skin) while you prepare the remaining cuttlefish in the same way. Then peel away the dark skin with your fingers, starting at a bottom edge.

(continued)

Prepare the dish:

Slice the cuttlefish crosswise into strips about ½ inch wide and 2½ inches long.

Sauté the garlic and onion in the olive oil until soft. Add the parsley and the strips of cuttlefish and their tentacles and sauté over a medium-high flame for 5 to 6 minutes. Pour on the wine, then the tomato paste dissolved in ¼ cup of the broth. Bring to a simmer, cover, reduce heat, and cook gently for 30 minutes, stirring often. If the liquid cooks off, add a few tablespoons of the remaining broth as necessary. Taste for salt before serving.

WINE SUGGESTION

A rich, distinctive white wine makes the best partner to this dish; Tocai is fine, as is top-of-the-line Sauvignon, and so are Vintage Tunina and Gavi.

Ligurian Fish Stew
[ZUPPA DI PESCE ALLA LIGURIANA]

A marvelous, aromatic, tomato-less fish stew, very different from the southern version that you'll find on page 278. Try to select a mixture of fish of different tastes and textures. Weakfish (sea trout), flounder, and bluefish are fine; whiting, monkfish, or striped bass can also be used. If you use monkfish or blowfish tails, don't also use sea scallops; the textures and flavors are too similar. If you have your fish dealer prepare the fish for you, don't forget to have him give you the heads and bones for the stock this recipe requires. Allow 40 to 45 minutes' cooking time, exclusive of cleaning the fish.

————————◆————————

1½ pounds mixed whole fish: weak-fish, fluke or flounder, bluefish, eel, scallops, etc.
½ carrot
½ small onion
½ celery stalk
8 to 12 mussels
¾ pound squid
2 hearts of romaine lettuce
3 anchovy fillets
1 garlic clove

⅓ cup olive oil
1 tablespoon minced white of leek (or substitute onion)
1 bay leaf
¼ teaspoon dried thyme
Salt
Freshly ground black pepper
⅓ cup dry white wine
4 slices day-old country bread, toasted in the oven
1 tablespoon chopped parsley

Bone the fish and cut the flesh into serving-size pieces—steaks and fillets, according to the size and shape of the fish. Put the fish heads, tails, and trimmings into a pot with a quart of water. Coarsely chop the carrot, onion, and celery and add them to the pot. Bring to a boil and simmer, covered, for 30 minutes, then strain and reserve the broth.

Scrub the mussels and steam them open in a pot with ¼ cup water. Remove them from their shells, debeard, and rinse them carefully; set them aside. Strain the mussel cooking liquid into the fish broth.

Clean the squid and cut them into rings. Chop the lettuce; you should have 1½ to 2 cups, loosely packed. Mince the anchovy fillets. Peel and halve the garlic.

In a large casserole, heat ¼ cup of the olive oil. Add the squid rings and sauté 5 minutes. Then add the minced leek or onion, the chopped lettuce, the bay leaf, and the thyme. Salt lightly, pepper heavily, and cook gently for 20 minutes, uncovered, stirring from time to time.

Turn heat to high, add the wine, and stir constantly until it is entirely evaporated. Stir in the minced anchovy and the pieces of fish. Sauté 2 to 3 minutes, then add the fish broth. Stir well and simmer 10 minutes.

Heat the remaining olive oil in a small skillet with the garlic halves. When the garlic is golden, press and discard it.

Add the mussels to the fish stew and simmer 2 more minutes. Pour the garlic-flavored oil into the stew.

Line a serving bowl with the toasted bread slices. Pour in the stew, garnish with chopped parsley, and serve at once.

WINE SUGGESTION
Crisp, dry, white wine, and a lot of it, well chilled, goes perfectly with this dish; Soave, Bianco di Custoza, Pinot grigio, Sauvignon—all are contenders.

Chicken with Morels
[POLLO CON SPUGNOLE]

The French virtually have a patent on the magical combination of chicken with morels, those wonderful springtime mushrooms that smell and taste of the forests they come from. But Italians have been reaping the fruits of their forests for quite a few years now, and they know a good way to cook a chicken when they see one. Actually, this recipe works well with any mushrooms, wild or cultivated, fresh or dried, but with fresh morels it achieves its loveliest balance of robustness and delicacy. We give directions for dried morels, as they are far more common; if you are lucky enough to obtain fresh, use half a pound of them—more if you really love them.

---

2 cups milk (made from nonfat dry milk powder is OK)
1½ ounces dried morels
1 chicken, about 3 pounds
2 tablespoons butter
2 tablespoons olive oil
Salt
Freshly ground black pepper
½ cup chopped onion

1 tablespoon flour
½ cup dry white wine
1 to 2 tablespoons brandy or grappa, optional
1 tablespoon tomato paste
1 cup chicken broth (page 45)
2 tablespoons chopped parsley
2 tablespoons chopped fresh basil

Heat the milk to a simmer and pour it over the morels in a bowl. Let them sit for 30 minutes, then drain and rinse the mushrooms, halve each one lengthwise, rinse again, and set aside.

Rinse the chicken, cut it into 12 pieces, and dry them with paper towels. Heat the butter and oil in a pan large enough to hold all the chicken pieces in a single layer. Brown the chicken pieces, sprinkling them with salt and pepper as you turn them. Remove them from the pan and set them aside.

Add the onion and morels to the pan and sauté over medium heat for 5 minutes, stirring occasionally. Sprinkle on the flour, salt, and pepper, and continue to cook, stirring, for 2 to 3 minutes longer. Add the white wine and let it reduce to about half. For a more aromatic dish, you can also add a tablespoon or two of brandy or grappa at this point.

Return the chicken pieces to the pan. Dissolve the tomato paste in the broth and add it, stirring well. Cover and simmer for 20 to 30 minutes, until the chicken is done. Check from time to time, and if the sauce seems too thin, set the cover ajar for a time.

Defat the sauce if desired, sprinkle with the chopped fresh herbs, and serve.

WINE SUGGESTION

A good red wine is what we want here. Ideal choices would be a Nebbiolo or a Barbaresco, or perhaps a Nebbiolo-based wine from the eastern Piedmont—Gattinara or Ghemme or one of their cousins.

Sauté of Chicken with Salami, Mushrooms, and Chicken Livers

[POLLO ALLA FRIULANA]

The strong, bright seasonings in this recipe will infuse some flavor into even the blandest supermarket chicken. This is no-nonsense, hearty food, not meant for people who choose chicken because it's undemanding on the taste buds. About an hour's preparation and cooking time.

---

1 ounce dried *porcini*	⅓ cup finely chopped onion
1 chicken, 2½ to 3 pounds	1 tablespoon chopped parsley
½ pound chicken livers	1 bay leaf
¼ pound Genoa-style *salami*	½ cup dry white wine
4 tablespoons butter	

Put the dried mushrooms in a bowl and pour 1 cup boiling water over them. Let them sit for 30 minutes, then drain them, reserving the water. Rinse them thoroughly, cut them into thin strips, and rinse again to remove all traces of grit. Line a sieve with a dampened paper towel and strain the mushroom-soaking liquid into a small bowl.

Rinse and pat dry the chicken. With knife and poultry shears, cut it into about 20 small pieces. Dry each piece with paper towels. Clean the chicken livers and chop them together with the *salami*.

In a large, heavy-bottomed casserole, melt the butter. Add the onion, parsley, bay leaf, and chicken pieces. Let them cook together gently for 10 minutes over moderately low heat, turning the chicken pieces frequently to brown them on all sides.

Raise heat, pour in the wine, and stir until it evaporates. Lower heat, add the liver, *salami*, mushrooms, and ¼ cup of the mushroom soaking liquid. Salt very lightly and pepper generously. Stir all well together, bring to a simmer, cover, and cook gently for 30 minutes, checking occasionally and adding a few spoonfuls of the mushroom-soaking water if the dish appears to be drying out.

Serve at once.

WINE SUGGESTION

A big white wine or a medium-bodied red. Good choices include Pinot bianco, Tocai, and Traminer for whites; Merlot, Cabernet, or Dolcetto for reds.

Sautéed Rabbit with Peppers

[CONIGLIO AI PEPERONI]

This classic Piedmontese dish can be made with chicken instead of rabbit, but since it's easier to get a rabbit with flavor of its own than a chicken that tastes like anything—even the frozen rabbits that supermarkets carry are much tastier than most chickens—it would be a shame not to try this recipe at its best. It takes only a little more than 1 hour to prepare.

1½ ounces *prosciutto* in a chunk	4 parsley sprigs
3 tablespoons butter	¾ cup broth (page 45)
3 pounds rabbit, cut into serving pieces	4 large red or yellow bell peppers
Salt	¼ cup olive oil
Freshly ground black pepper	2 garlic cloves, minced
2 bay leaves	4 anchovy fillets, chopped
1 rosemary sprig	⅓ cup red wine vinegar

Chop the *prosciutto* and sauté it in the butter in a large casserole for 5 minutes. Rinse and dry the pieces of rabbit and brown them in the casserole. Add salt, pepper, the herbs, and the broth. Cover and cook gently until the rabbit is just tender, about 45 minutes.

Turn two gas stove burners to their highest flame. Set the peppers directly on the grates. As the skin blackens in the flame, turn the peppers with tongs until their entire surfaces are black. Then drop them in a brown paper bag, close the bag, and leave them for at least 5 minutes. Under a thin stream of running water, scrape away all the blackened skin of each pepper with a paring knife. Then cut it open, remove all seeds and membrane, blot it dry with paper towels, and cut it into strips about 2 inches long and ½ to 1 inch wide.

In a small pan, heat the olive oil. Sauté the garlic until golden, add the anchovy pieces, and cook over low heat until they dissolve (a minute or two). Turn heat to high, add the vinegar, and reduce the liquid to about 2 tablespoons.

When the rabbit is just tender, stir in the peppers and the garlic and anchovy mixture. Cook, covered, 20 minutes longer, stirring occasionally. Check from time to time, and if the sauce seems too thin, set the cover ajar for a time.

WINE SUGGESTION
This dish takes a great Piedmontese red wine (Barbaresco or Barolo) or a youngish (five or six years old) Amarone.

Herbed Baked Rabbit with Piquant Anchovy Sauce

[CONIGLIO AL FORNO CON PEVERADA]

Peverada is a vibrant sauce that goes well with many mild-flavored baked or roasted meats. The piquancy of its anchovy, onion, wine vinegar, and lemon juice is counterpointed by the lushness of its poultry livers and olive oil. In this recipe, that harmony of tastes is intensified by the rosemary, sage, and thyme that bake with the rabbit. The lard is also an important flavor component, so don't, by any means, substitute hydrogenated vegetable shortening. If you have no lard, olive oil would be an acceptable alternative.

FOR THE PEVERADA

¼ cup chopped onion
2 tablespoons olive oil
The rabbit's liver, or 3 ounces chicken
 livers
1 clove garlic

3 anchovy fillets
Salt
Freshly ground black pepper
Juice of ½ lemon
1 tablespoon wine vinegar

1 teaspoon dried rosemary
1 tablespoon sage
1 teaspoon dried thyme
2 ounces lard

2½ pounds rabbit, cut into serving
 pieces
½ cup dry white wine
1½ teaspoons chopped parsley

Make the peverada:

Soften the onion in a small, heavy-bottomed pan with the oil. Mince the liver together with the garlic and anchovy into a paste. Add the paste to the pan; salt lightly and pepper generously. Stir until the mixture loses its raw red color, then add the lemon juice and vinegar. Stir, cover, and cook over low heat for 45 minutes. Set aside until the rabbit is cooked.

Prepare the rabbit:

Preheat the oven to 375 degrees F. Finely chop the rosemary, sage, and thyme. Rub a heavy-bottomed broad baking dish with the lard and lay in the rabbit pieces. Strew any remaining bits of lard on the rabbit. Sprinkle with salt, pepper, and chopped herbs. Pour the wine over all.

Put the dish in the oven. After 15 minutes, reduce heat to 350 degrees and baste the rabbit with its cooking juices. Continue baking for 1 hour, basting every 15 minutes. Be sure liquid does not completely evaporate before rabbit is cooked (add water if necessary).

When the rabbit is tender, remove the pieces to a serving dish. Add the rabbit cooking juices to the warm *peverada*, stir in the chopped parsley, and pour it over the rabbit.

WINE SUGGESTION:
Same choices as for preceding recipe.

Duck Braised in Barolo

[ANATRA AL BAROLO]

The best duck for this dish is a relatively lean one like a mallard or a young muscovy. That is why a 2-pounder will feed 4 people in an Italian-style meal. If you can get only the pekin (Long Island duckling), which is an extremely fatty duck, you'll need at least a 5-pounder. Also, you'll have to defat the cooking pan carefully, though at least you'll then have a lifetime supply of duck fat to use for sautéing potatoes. Truly, it would be best to save this recipe for an occasion when the right kind of duck is available. About 2 hours' preparation and cooking time.

1 mallard duck, about 2 pounds	2 bay leaves
½ lemon	6 sage leaves
⅓ cup chopped onion	½ teaspoon rosemary leaves
⅓ cup chopped carrot	Salt
⅓ cup chopped celery	Freshly ground black pepper
2 tablespoons butter	1 cup Barolo or other hearty red wine
3 tablespoons olive oil	Chicken broth (page 45)

Rinse the duck inside and out, pat it dry with paper towels, and rub its interior with the cut half of the lemon.

Sauté the onion, carrot, and celery in the butter and oil until soft. Add the duck's liver and cook, stirring, for a minute or two. Add the duck, all the herbs, and a light sprinkling of salt and pepper. Brown the duck all over.

Tip the casserole and draw off most of the rendered fat. Pour on the wine, and when it comes to a boil, lower heat, cover, and cook gently, turning the duck every 15 minutes or so. From time to time, as the wine evaporates, add a ladleful of hot broth. Continue cooking for about 1½ hours, until the duck is tender.

Remove the duck and keep it warm. If there is hardly any liquid left, add another ladleful of broth and deglaze the pan. Degrease the sauce, pass it through the fine blade of a food mill, and reheat it in the pot. Cut the duck into quarters and pour the sauce over it before serving.

WINE SUGGESTION
With this duck serve (what else?) a good Barolo, preferably one at least seven years old.

Guinea Hen with Cabbage and Mushrooms
[FARAONA ALLE VERZE CON FUNGHI]

This is another recipe we have adapted from Ristorante San Domenico, in Imola. The savory preparation is also excellent for pheasant, partridge, or squab. The mushrooms contribute a great deal of flavor, so if you are driven to using cultivated ones, try beefing them up with a small quantity of dried *porcini*. In that case, you could also substitute up to a cup of the strained *porcini*-soaking liquid for an equal amount of broth. This dish takes about 2 hours from beginning to end.

1 guinea hen, 2 to 2½ pounds	2 to 2½ pounds savoy cabbage
6 tablespoons extra-virgin olive oil	½ pound fresh *porcini* or *shiitake* or
2 tablespoons butter	*cremosina* mushrooms
4 garlic cloves	3 cups broth (page 45)
2 teaspoons rosemary leaves	

Preheat the oven to 300 degrees F. Rinse and pat dry the guinea hen. Put 2 tablespoons of the olive oil and all the butter into a deep-sided casserole just large enough to hold the hen. Lay the hen in and set the dish, uncovered, in the oven for 1 hour, turning the bird every 10 minutes to brown on all sides.

Put the remaining olive oil into a small pan with the peeled whole garlic cloves and the rosemary. Heat very gently for about 15 minutes, not allowing the garlic to color. Then set aside until ready to use.

Wash, core, and coarsely chop the cabbage. Cut the stems off the mushrooms and discard or reserve for other uses. Quarter the caps.

Strain the flavored oil into a deep ovenproof pan large enough to hold all the cabbage. Over a medium-high flame, sauté the mushrooms for 2 minutes, stirring constantly. Add the cabbage and the broth. Mix well, cover, reduce heat to low, and simmer gently 30 minutes.

When the guinea hen is tender, remove it and cut it into serving pieces.

Bury them in the cabbage and put the entire pan in the oven for 10 minutes before serving.

WINE SUGGESTION
Red wine of good quality matches best here; almost any of the Nebbiolo wines would make a good choice.

Sautéed Breaded Veal Chops
[COSTOLETTE ALLA MILANESE]

The translation of *costolette alla milanese* does an injustice to this extraordinarily delicate dish. It is nothing like the rather heavy, solid food that the English-language description suggests, or what, regrettably, too many Italian-American restaurants offer—a German-style breaded veal steak. The true *costolette alla milanese* uses only the best, palest, young veal; only freshly made bread crumbs for the coating; and only pure butter for the sautéeing. It requires rib chops (sometimes called rib steaks) cut ½ to ¾ inch thick. In Italy, that's the thickness of a single rib bone. Our rib veal chops, being from larger animals, are about twice that thick, so ask your butcher to knock off the bottom bone, leaving only the curving rib bone; trim off all possible fat, baring an inch or two of the rib bone above the eye of the chop; butterfly the meat back to the rib, then split the rib lengthwise (the butcher's bandsaw does this easily) to give 2 thin rib chops; and pound the meat to flatten it.

Half a loaf of day-old Italian bread, crusts removed	¼ pound butter
1 egg	Salt
4 thin rib veal chops, cut as described above	1 lemon

Cut the bread into chunks and reduce it to fine bread crumbs in a food processor or blender. (If the bread is very fresh, you may need to stale it in the oven for half an hour so it will make fine enough crumbs.) You will need about 1½ cups. Spread them out on a plate.

Beat the egg on another plate.

Pat the veal chops dry with paper towels. Pound them lightly again to thin them out. Holding them by the rib bone, dip each one first into the egg, then into the bread crumbs, pressing down with your hand on the crumbs to make them adhere. This can be done in advance and the chops set on a rack in the refrigerator.

Turn the oven to low and set a serving plate in it. In a heavy-bottomed
sauté pan large enough to hold a single chop, melt 2 tablespoons of the butter.
As soon as the foam subsides, put in a chop and cook over medium heat for
3 to 4 minutes on each side, until the crumb coating is golden. Transfer the
chop to the dish in the oven while cooking the remaining chops, using 2
tablespoons butter for each one.

When all four are done, salt them lightly, distribute lemon wedges around
the dish, and serve.

WINE SUGGESTION
Gattinara or Carema make especially good accompaniments to this dish,
but any medium-bodied red wine of good quality will also serve.

Rolled Pan Roast of Veal
[ROTOLO DI VITELLO]

This appetizing and simple rolled breast of veal makes a very interesting contrast
to the more elaborately filled southern stuffed veal roll on page 286. If the
veal breast is very thick, butterfly it before pounding it, or substitute an equal
weight of veal round, butterflied and pounded. This recipe requires about 2
hours from start to finish (including the time needed to soak the mushrooms).

———————◆———————

1½ ounces dried *porcini*	1 teaspoon rosemary
1½ pounds boneless veal breast, in one piece	1 teaspoon sage
	1 garlic clove, slivered
Salt	2 tablespoons butter
Freshly ground black pepper	1 tablespoon olive oil
2 ounces thinly sliced *prosciutto* or *speck*	½ cup dry white wine
	1 cup broth (page 45)
1 tablespoon chopped parsley	1 tablespoon cornstarch, optional

Put the dried mushrooms in a bowl and pour 1½ cups boiling water over
them. Let them sit for 30 minutes, then drain them, reserving the water. Rinse
them thoroughly, chop them fine, and rinse again to remove all traces of grit.
Lay a dampened paper towel in a small sieve and strain the mushroom soaking
liquid through it.

Pound the piece of veal to thin it slightly. Salt and pepper it and lay the
prosciutto slices over the entire surface. Spread the chopped mushrooms,
parsley, rosemary, sage, and garlic over the top. Roll and tie it.

(continued)

In a heavy casserole, melt the butter and oil and brown the veal roll on all sides. Pour on the wine and let it evaporate almost completely. Sprinkle the meat with salt and pepper, add ¼ cup of the broth, cover, and cook slowly 1 to 1½ hours, adding the rest of the broth a little at a time as needed. Thicken cooking juices with cornstarch dissolved in 2 tablespoons water, if desired.

WINE SUGGESTION

A full-bodied white or a gentle red wine will both do well with this dish. Choose from Tocai or Pinot bianco for the whites or Dolcetto or Merlot for the reds.

Braised Veal Shanks

[OSSO BUCO ALL'ANTICA]

This is a traditional northern preparation of veal shanks without the tomato that characterizes the more familiar *osso buco alla milanese*. The unctuousness of the shank meat and especially of the marrow dominates the flavor of the dish. About 2½ hours' total preparation time, most of which is taken up by gentle simmering of the shanks.

½ ounce dried *porcini*
Flour
2 veal shanks, each cut into 3 or 4 pieces
4 to 6 tablespoons olive oil
¼ pound fresh mushrooms, sliced ¼ inch thick
4 garlic cloves, finely chopped
½ cup finely chopped onion
½ cup finely chopped celery

12 fresh sage leaves, or ½ teaspoon dried
2 sprigs fresh rosemary, or 1 teaspoon dried, crumbled
1 cup dry white wine
Peel of ½ lemon
2 tablespoons chopped parsley
1 teaspoon salt
Freshly ground black pepper

Put the dried mushrooms in a bowl and pour 1 cup boiling water over them. Let them sit for 30 minutes, then drain them, reserving the water. Rinse them thoroughly, coarsely chop them, and rinse again to remove all traces of grit. Lay a dampened paper towel in a small sieve and strain the mushroom soaking liquid through it.

Flour the pieces of veal shank and brown them, a few at a time, in 4 tablespoons of the olive oil in a large casserole. Remove them to a dish as they are done. Add more olive oil if necessary and sauté the chopped and sliced mushrooms, garlic, onion, celery, sage, and rosemary until well soft-ened, 5 to 10 minutes.

Add the wine and reduce it to half, scraping up browned bits adhering to the pan. Add the strained mushroom soaking liquid, the lemon peel, parsley, and salt and pepper to taste. Return the veal shanks to the pan and simmer, covered, for 1½ hours. Remove the pieces of lemon peel and the rosemary stems before serving.

WINE SUGGESTION

The ideal wine with this dish is one with enough tannin or acidity to counterpoint the succulence of the veal shanks. If you want a red wine, Barbera would be ideal (a young Nebbiolo might also serve); if you prefer white wine, try a Traminer aromatico or a young, relatively inexpensive Chardonnay.

Lamb with Fresh Horseradish
[AGNELLO AL CREN]

This improbably delicious dish could be called "lamb braised backward." You drop the meat into boiling liquid, simmer it for 30 minutes, then uncover the pot and boil off the liquid. Why the lamb remains meltingly tender, how it goes from pallid gray to a richly appetizing brown, and how it emerges perfectly seasoned and needing not a grain of salt, are all among the minor mysteries of Italian cooking technique. It definitely does all these things, however, and the dish gets a final boost into culinary stardom by a last-minute dressing with browned butter, grated horseradish, and chopped parsley. The horseradish should be fresh, and grated at the last minute. If you're forced to use prepared horseradish, drain it and rinse it well, and reduce the vinegar to 1 tablespoon.

1½ to 2 pounds lean boneless lamb from the leg
6 tablespoons butter
1 medium onion, thickly sliced
½ teaspoon dried thyme
1 bay leaf

¼ teaspoon freshly ground black pepper
3 tablespoons red wine vinegar
¾ cup broth (page 45)
1 small fresh horseradish root
3 tablespoons minced parsley

Trim all visible fat from the meat and cut it into 2-inch chunks. In a large casserole, place 3 tablespoons of the butter, the sliced onion, thyme, bay leaf, pepper, vinegar, and broth. Bring to a boil and add the pieces of lamb, stirring to coat them with the liquid. Cover and cook gently for 30 minutes, regulating heat to maintain a steady but gentle simmer. Stir occasionally.

Uncover the pan, raise heat to medium-high, and simmer briskly until liquid evaporates, 20 to 30 minutes. Stir often to keep the lamb from sticking. When the pan juices start to sizzle, lower heat and continue to cook, stirring, until lamb is well browned. (At this point the casserole can be set aside, loosely covered, until needed. Remove the bay leaf and reheat lamb thoroughly before proceeding.)

Peel and grate ¼ cup of horseradish root. In a small sauté pan, melt the remaining 3 tablespoons butter and simmer until it begins to brown. Off heat, stir in the horseradish and the parsley. Arrange lamb in a hot serving dish. Pour the sauce over it, toss well, and serve.

WINE SUGGESTION

With this dish you can serve either a soft red wine—Merlot or Cabernet from Friuli would be ideal—or a full-bodied white. In the latter case, Tocai is fine.

Lamb Shanks with Beans
[MONTONE CON FAGIOLI]

Originally intended for mutton and here adapted to lamb shanks, this dish makes great winter fare, with unaffected good flavor. It takes about 2 hours, plus the time to soak the beans.

¾ pound dried Great Northern beans	Salt
¼ pound *pancetta*	Freshly ground black pepper
3 tablespoons olive oil	2 tablespoons flour
½ cup minced onion	¾ teaspoon dried thyme
4 large lamb shanks (4½ to 5 pounds), sawn in half	1 bay leaf
	2 garlic cloves

The day before serving, pick over the beans and soak them overnight in a generous quantity of cold water.

The next day, drain the beans. Chop or grind the *pancetta*. Bring a kettle of water to the boil. Heat the olive oil in a large, heavy-bottomed casserole and add the onion and *pancetta*. Sauté over medium heat for about 5 minutes, until onion is soft and *pancetta* partly rendered.

Add the lamb shanks and brown them on all sides. Salt and pepper the pieces, then sprinkle on the flour and mix it well into the oil. Sauté another minute.

Add the thyme, bay leaf, whole garlic cloves, and the drained beans. Pour on enough boiling water to cover the beans by 1 inch. Bring to a boil, reduce to a simmer, cover, and cook 1½ hours, or until lamb shanks are tender. Check the liquid level from time to time and add a little more water if necessary. Taste for seasoning before serving.

WINE SUGGESTION
Dolcetto or Barbera make perfect companions to this unpretentious dish.

Calf's Tongue in Red Wine
[LINGUA DI VITELLO AL VINO ROSSO]

This method of cooking calf's tongue gives that delicate meat a more forceful flavor than usual, while leaving its pleasing texture intact. Many people enjoy this preparation even more with beef tongue, which requires an additional hour of boiling before peeling and proceeding with the recipe. The cooking techniques are very simple, and the dish can be done entirely in advance and reheated very satisfactorily.

1 calf's tongue, about 2 pounds	1 cup red wine
Salt	2 tablespoons minced parsley
1½ cups broth (page 45)	½ teaspoon dried thyme
3 tablespoons olive oil	1 bay leaf
2 tablespoons flour	Freshly ground black pepper

Drop the tongue into a generous quantity of boiling salted water and boil for 30 minutes. Drain it and let it cool. Peel away all the skin with a sharp-pointed paring knife. Trim off all gristle and fat from the base of the tongue.

Bring the broth to a simmer. Heat the olive oil in a deep casserole. Brown the tongue lightly on all sides, then remove it to a plate. Sprinkle the flour on the oil and cook, stirring, over a low flame for 2 minutes. Then add the wine and broth and bring to a boil.

Return the tongue to the pot, along with the parsley, thyme, and bay leaf. Salt and pepper lightly. Bring to a boil, reduce to a simmer, cover, and let cook 1½ hours, turning the tongue every 30 minutes. If the sauce gets too thick, add a few tablespoons of hot water.

(continued)

To serve, carve the tongue into ½-inch slices and strain the sauce over them.

WINE SUGGESTION
A soft red wine like Merlot or Dolcetto makes an ideal match.

Calf's Liver with Sautéed Onions
[FEGATO ALLA VENEZIANA]

The only secrets of this brilliant dish lie in getting the palest, youngest possible calf's liver and cooking the onions very slowly, wilting them just as you would for an onion soup. The marriage of these two ingredients creates a luscious harmony. Many versions of this dish call for lemon juice or vinegar, but we find that such an acid brightener isn't needed if you cook the liver *in* the long-simmered onions.

1 pound calf's liver, sliced ¼ inch thick	1 pound Bermuda onion, thinly sliced
Salt	2 tablespoons butter
Freshly ground black pepper	5 tablespoons olive oil
	1 tablespoon chopped parsley

Rinse the liver and trim off any bits of gristle or tube. Cut it into 2½-inch squares. Salt and pepper them lightly.

In a large-diameter sauté pan, sauté the onions in the butter and oil over the lowest possible heat, uncovered, for 30 minutes. Stir often and do not let the onions brown. Salt and pepper the onions lightly.

Raise heat to medium, add the liver, and cook 3 minutes, mixing constantly, so the liver pieces brown but don't harden. Stir in the parsley and serve at once.

WINE SUGGESTION
Friulian Cabernet or Merlot would make a fine companion to this dish.

Oxtails
[CODA DI BUE]

This dish offers excellent flavor and a rich, dark sauce from the long simmering of the oxtails—perfect fare for fending off the chills and damps of winter. Most of the cooking can be done in advance, leaving only about 20 minutes to finish the dish.

1 ounce dried *porcini*	½ teaspoon salt
4 tablespoons olive oil	¼ teaspoon pepper
3 tablespoons minced onion	1 ounce pork skin, diced
2 tablespoons minced carrot	1 oxtail, 2 to 2½ pounds, cut up
2 tablespoons minced celery	1 cup red wine
1 tablespoon minced parsley	1½ tablespoons butter
2 bay leaves	1 tablespoon flour

Put the dried mushrooms in a bowl and pour 1 cup boiling water over them. Let them sit for 30 minutes, then drain them, reserving the water. Rinse them thoroughly, coarsely chop them, and rinse again to remove all traces of grit. Lay a dampened paper towel in a small sieve and strain the mushroom soaking liquid through it.

Warm the olive oil in a casserole and add the minced vegetables, parsley, and bay leaves. Sauté 5 minutes over low heat. Add the salt, pepper, diced pork skin, and pieces of oxtail. Raise heat somewhat and cook together, stirring, for 5 more minutes.

Add the red wine and cook until it is almost entirely evaporated. Add the strained mushroom soaking liquid. Bring to a boil, reduce to a simmer, cover, and cook for 1½ hours, stirring occasionally. If stew becomes too dry, add a little broth or hot water.

Knead the butter and flour together into a paste. Remove the oxtail pieces from the pot and keep them warm. Remove and discard the bay leaves. Stir in the butter-flour paste and simmer 2 to 3 minutes. Add the chopped mushrooms and the oxtail pieces. Cover and simmer for 15 minutes. Serve at once.

WINE SUGGESTION
Robustness rather than elegance is what is needed here. Dolcetto seems a natural choice.

Roast Loin of Venison

[SELVAGGINA IN PAIZ]

Game is a much less exotic item in Italy than it is in the United States, and in the North, venison in season appears regularly on restaurant and home tables. This excellent preparation is typical of many northern game dishes: bathing in a wine-based marinade followed by gentle roasting with a flavorful source of additional fat to keep the lean meat moist. After the day of marinating, roasting time is only 1 hour.

FOR THE MARINADE

1 bottle dry white wine
1 small carrot, roughly chopped
1 celery stalk, roughly chopped
1½ tablespoons chopped parsley
1 stick cinnamon bark, about 2 inches long
1 tablespoon rosemary leaves

1 quarter-size piece of fresh ginger, chopped
8 cloves
1 teaspoon salt
½ teaspoon freshly ground black pepper

---

2 pounds loin of venison

¼ pound sliced *pancetta*

The day before serving, bring the wine to a boil. Place the meat in a deep glass or crockery dish and scatter all the remaining marinade ingredients around it. Pour on the boiling wine, weight the meat so it is fully covered by the wine, and let it cool to room temperature. Then refrigerate the dish for 24 hours, turning it once or twice during the time.

On serving day, preheat the oven to 350 degrees F. Drain and pat dry the venison. Place it on a rack in a roasting pan and cover it with the slices of *pancetta*. Roast for 1 hour.

WINE SUGGESTION

Game wants your biggest red wines; Barolo or Amarone are the logical choices here. Either of those wines will benefit greatly from being allowed to breathe for a few hours before drinking.

Bollito Misto

In English, "mixed boiled meats" doesn't sound very appetizing. In Italian, *bollito misto* always means a high treat. Americans traveling in Italy during the cool months are always surprised to see how many Italians choose a dinner of simple boiled beef or boiled chicken. In the best restaurants, the *carrello di bolliti*—the cart of boiled meats—always holds a place of honor, and often the most popular *secondo* of the winter is the *grande bollito misto*: an assortment that may include beef (short ribs—leaner in Italy than here—are a favorite cut), veal shank, a richly flavored stewing hen, fresh veal or beef tongue, *guanciale* (pork cheek—delicious though ugly), calf's head, and *cotechino* or *zampone*. These are always accompanied by puréed potatoes and several sauces, usually a mellow red one, a sharp green one, and *mostarda di Cremona*—a beautiful relish of whole fruits preserved in a clear syrup that is simultaneously fruit-sweet and mustard-tangy (happily now being imported). This recipe is the essence of simplicity; if you can boil water you can make a *bollito*, and if you have the smallest tinge of gastronomic imagination you can vary it at will. For example, strengthen the broth by adding some already-made stock to the pot, or add a parsley root or small leek. Or add a fresh tongue or a veal shank to enlarge the dish for extra diners; since the beef takes longer to cook than other meats, just add them later. Allow 2 to 3 hours for beef tongue, 1½ hours for veal shank, and about 45 minutes for calf's tongue. Or separately prepare our *cotechino* and lentil recipes (pages 38 and 130), and serve an assortment of *bolliti* accompanied by the lentils. Note too that many Italians take a bowl of the *bollito* broth with a few noodles or *tortellini* as their *primo* before tackling the meats. Any way you do it, it's simple and far more delicious than the bare-bones recipe makes it seem. Total cooking time for the meats given below is the time it takes the beef to reach tenderness: 2 to 2½ hours.

---

2 pounds beef brisket
2 celery stalks
1 large carrot, split lengthwise
1 medium onion
1 to 2 tablespoons tomato paste

1 chicken, 2½ pounds (or half a large stewing hen)
1 recipe tomato sauce for meats (page 34)

Bring 8 quarts of water, or part water and part broth, to a boil in a very large pot. Add the brisket, celery, carrot, onion, and tomato paste. Adjust heat to maintain a steady brisk simmer and cook, in all, about 2½ hours.

After the beef has been cooking for 1½ hours, add the whole chicken to the pot. (If you are using a stewing hen, add it sooner: it will need about 2 hours.) Cook until the meats are tender, about 1 hour. Just before serving, heat the tomato sauce in a small pot.

To serve, arrange the meats on a deep serving platter and moisten them with a little of the broth. Carve directly from the platter, or from a carving board. Serve a side bowl of broth to each diner, and pass the tomato sauce.

WINE SUGGESTION
A full-flavored, smooth red wine is perfect with bolliti. *Gattinara or its near neighbors make good choices.*

La Finanziera

This dish virtually defines Piedmontese cooking in its richness and variety as well as in the humble ingredients that it transforms into culinary glamour. It is a real tour de force, but the effort is well worth it. We give a recipe here for 8 diners, since if you're going to go to all this trouble you might as well have several friends over to share the glory of it. The name of the dish doesn't seem to have any connection (save in similar onomastic inspiration) with French preparations *à la financière*: Both denote a dish rich and varied enough to please exacting palates. Our recipe is of necessity an adaptation, since utterly authentic versions use parts of the cow and the chicken that the FDA thinks are fit only for cat food. If you are ever traveling in the Piedmont, taste some *finanziera* and see how well your cat is dining.

―――――――◆―――――――

FOR THE FORCEMEAT BALLS

½ pound veal stew meat
2 ounces *prosciutto*
1 large shallot
1 slice firm white bread, crust removed
½ teaspoon salt

⅛ teaspoon freshly ground black pepper
Nutmeg
2 tablespoons chopped parsley
1 egg

―――――――◆―――――――

1 pound veal sweetbread
1 veal kidney (about ¾ pound)
½ pound chicken livers
1 chicken breast (½ to ¾ pound)
6 ounces pickled mushrooms
3 ounces cornichons

1 cup meat broth (page 45)
6 tablespoons butter
6 tablespoons olive oil
Flour
½ cup red wine vinegar
⅓ cup dry Marsala

Make the forcemeat balls:
In a meat grinder, grind the veal, *prosciutto*, and shallot to a fine paste.

Crumble the bread, and add it to the veal mixture, along with the salt and pepper, a small grating of nutmeg, the parsley, and the egg. Mix all together well, then roll the mixture into 1-inch balls. Set them aside.

Prepare the meats, keeping each kind separate:
Blanch the sweetbread in acidulated water for 5 minutes. Cool under cold running water. Trim it and cut it into 1-inch chunks. Trim the kidney and the chicken livers and cut them into similar-size pieces. Skin the chicken breast and cut it into julienne strips.

Proceed with the dish:
Cut the mushrooms to match the meats; slice the cornichons. In a pot large enough to hold all the meats comfortably, bring the broth to a simmer.

Melt 2 tablespoons of the butter together with 2 tablespoons of the olive oil in a large sauté pan. When very hot, put in the strips of chicken and cook quickly over medium-high heat, stirring to separate the strips. Salt and pepper lightly. After about 2 minutes, as soon as they are opaque, take them out and put them into the main pot with the broth. (Keep this on the barest simmer throughout.) Lightly flour the forcemeat balls. Add another tablespoon each of butter and oil to the pan and brown the meatballs in it. Transfer them to the pot.

In succession, flour and brown the sweetbreads, the livers, and the kidneys, adding more butter and oil as necessary, lightly salting and peppering the meats, and transferring them to the pot when done.

When all the meats are in the pot, deglaze the sautéing pan with ¼ cup of the vinegar and add the contents of the pan to the pot. Add the preserved mushrooms and cornichons. Simmer gently, covered, 10 minutes. The dish can be prepared in advance up to this point. When ready to proceed, bring the pot back to a simmer. Add the remaining wine vinegar and the Marsala and cook, uncovered, 5 more minutes. Serve at once.

WINE SUGGESTION
Barbaresco and Barolo never taste so good as they do alongside finanziera, *and vice versa.*

Calf's Liver Sausage Rolls
[INVOLTINI ALLA CANAVESE]

These succulent little meat packages hold a sophisticated medley of sweet, sharp, and savory flavors. They positively cry out for a bottle of good red wine. The few spoonfuls of tomato sauce used in the cooking can be any type you have on hand; either our basic southern (page 31) or basic central (page 32) sauces would be fine. Since making up the *involtini* is somewhat time-consuming, we'd suggest doubling the recipe and freezing the extras, because once you taste them, you'll want to have them again. The second time, rather than braising them in broth and tomato sauce as directed below, try grilling them over a charcoal or wood fire. Either way, they're the best incentive we know to find a butcher who will supply you with caul fat (see discussion on pages 35–36).

―――――――――♦―――――――――

½ pound pork caul fat	1½ ounces grated *parmigiano*
½ pound calf's liver	5 juniper berries, chopped
2 ounces dried currants or raisins	3 tablespoons butter
½ pound plain sausage (page 36) or	½ cup broth (page 45)
Italian-style sweet sausage	3 to 4 tablespoons tomato sauce

Soak the caul fat in cold water for 30 minutes to clean and soften it. Spread it out on a board, trim off any large chunks of fat, and cut it into pieces 4 to 5 inches square.

Trim any tubes or fat from the liver. Soften the currants in warm water for 10 minutes, then drain them. (If using larger raisins, chop them.) Skin the sausages and crumble the meat. Put the liver through a meat grinder or pulse it briefly in a food processor. Mix it with the sausage meat. Mix in the grated cheese, the chopped juniper berries, and the currants.

Take a square of caul fat and place 1 tablespoon of the meat mixture along an edge. Roll into a tube, tucking the ends under and making a little sausage shape about 4 inches long and 1¼ inches in diameter. Make up *involtini* in that manner with the remaining caul and meat mixture.

Melt the butter over medium-high heat in a sauté pan. Add the *involtini* and sauté them for about 4 minutes, until they are lightly brown on all sides and a little firmer. Lower the heat if they start to stick.

Defat the pan if necessary, then add the broth. Raise heat and boil slowly until the broth is almost entirely evaporated. Stir in the tomato sauce. Turn the *involtini* in it, cover, and cook at low heat for 8 minutes.

Barbera, Dolcetto, Merlot—anything up to and including Nebbiolo would do well with *these* involtini.

Baked Eggplant Parma Style
[PARMIGIANA DI MELANZANE]

A very elegant and up-to-date northern version of the dish Americans know as eggplant parmigiana. This recipe, made entirely without the cheese of the same name, is a reminder that *i parmigiani* (citizens of the city of Parma) are some of the best cooks in Italy. Leftovers, should there be any, can be served at room temperature as an excellent *antipasto*.

———◆———

2 large eggplants (about 2½ pounds)
Salt
1 cup olive oil
1 to 1½ pounds tomatoes

4 tablespoons finely chopped fresh basil
Freshly ground black pepper
12 ounces *fontina*, sliced
8 ounces *gorgonzola*

Peel the eggplants and slice them lengthwise into ¼-inch pieces. Salt them generously and let them stand in a colander in the sink for an hour, then blot them dry and proceed.

Heat the olive oil in a heavy skillet. When it is almost smoking, fry the eggplant slices, a few at a time, until nicely browned. Drain on paper towels.

Preheat the oven to 375 degrees F. Peel, seed, and chop the tomatoes. Stir into them the basil and several grindings of pepper. Crumble the *gorgonzola*.

Lightly oil a shallow baking dish. Make layers of the eggplant slices, a small amount of tomato mixture, slices of *fontina*, and crumbles of *gorgonzola*. Reserve a generous amount of the two cheeses for the topmost layer.

Bake for 20 to 25 minutes, until cheeses are nicely runny and bubbling. Remove from oven and let sit at least 15 minutes before serving.

WINE SUGGESTION

A *crisp white wine will do here—Soave or Pinot grigio suggest themselves—but even better would be one of Verona's charming light red wines, Bardolino or Valpolicella.*

———◆———

CONTORNI

In Northern cooking, vegetable dishes play very much the same role as in American and French cuisine. That is, they are side attractions, supporting players to the central star—the fish or fowl or flesh that occupies center stage. In contrast to most of the rest of Italy, only a few northern *contorni* are capable of standing on their own as luncheon dishes or *antipasti*. This, however, is not at all to say that northern vegetable cookery is uninteresting. Far from it; some of these dishes would rank as leaders of their class in any cuisine.

Asparagus with Hard-Boiled Egg Yolk Mayonnaise
[ASPARAGI ALLA BASSANESE]

An elegant "sunburst" presentation for spring's first pencil-thin stalks of young asparagus. Italians are firmly convinced that thin asparagus have more concentrated flavor than fat ones, but it is not an extraditable offense to make this dish with thick stalks if they are your preference. The dish could also be served as an *antipasto*.

1½ pounds thin asparagus	½ teaspoon fresh lemon juice
4 hard-boiled egg yolks	Salt
⅔ cup olive oil	

Trim the asparagus spears to the same length. Wash them well and tie them in a bundle. Steam them or cook them in an asparagus cooker in boiling water up to within 2 inches of the tips. Cook 12 minutes (or more, depending on their thickness), until tender. Drain and let cool to room temperature.

In a medium-size bowl, mash the hard-boiled egg yolks to a very smooth paste with the back of a spoon. Pour on the olive oil in a thin stream of droplets, as in making mayonnaise, stirring constantly so that the yolks take up all the oil. Then add the lemon juice and a sprinkling of salt.

Choose a very large round serving plate. Arrange the asparagus in a sunburst pattern, tips facing inward. Pour the sauce in a ring around the necks of the asparagus spears. Diners are to pick up the spears in their fingers and dip the tips in the central pool of sauce. The tough part of the stem at the base is not eaten.

If the asparagus are to be used as an antipasto, *accompany them with a light, acidic white like Pinot grigio. If served as* contorno, *serve the wine suggested by your* secondo.

Cabbage in Casserole

[CAVOLO IN CASSERUOLA]

This simple treatment produces an unusually subtle dish of cabbage, imbued with a harmony of flavors from the *pancetta*, rosemary, and onion. It takes about 45 minutes, including the time to shred the cabbage.

1¼ to 1½ pounds cabbage, preferably savoy	1½ teaspoons rosemary leaves
2 ounces *pancetta*	Salt
½ cup broth (page 45)	Freshly ground black pepper
¼ cup olive oil	1 tablespoon tomato paste dissolved
½ cup chopped onion	in ½ cup warm water

Wash and trim the cabbage. Quarter it, remove the core, and slice it into strips ½ to 1 inch thick. Cut the *pancetta* into ¼-inch cubes or matchsticks. Bring the broth to a simmer.

Warm the olive oil in a large casserole. Add the onion and rosemary and sauté over low heat until the onion is soft, about 5 minutes. Add the *pancetta* and continue cooking, stirring occasionally, for 5 to 10 minutes, or until the *pancetta* colors and is partly rendered.

Add the cabbage, salt and pepper it generously, and stir to coat it well with the other ingredients. Then raise the heat to medium and stir in the tomato paste dissolved in the water. When the tomato water is almost completely absorbed, add the hot broth and continue cooking, partly covered, for about 20 minutes longer, stirring occasionally. The dish is done when the cabbage has absorbed all its liquid and is tender to the bite. (If the liquid disappears before the cabbage is tender, add hot water by tablespoonfuls.)

WINE SUGGESTION

Follow the wine suggestion for your secondo.

Deep-Fried Fennel

[FINOCCHI FRITTI]

Fennel is available fresh during most of the year, and its bright, refreshing taste is especially welcome in the cold months when other vegetables are far from their best. Stalks of fennel, washed and trimmed, often appear raw as part of a simple *antipasto*, but the cooked vegetable also has great charm. This almost universal Italian preparation takes about 20 minutes from start to finish. The cooked fennel may also be served at room temperature as part of a mixed vegetable *antipasto*.

2 large or 4 small bulbs fennel	1 egg
Salt	3 tablespoons milk
Oil for deep-frying	2 tablespoons flour

Trim and wash the fennel. Cut it into lengthwise wedges about ½ inch across the thickest part. Drop the pieces into boiling salted water and boil for 5 minutes. Drain and pat them dry.

Heat frying oil to 375 degrees F. In a broad dish, whisk together the egg and milk, then gradually beat in the flour to make a smooth batter.

Coat the pieces of fennel with the batter and fry them in the oil until golden. Drain on paper towels and serve immediately.

WINE SUGGESTION

A *dry white wine like Soave or Pinot grigio goes well with fennel in an* antipasto; *for use as a* contorno, *follow the wine suggestion for your* secondo.

Stewed Lentils

[LENTICCHIE IN UMIDO]

Lentils are wonderful with all sorts of boiled or dry-cooked meat. They are almost obligatory as an accompaniment to *cotechino*. This recipe takes slightly more than 2 hours to make, but it needs very little attention during that time. Any leftovers make a pleasant cold side dish, with a generous topping of crisp chopped onion and perhaps a lacing of extra-virgin olive oil.

½ pound lentils (1 cup)
1½ cups broth (page 45) or, preferably, *cotechino* cooking liquid (page
38)
6 tablespoons chopped onion
6 sage leaves
½ cup chopped carrot

½ cup chopped celery
2 garlic cloves, peeled and lightly
crushed
½ cup olive oil
Salt
Freshly ground black pepper

Pick over the lentils, rinse, and drain them. Put them in a pot, cover them with cold water, and bring to a boil. Boil gently for 1 minute, then let sit in the water for 1 hour. Drain.

Bring the broth to a simmer.

Sauté all the vegetables and the sage in the olive oil for 5 minutes. Add the lentils and sauté, stirring, for 2 minutes. Add the hot broth, cover, turn heat very low, and cook for 1 hour, or until lentils have absorbed all their broth. Taste for seasoning and add salt and pepper to taste. Stir thoroughly and serve.

WINE SUGGESTION
Serve the wine suggested for your secondo.

Grilled Mushrooms

[FUNGHI GRIGLIATI]

This recipe is an adaptation of the Italian way of dealing with fresh *funghi porcini,* and if you are lucky enough to ever find *porcini* in your market or woods by all means use them. We have found that *shiitake,* an oriental mush-room now widely cultivated in the United States, responds well to the same treatment and gives a significant echo of *porcini*'s taste and texture. *Cremosini* are an Italian mushroom that turns up frequently if irregularly in markets. They are shaped like our domestic cultivated mushrooms, but are usually larger, and with a dark brown cap and dark gills. Both are very tasty, and this recipe can be executed successfully using either one. In fact, this recipe also works pleasingly with large caps of the ordinary cultivated mushrooms. Mush-room dishes like this one are often served for lunch or as a light *secondo.*

8 large mushrooms, 4 each of *shiitake*
and *cremosini*

1 large garlic clove
⅓ cup olive oil

(continued)

Wash or wipe clean the mushrooms. Trim off stems and reserve for other uses. Slice the garlic thin and sauté it gently in the oil until it turns golden.

Preheat the broiler. Set the mushrooms, cap side down, on the broiler pan 3 to 4 inches from the heat and brush them generously with the garlic-scented oil. Broil 3 to 5 minutes, then turn them, brush the top sides generously with the oil, and broil another 3 to 5 minutes. Serve immediately.

WINE SUGGESTION
If the mushrooms are standing on their own, serve a medium-bodied red wine such as a good Dolcetto or even a Nebbiolo. If they are a contorno, *follow the wine suggested for your* secondo.

Venetian Pan-Fried Potatoes
[PATATE ALLA VENEZIANA]

In Venice, these simple potatoes sometimes accompany calf's liver, but more often turn up alongside roast meats and grilled fishes.

2 pounds boiling potatoes	⅔ cup thinly sliced onion
4 tablespoons butter	1 teaspoon salt
4 tablespoons olive oil	2 tablespoons chopped parsley

Peel potatoes and cut them into chunks 1 to 1½ inches thick.

Melt the butter in a sauté pan with the oil; add the onions and sauté over low heat until they begin to soften, about 5 minutes. Add the potatoes and continue cooking gently, uncovered, stirring often, about 40 minutes, or until they are done. Add salt and parsley, mix well, and serve.

WINE SUGGESTION
Follow the suggestions for your secondo.

Ligurian Potato-Cheese Pie
[TORTINO ALLA LIGURIANA]

This rich and delicious recipe plays havoc with resolutions to eat lightly. It really serves more than 4 persons, but the quantities given fit neatly into a standard pie plate, and the leftovers are excellent, especially if you don't refrigerate them. Besides, diners always eat more of this than they think they possibly can, so leftovers are rarely a problem. Serve these potatoes with roasted meats, grilled steaks or chops, or even with complexly sauced meats.

2 pounds baking potatoes
7 ounces *fontina*
5 teaspoons flour
⅓ cup milk
7 tablespoons butter
4 to 5 tablespoons bread crumbs

2 tablespoons olive oil
2 whole eggs plus 1 yolk
Salt
Freshly ground black pepper
5 teaspoons grated *parmigiano*

Cook the potatoes in their skins in salted water until three-quarters done. Drain, peel, and cut them into ½-inch slices.

Cut the *fontina* into ½-inch dice. Dissolve the flour in the milk. Butter a 9-inch pie plate and coat with bread crumbs. Preheat the oven to 375 degrees F.

Melt 4 tablespoons of the butter in a large casserole with the oil. Add the *fontina* and the flour-milk mixture and stir over low heat until the cheese melts. Off heat, mix in the potatoes, then the eggs, the extra yolk, and generous quantities of salt and pepper.

Put the potato mixture into the prepared pie plate, spreading it evenly. Sprinkle the top with 2 to 3 tablespoons of bread crumbs and the grated *parmigiano*. Dot with the remaining butter. Bake for 45 minutes, or until the surface is crisp and golden brown. Unmold or serve directly from the baking dish.

WINE SUGGESTION
Follow the suggestion for your secondo. *The cheese and potatoes in this pie interact splendidly with all sorts of red wines.*

Grilled Radicchio di Treviso
[RADICCHIO ALLA GRIGLIA]

Radicchio di Treviso is a relatively new arrival on the American scene. Its closest analogue among more familiar vegetables is probably Belgian endive, but we think *radicchio* is tastier—vivid yet subtly bitter-savory. Raw *radicchio* makes a superior single-ingredient salad, but quickly grilled it's magnificent. You must use the Treviso variety of *radicchio*; look for something that resembles a small romaine lettuce that has been crossed with a beet—long heads of deep ruby-to-maroon, white-veined leaves arranged like an old-fashioned feather duster. There is another variety called *radicchio di Verona*, which is round-headed, resembles a small, loose red cabbage, and tastes pretty much like cabbage too.

---

4 heads *radicchio di Treviso* (¾ to 1 pound)	Salt
	Freshly ground black pepper
3 tablespoons olive oil	

Halve the *radicchio*, leaving some stem attached to each piece. Wash and drain the halves, then pat them dry with paper towels.

Preheat a griddle or large cast-iron frying pan to very hot: a few drops of water flicked onto the surface should bead up and skitter away instantly.

Rub each half head of *radicchio* with olive oil, using 2 teaspoons or less per half. Place them on the hot griddle and cook 1 to 3 minutes per side until the edges of the leaves brown and the whole head wilts; turn once only. Sprinkle lightly with salt and pepper while cooking. Serve at once.

WINE SUGGESTION
Follow the suggestion for your secondo.

Salad with Pancetta and Balsamic Vinegar
[INSALATA BALSAMICA]

The cooking technique and desired effect of this recipe are similar to those of the French dandelion salad, *pissenlits au lard*. In both cases the greens are dressed with and lightly wilted by the hot fat—though *insalata balsamica* has the advantage of then caressing them with the wonderful balsamic vinegar produced in and around Modena, a vinegar unlike any other in the world. It is thick, dark, and intensely flavored, the result of years of aging and concentrating in a succession of barrels made from different varieties of wood.

---

4 cups (loosely packed) chicory, young dandelions, escarole, and/or hearts of Bibb lettuce	2 teaspoons olive oil
	Salt
	Freshly ground black pepper
1 scallion, chopped	2 teaspoons balsamic vinegar
2 ounces *pancetta*, diced	

Wash, drain or spin dry, and shred the greens.

Slowly render the chopped *pancetta* in an enameled sauté pan with the olive oil until completely crisp—about 15 minutes. Remove the crisped bits with a slotted spoon and put them in a large salad bowl. Add the salad greens and the scallion, and sprinkle lightly with salt and pepper.

Just before serving, reheat the oil and rendered *pancetta* fat. Toss the salad with the fats, then with the balsamic vinegar. Serve immediately.

WINE SUGGESTION

Balsamic vinegar doesn't behave as churlishly with wine as other vinegars do, so you may continue to drink with this salad whatever remains of your secondo's wine. Should you choose to serve this dish as an antipasto, *try accompanying it with a good Pinot bianco or Sauvignon.*

DOLCI

Dolci means "sweets" in Italian, but sweet they rarely are. Most Italian desserts taste of fruit and nuts, even of wine and spices, rather than of sugar. And most Italian meals don't conclude with a dessert. That's usually reserved for very special occasions. So the Italian dessert repertoire is not enormous, and the recipes that follow are pretty representative of the mainstream of it—fruits, fresh and cooked, puddings of a sort (the category of *budino* covers a lot of territory), a few "pastries" that are really often close to flavored breads. Each of them is tasty and wholesome, and each could be accompanied by a glass of fruity Asti Spumante—which is unqualifiedly Italy's favorite dessert wine —or by a glass of sweet, still Moscato.

———— ♦ ————

Baked Stuffed Peaches
[PESCHE RIPIENE ALLA PIEMONTESE]

A classic Piedmontese dessert, playing the lush sweetness of summer peaches against the almond essence of amaretti cookies, with just a touch of bitter chocolate to blend them. We use the optional sugar only when we can't find bursting-ripe peaches. About 10 minutes preparation time, 30 minutes baking.

———— ♦ ————

4 large ripe freestone peaches	1½ tablespoons granulated sugar, optional
12 amaretti cookies	1 teaspoon brandy
1½ teaspoons unsweetened cocoa	Butter for baking dishes

Preheat the oven to 350 degrees F. Wash and dry the peaches but do not peel them. Cut them in half and remove the stones. With a teaspoon, scoop out some of the pulp, enlarging the cavities but leaving a wall about ½ inch thick all around.

Mince the removed pulp and put it in a small bowl. Crumble in the amaretti cookies and stir them into the peach pulp along with the cocoa, the sugar if desired, and the brandy. Stuff the peaches with the mixture.

Butter 4 individual gratin dishes and set 2 stuffed peach halves in each. Bake 30 minutes. Serve hot, warm, or at room temperature.

Raspberries, Blueberries, and Strawberries in Grappa

[LAMPONE, MIRTILE, E FRAGOLE AL LANGHE]

This deceptively simple recipe amounts to considerably more than just a bowl of berries. Choose a young, unaged grappa, clear as water—preferably from the Piedmont, of course. And try an ice-cold glass of the same grappa (not poured over ice, but the whole bottle left in the freezer for half an hour or so) as a *digestivo* after you've finished your coffee.

———————————•———————————

1 cup raspberries
1 cup blueberries
1 cup strawberries

2 tablespoons confectioners' sugar
2 tablespoons grappa

Wash and stem the berries. Quarter the strawberries unless they are very small. Gently mix all the berries in a bowl with the sugar and the grappa. Refrigerate for about 1 hour before serving.

Lario Lemon Cream

[CREMA DEL LARIO]

The lively mixture of cream and lemon in this simple, charming dish is a delightful surprise to the palate. Contrary to what you might expect, the whipped cream does not break down when you add the lemon juice; it absorbs it with alacrity. Grappa fans are urged to substitute a young, clear grappa for the brandy.

———————————•———————————

1 cup heavy cream
4 tablespoons granulated sugar
½ teaspoon grated lemon peel

Juice of ½ lemon
3 tablespoons brandy

Whip the cream into stiff peaks. Delicately fold in first the sugar, then the grated lemon peel, then the lemon juice, and last the brandy.

Distribute the cream over 4 dessert dishes and chill for at least 1 hour before serving (to dissolve the sugar).

May be served with a crisp cookie.

Monte Bianco

Monte Bianco is the Italian name for the mountain most maps give as Mont Blanc. Italian cooks insist that the French version of this famous chestnut dessert is the translation and theirs the original. Whichever came first, it makes a grand dessert in Italian, French, or English. (Chestnut lovers should look into the southern *scherzo* of this dish on page 307.) Dried chestnuts, available in specialty-food stores, are much easier to work with than fresh, which are difficult to shell and skin. If you are using fresh chestnuts, however, double the weight called for in the recipe.

6 ounces dried chestnuts	1½ tablespoons butter
1 quart milk	4 tablespoons confectioners' sugar
1½ ounces unsweetened baking chocolate	1 cup heavy cream
	¾ teaspoon vanilla extract

Rinse the chestnuts. Put them in a large pot with 3 cups of the milk and bring to a boil. Boil 2 minutes, then turn off heat and let nuts sit in the milk for at least 2 hours.

Drain and rinse the chestnuts, discarding the milk. Pick over the chestnuts carefully, removing any remaining brown skins and cutting out any unsound parts. Put the nuts in a clean pot with fresh milk to cover. Bring to a boil and simmer briskly, uncovered, about 15 minutes, until milk is entirely absorbed.

Melt chocolate and butter in a double boiler. Add 3 tablespoons of the sugar and stir until dissolved. Off heat, purée the chestnuts through the coarse blade of a food mill into the chocolate. Mix well, adding 2 to 3 tablespoons of cream, if necessary, to achieve a smooth consistency.

Pass the mixture through the food mill again, letting it fall freely onto a serving plate. With your fingers, lightly comb the shreds into a conical mound.

Whip the remaining cream with the vanilla and remaining 1 tablespoon sugar. Cover the upper third of the chestnut mound with whipped cream, drawing it up into a peak to resemble a snowcapped mountain. Serve at once.

Bonet

Bonet is not only one of the most popular desserts of the Piedmont, it is several of the most popular desserts of the Piedmont. Its local variations range all the way from a light chocolate pudding up to this elaborate caramelized coffee custard unmolded onto a chocolate almond cake base. Allow about 3 hours to prepare this *bonet*.

FOR THE CAKE BASE

¼ pound butter
½ cup granulated sugar
2 eggs, separated, plus 1 egg white

2 teaspoons unsweetened cocoa
¼ cup flour
4 amaretti cookies, pulverized

FOR THE CUSTARD

1½ cups sugar, in all
2 cups milk
6 eggs at room temperature

6 tablespoons unsweetened cocoa
1 cup *espresso* or other strong coffee

Make the cake:

Preheat the oven to 350 degrees F. Butter and flour a 9-inch springform pan. Cream the butter and sugar until light. Add the egg yolks and beat very thoroughly. Gradually mix in cocoa, flour, and pulverized amaretti. Beat the three egg whites until stiff but not dry and fold them into the batter. Pour it into the prepared pan and bake 20 minutes, or until cake is still slightly soft in the center. Cool the cake on a rack, leaving it in the pan.

Make the custard:

Caramelize a 9-inch round 6-cup mold, using 1 cup of the sugar, as follows: Put the sugar in a small pan. Add ¼ cup water but do not stir. Turn heat to high and cook, swirling the pan occasionally, until the sugar dissolves. Continue to boil the syrup until it turns a light golden brown. Pour this caramel into the mold and tilt it in all directions to coat it completely.

Preheat the oven to 350 degrees F. Bring a kettle of water to a boil. Heat the milk to just below boiling point. Beat the eggs and the remaining ½ cup of sugar together well. Beat in the cocoa. Still beating, gradually add the coffee and the milk. Pour the mixture into the caramelized mold.

Set the filled mold in a baking pan and add boiling water to a depth of 1 to 2 inches. Bake 1 to 1¼ hours, until a knife blade inserted into the center of the custard comes out clean. Transfer the mold to the refrigerator and chill thoroughly.

Assemble the bonet:

Have a serving plate ready. Remove the sides of the springform pan from the cake. Loosen it from the bottom of the pan, but let it remain sitting on the bottom. Dip the custard mold briefly in hot water to loosen it. Quickly place the cake upside down on top of the custard mold, take off the bottom of the springform pan and replace it with the serving plate, then invert plate, cake and custard, removing the custard mold. Serve at once.

Ladyfingers

[SAVOIARDI]

We call them ladyfingers, the French call them cats' tongues, and Italians name them for the ancient province where they originated. Of the three, only the Italian name makes any sense; the English is ridiculous and the French unthinkable. *Savoiardi* are good with fruits or granita or sherbets. This recipe makes about 4 dozen.

Butter and flour for baking sheets	½ cup flour
3 eggs, separated, plus 1 extra egg white	Pinch of salt
¾ cup granulated sugar	¼ cup confectioners' sugar

Preheat the oven to 325 degrees F. Butter and flour two large baking sheets.

Beat the egg yolks together with ½ cup of the granulated sugar until the mixture is pale yellow and very thick. Put the flour and salt into a sifter and gradually sift it over the egg-sugar mixture, stirring it in until smooth.

Beat the 4 egg whites until stiff but not dry. Stir a big spoonful of them into the batter, then delicately fold in the rest. Transfer the batter to a pastry bag fitted with a round or fluted tip.

Pipe the batter onto the prepared baking sheets in strips about 4 inches long and ⅜ inch wide, leaving 1-inch spaces between strips.

Mix the remaining ¼ cup of granulated sugar together with the confectioners' sugar. Put it in a small sieve and sift half of it over the cookies. Let them sit 10 minutes to absorb the sugar, then sift on the rest. Let sit 2 minutes.

Put the sheets in the oven and bake 10 minutes, or until the *savoiardi* are very lightly golden. Let them cool 2 minutes on the pans, then transfer them to racks.

Barolo Chocolate Cookies

[ALBESI AL BAROLO]

An unusual combination of ingredients in these "little Albans" results in a very good, crisp cookie. Actually, good isn't right; they're great, with a rich, deep, unsweet chocolate flavor that almost transforms into coffee. Though this recipe requires about 5 hours, most of it is just waiting for things to ripen.

½ cup shelled hazelnuts (2 ounces; about 4 ounces whole nuts)
¾ cup granulated sugar
½ teaspoon baking soda
1 tablespoon unsweetened cocoa

1 egg white
2 tablespoons Barolo or other dry red wine
Butter
4 ounces semisweet baking chocolate

Reduce the hazelnuts to a powder by pulsing them in a food processor (be careful not to let them become butter). Add the sugar, baking soda, and cocoa and blend them together well.

Transfer the mixture to a bowl and mix in the unbeaten egg white and the red wine, to obtain a very thick batter.

Line 4 cookie sheets with buttered parchment paper. Transfer the batter to a pastry bag fitted with a plain round tip and pipe the dough out in 1-inch rounds, leaving 3 inches of space between cookies. (Or drop the batter by half teaspoonfuls onto the paper.) There should be about 4 dozen rounds. Set the cookie sheets aside for 1 to 2 hours.

Preheat the oven to 325 degrees F. Bake each sheet 10 minutes, until the cookies are large, flat, bubbling, and still just a little bit soft. Remove the sheet from the oven and let it sit for a minute, then carefully detach the cookies from the paper with a spatula. Cool them on a rack.

Melt the chocolate in a small, heavy-bottomed pan. Using a butter knife, delicately (because the cookies are very fragile) spread the bottom of one cookie with a thin layer of chocolate and sandwich another cookie to it. Let the *albesi* sit at least 2 hours before serving.

They keep well for several days.

WINE SUGGESTION

Albesi *are one of those rare desserts that just love a red wine, and Barolo is the obvious choice. It's worth saving a glass of your dinner red to sip with these little black beauties.*

Miascia

We wish we could tell you what *miascia* means, but we've not been able to find out; a reasonable guess says it means mixture or medley, which would certainly be an accurate description of its ingredients. Whatever it may mean, it's a fine, old-fashioned country cake, with an unusual vibrancy from the presence of the rosemary leaves. About an hour's preparation time, then an hour's baking.

---

4 ounces day-old country bread, hard crusts removed	¼ teaspoon salt
1 cup milk	1 tablespoon flour
1 tablespoon golden raisins	1 tablespoon cornmeal
½ cup seedless grapes	1 egg
1 apple	3 tablespoons butter
1 pear	1 tablespoon olive oil
Grated peel of ½ lemon	1 teaspoon chopped fresh rosemary leaves
¼ cup plus 1 tablespoon granulated sugar	

Cube the bread, lay it in a broad deep bowl, pour on the milk, and let it soften for 1 hour. Soften the raisins in warm water for 15 minutes. Wash and drain the grapes.

Preheat the oven to 350 degrees F. Peel and slice the apple and the pear. Add them to the bowl of bread and milk, along with the lemon peel, the ¼ cup sugar, salt, flour, cornmeal, raisins, grapes, and egg. Mix all together well.

Butter a 9-inch round baking dish. Pour in the mixture and smooth the surface. Dot the butter over the top and sprinkle on the olive oil, the remaining tablespoon of sugar, and the chopped rosemary. Bake for 1 hour. Let cool before serving.

Paradell

Paradell resembles *miascia* both in the untranslatability of its name and in the down-home comfort of its taste. This quickly made dessert—about 15 minutes to cook once the batter has rested—is really a giant pancake with fruit, not unlike the French *clafoutis*.

3½ tablespoons butter	¾ cup flour
2 eggs	2 large cooking apples
⅛ teaspoon salt	Confectioners' sugar
⅓ cup milk	

Melt 2 tablespoons of the butter and let it cool. In an electric mixer, blender, or food processor, beat the eggs together with the salt, milk, and melted butter.

Gradually incorporate the flour and beat until very smooth. Let the batter sit
for about 1 hour.

Peel, core, and slice the apples thin. Mix them into the batter.

Melt 1 tablespoon of the remaining butter in a 9-inch nonstick sauté pan and spread the apple batter evenly in it. Cook at moderate heat for 5 to 6 minutes, until the bottom is firm and golden. Slide the *paradell* out onto a plate. Film the bottom of the pan with the remaining butter, then quickly set the pan upside down on top of the plate with the *paradell* and invert the two. Cook the other side of the *paradell* another 5 minutes, or until golden.

Serve immediately with a liberal dusting of confectioners' sugar over the top.

Sage-Scented Tea Bread

[PANE ALLA SALVIA]

A specialty of Genoa, *pane alla salvia* falls into the general category of sweet tea breads, but it is also an ideal companion to a cup of strong espresso, any time of the day. The whole recipe takes an hour or less.

2 tablespoons butter	½ teaspoon salt
1 cup flour	1 tablespoon fresh sage leaves, minced
1 cup yellow cornmeal	1 egg
6 tablespoons granulated sugar	1 cup milk
4 teaspoons baking powder	

Preheat the oven to 375 degrees F. Melt the butter and let it cool. Mix together the dry ingredients. Add the egg, milk, and melted butter and beat to a smooth consistency.

Generously butter a 2-quart baking dish (a shallow square is traditional: 8 inches by 1½ inches). Pour in the batter and smooth it out. Bake 40 minutes, or until a knife blade inserted near the center comes out clean. Let cool somewhat, unmold, and serve warm or at room temperature.

La Gubana

A festive and much-loved dessert in Friuli, *la gubana* is a richly fruit-and-nutted coffeecake that grows subtle and sophisticated from a generous moistening with slivovitz—clear, unaged plum brandy—just before serving. The slivovitz is definitely a Yugoslavian touch; if you can't find any, an Alsatian *alcool blanc* like quetsch or mirabelle would be fine, or try using a clear young grappa. It's a lengthy preparation, though not complicated, so it's best to plan on an entire day for the project.

—————————◆—————————

FOR THE DOUGH

3 packages active dry yeast	¾ cup granulated sugar
½ cup warm milk	¼ pound butter, melted and cooled
6 cups flour	2 teaspoons salt
3 eggs, beaten together	

FOR THE FILLING

4 ounces shelled hazelnuts	1 tablespoon fresh bread crumbs
1 ounce blanched almonds	3 tablespoons butter
1 ounce pignoli	1 egg, separated
6 ounces golden raisins	1 to 2 tablespoons brandy
3 ounces mixed dried fruits	

FOR FINISHING AND SERVING

1 egg yolk	Slivovitz or other plum brandy or
Granulated sugar	grappa

Make the dough:

Begin by making a sponge. Dissolve the yeast in the milk and add 1 cup of the flour. Beat in an electric mixer for 2 minutes. Leave in mixer bowl, covered with a towel, and let rise in a warm place for 1 to 2 hours, until light and filled with air bubbles.

Mix remaining ingredients into sponge to obtain a soft but not sticky dough. (Use a little more flour or milk as necessary.) Knead 10 minutes. Cover again and let rise in a warm place until double in bulk, 2 to 3 hours.

Make the filling:

Soften raisins and dried fruits by steaming them over boiling water for 5 minutes. Drain well. Finely chop the hazelnuts, almonds, and dried fruits together. Put them in a large bowl together with the raisins and pignoli.

Brown the bread crumbs in the butter. Stir them into the fruits and nuts and mix all together well. Mix in the egg yolk and brandy. Just before spreading the filling on the dough, whip the egg white until stiff and gently stir it into the filling.

Form, bake, and serve:

Deflate the dough. Roll it out into a rectangle about 12 inches by 24 inches. Spread the filling over the entire surface, leaving narrow margins all around. Roll snugly from the long side, pinching the trailing edge to seal in the filling. Keep rolling the cylinder of dough under your hands, using gentle pressure to extend it to about 36 inches in length. Form it into a spiral on a buttered baking sheet, tucking the end in snugly. Drape a towel over it and let it rise once more to double in bulk, about 1 hour.

Preheat the oven to 400 degrees F. Paint the surface of the *gubana* with egg yolk and sprinkle it with sugar. Bake 15 minutes, then turn the oven down to 375 degrees. Bake 30 minutes longer. Check after the first half hour in the oven, and if the top is browning too fast, lay a piece of aluminum foil loosely over it. Test for doneness after a total of 45 minutes in the oven. Cool on a rack.

Serve still warm or at room temperature. Over each slice, pour 2 to 3 tablespoons of slivovitz. Don't omit this step. Without the slivovitz (or another plum brandy, or grappa) the *gubana* is only an excellent coffeecake. With it, it becomes a much more interesting creature, and as likely to become your favorite dessert as it is Friuli's.

Almond Torte

[TORTA ALLE MANDORLE]

Rye bread may seem an unlikely ingredient in a dessert, but it certainly works here. The medley of spices and other flavors results in a very sophisticated version of the ubiquitous almond torte. This recipe needs 30 to 45 minutes' preparation time and 30 minutes' baking.

Butter and bread crumbs for baking dish	1¼ cups granulated sugar
5 ounces blanched almonds	Grated peel of 1 lemon
4 eggs	⅛ teaspoon ground cloves
4 ounces fresh rye bread, without crust	⅛ teaspoon ground cinnamon
¼ cup rum	Confectioners' sugar, optional

(continued)

Preheat the oven to 350 degrees F. Butter a 9-inch round baking dish and coat with bread crumbs. Grate the almonds into fine fluffy pieces. Separate 1 of the eggs. Shred the rye bread into small crumbs. Spread them on a plate and sprinkle them with the rum.

Beat together 3 eggs and the extra yolk. Gradually add the sugar, beating well. Add the grated almonds, soaked bread crumbs, lemon peel, cloves, and cinnamon. Beat very well.

Whip the remaining egg white into soft peaks and fold it into the mixture. Pour it all into the prepared dish, smooth the surface, and put it into the preheated oven. Bake 30 minutes, or until a knife blade inserted into the center of the torte comes out clean. Unmold and cool on a rack. Sprinkle confectioners' sugar over the top before serving, if you like.

WINE SUGGESTION

If you can possibly find it—and once you've found it, if you can possibly afford it—serve with this lovely dessert a glass of Friuli's rare Picolit, an amber-yellow dessert wine of tremendous delicacy and charm. Otherwise, try a still Moscato.

THE CENTER

THE CENTRAL ITALIAN MENU

ANTIPASTI

Focaccia with Salt • Small Seasoned Focaccia
Garlic Bread with Tomato
Chicken-Liver Crostini I and II • Prosciutto and Cheese Crostini
Fresh Favas with Pecorino • Antipasto Mushrooms
Braised Artichokes with Parsley, Garlic, and Mint
Eggplant Nests • Roasted Stuffed Tomatoes
Baked Peppers with Piquant Sauce
Spiced Ricotta Spread • Poached Whiting

PRIMI

Bread Soup • Vegetable Soup • Ribollita
Spaghetti with Summertime Sauce • Summer Macaroni
Pasta with Beans • Penne with Artichokes
Linguine with Clam Sauce • Spaghetti with Tuna Sauce
Tonnarelli with Prosciutto and Peas
Spaghetti alla Carbonara • Spaghetti with Amatriciana Sauce
Macaroni with Lamb Ragù
Rigatoni with Prosciutto, Mushrooms, and Chicken Livers
Ravioli with Tomato Sauce
Potato Gnocchi with Tomato Sauce • Gnocchi with Puréed Pepper Sauce

SECONDI

Baked Striped Bass • Braised Squid • Deep-Fried Salt Cod
Fricasséed Chicken • Chicken with Peppers • Braised Chicken
Spit-Roasted Squabs
Veal Scallops with Prosciutto, Chicken Liver, and Anchovies
Beef Stew with Onions • Perugian Beef Rolls
Lamb Sauté with Wine and Vinegar

Crown Roast of Pork • *Roast Suckling Pig*
Roast Leg of Boar • *Sausages with Rape*
Braised Oxtails • *Braised Beef Tripe*
Mozzarella Soufflés

CONTORNI

Country-Style Artichokes • *Deep-Fried Artichokes*
Green Beans Sautéed with Tomato • *Green Beans with Fennel*
Fresh Shell Beans • *Sautéed Escarole*
Sautéed Tuscan Mushrooms
Roasted Potatoes with Bay Leaves • *Roasted Rosemary Potatoes*
Braised Zucchini • *Zucchini Tartlets*

DOLCI

Winter Fruit Compote
Ricotta and Strawberry Parfait • *Deep-Fried Ricotta*
Hazelnut Macaroons • *Hazelnut Cookies* • *Biscotti di Prato*
Rocciata • *Apple Tart* • *Jam Tart*

THE COOKING OF CENTRAL ITALY

I f you are one of the thousands of Americans who have managed to spend two or three weeks' vacation in Italy, the cuisine of central Italy is probably the Italian cooking you remember best. The Italian triple-play vacation—Rome-Florence-Venice—that constitutes most travelers' introduction to Italy also amounts to a reasonable introduction to the culinary style of the Center of Italy—and it is a center in more ways than only geographical.

The cooking of Italy's central provinces varies much more than that of the North. It is on the whole a lighter cuisine, with meat portions smaller, vegetables and fresh cheeses—such as Rome's beloved *ricotta*—more prominent. It manages to embrace extremes both of austerity and of richness, though an American view and an Italian view of which is which are likely to turn out completely opposite.

Take for example a Tuscan specialty, the fabled *bistecca fiorentina*, a large T-bone steak cut from Italy's best beef cattle, the Chianina. It is always prepared simply: grilled over a wood fire and served with the merest film of good olive oil—it's a very lean meat—plus lemon wedges and freshly ground pepper. That may make an American mouth water, but it's not what we have in mind when we think of luxurious dining. To the Italian palate and imagination, however, that large a piece of meat—especially a cut tender enough to eat rare—is almost a one-dish definition of *gourmandise*.

On the other hand, a dish of wild pigeon—the already richly flavored bird stuffed with a mixture of its own liver and a generous mincing of fresh truffle, then braised in good red wine and fresh herbs—will surely seem to the American imagination a triumph of *haute cuisine*, while to an Umbrian, it's a robust country dish—good eating but hardly a rarity.

The characteristic dishes of the Center reflect what the land and sea and seasons afford even more directly than those of the North. The hills, valleys, plains, and shores of Tuscany, Umbria (the only central Italian region without shores, actually), Lazio, the Marches, and the northern Abruzzi provide an abundance of good things, from boar, pigeon, hare, black truffles, and wild mushrooms to homely beans and greens and the thick, deep-green olive oil to dress them with.

Despite such specialties as the *bistecca*, meat occupies a less important place in the everyday menu of central Italy than it does in the North. Butter and cream don't disappear, but they play a much smaller role than olive oil and wine as recipe bases. *Polenta* loses its dominance here, though it will still appear occasionally (usually in the fall or winter, accompanying game). *Risotto* persists, but as an occasional dish rather than a staple.

Basically, this is the land of bread and pasta. Central Italy demonstrates the real meaning behind the cliché that bread is the staff of life. Good, hard-crusted country bread appears everywhere—at breakfast, in *antipasti*, in soups, in stuffings, even in desserts. Bread and wine appear on your restaurant table as soon as you sit (if you look around you will see at almost every table the performance of an ancient tribal rite: No one ever stops talking, no one ever loses eye contact, but every right hand automatically reaches out to take a slice of bread).

Simple *bruschetta* ranks among the most often enjoyed of *antipasti*, and for many country people may by itself make a light meal; a thick slice of bread, toasted in the oven or on the grill, rubbed while still warm with a clove of garlic—the raw garlic just melts into the golden bread—drizzled with extra-virgin olive oil and perhaps a pinch of salt, and served forthwith. Only those who have never tasted it will think it mean; like so much in Italian cooking, the whole is much more than the sum of its parts.

Pasta is ubiquitous and is always served as *primo* at the principal meal of the day. Echoes of the North persist, of course. Pasta here is frequently freshly made egg pasta, usually cut into noodles either broad or narrow—*fettuccine* or *fettucelle*, *papardelle* or *tonnarelli*, according to local dialect. Stuffed pastas also bear many names—*agnolotti*, *capellacci*, *ravioli*—but the most common stuffings are based on *ricotta*, with or without the addition of spinach. Commercial pasta—the dry, hard-wheat pasta of the South—also plays an important role, mostly in the form of the familiar *spaghetti*, but also as the much-loved *penne*.

Another southern touch shows up in the *arrabbiata* sauce that is almost indissolubly wedded to *penne*. What makes that sauce "rabid" is a little touch of *peperoncino rosso*, the small hot peppers so popular in the cooking of Abruzzi and points south. This is a tomato-based sauce, as is *salsa amatriciana* and many other of central Italy's favorite sauces. Nevertheless, the tomato does not dominate here as much as it does farther south. Many pasta sauces are executed *al bianco*, with just olive oil and white wine—or, like the famous *carbonara*, raw egg—as the liquid base, or with mushroom or meat juices providing the necessary moisture. Many, probably most, *secondi* use only a small amount of tomato as an accent, and a significant number use none at all.

Garlic is similarly employed. Even though by American standards it may be used frequently, it is almost never used heavily. Except in *bruschetta* and *spaghetti aglio e olio*, garlic serves mostly as an accent, often simply as a fragrance.

Throughout this area, *secondi* are usually very simply prepared. In Tuscany and much of Umbria, for instance, grilling over a wood fire is the most popular and frequent mode of cooking. Not only *bistecca*, but chops, cutlets, sausages, fowl of all sorts, even fish and shellfish cook directly on the flame. Where restaurants in France will make a major, self-congratulatory production of the fact that they grill *au feu de bois*, the practice is so common in Italy that it's never mentioned. It doesn't have to be; you taste it in the chickens, for instance, that come to table fragrant with the aroma of wood and wild herbs. In most cases, the flesh/fowl/fish has been lightly rubbed with olive oil, perhaps a squeezing of fresh lemon juice, and a crackling of fresh pepper, and allowed to "marinate"—there isn't enough liquid to call it that, but there's no other word—for about half an hour before grilling, while the fire burns through its first frenzy and makes a bed of evenly hot glowing embers. Then onto the grill, where it is watched carefully, turned once and once only—Italians swear turning meat or fish more than once toughens and dries it—and served promptly.

If a meat or a bird is too tough or a fish too big or too little to grill, they're likely to find themselves *in umido*, in some sort of moist preparation. Central Italians seem to prefer what we would call braises to what we would call stews, though the line is often a fine one, and individual cooks freely alter the quantity of liquid in any given dish to suit their own or their family's preferences (and every one of them will take an oath on their sainted mother's head that theirs is the only authentic way to make the dish in question). In dealing with such dishes in this book, we have given what we think to be the "mainstream" version of the recipe, but you obviously need not worry overmuch about preserving rigidly exact liquid measurements in your own cooking.

Vegetables, of course, vary with the season. Most Italian cooks eschew canned vegetables—the great exception is tomatoes—and remain distrustful of frozen ones. In central Italy, where the climate is mild over the year but unpredictable in the short term, *contorni* are a more reliable calendar than the weather, from the first asparagus and tiny peas of early spring to the last large caps of *funghi porcini* in late fall. In between, one enjoys a colorful and varied parade of vegetables: artichokes to be prepared in oil or in vinegar, to be steamed, stuffed, or fried; green beans, both broad and narrow; favas; zucchini and big yellow zucchini blossoms (stuffed with a bit of *mozzarella* and a smaller bit of anchovy and deep-fried—a dish to rhapsodize over); new potatoes to be roasted with fresh rosemary; and all the family of greens— spinach, swiss chard, escarole, and all their kin—that appear on menus and tables as generic but not inglorious *verdura*.

Desserts here, as everywhere in Italy, tend toward simplicity. Seasonal fruits appear in all their variety and all their Italian intensity of flavor. That, by the way, is a very real thing and not a piece of chamber-of-commerce hype. We've heard countless Americans swear they'd never really tasted a peach or pear until they ate them in Italy, and we're happy to add our own testimony to that effect. As Marcella Hazan remarks, the closest one comes in the United States to the lushness of flavor and texture of an Italian peach is a ripe mango. As for pears—well, one of our most avidly anticipated pleasures on an autumn visit to Italy is biting into a golden-ripe Anjou pear and feeling the still-firm flesh dissolve in the mouth into nectar. Perhaps one harvest in every five here comes up to what they achieve most years in Italy. The greatest cross an American cook who is trying to reproduce remembered Italian meals has to bear is California produce, big and pretty and bland. It promises so much and delivers so little!

Other desserts tend to be very local. Florentines love small hard nut cookies that they nibble with and dip in coffee—espresso, of course—or, even better, in the prized Vin Santo of the Chianti region just south of the city. Umbrians prefer *rocciata*, a sort of strudel packed with dried fruits and nuts and enough nutrition to keep a platoon marching for a week. Romans dote on *ricotta*— not just in their *ravioli*, but also made into a pudding, baked into a cake, formed into *bombe* (lightly sweetened balls of *ricotta* with a morsel of dark chocolate in their hearts, rolled in bread crumbs and deep-fried), or else served plain with sliced fruit or, simplest of all, by itself with a light sprinkling of sugar. Romans may take an elaborate pastry as a snack during the day, but after dinner they want a natural and simple dessert. During the brief season —a week or so in early June—when the fava beans are at their freshest and tenderest, they are what Romans will have for dessert, right out of the pod, perhaps with a shard of grainy *pecorino* cheese, and certainly with a glass of wine to wash it all down.

The cooking of central Italy derives as directly from basic country cooking as it depends on fresh country ingredients. The sophisticated cities of the region—Rome, Florence, Siena, Perugia—have preserved their lifelines to the countryside of farms and forests that, until very recent years, ran to within a kilometer or two of their bustling centers. It's not by accident that this *paese* was home to St. Francis: His ideals of simplicity and purity spring right from its heart. In this part of the world, to describe a dish as *un pasto dei poveri*— a dish of the poor—is not dismissal but praise of its honesty, flavor, and integrity.

Don't think, however, that central Italians are all naive peasants rejoicing in their poverty and simplicity. The Romans, who need a very sophisticated sense of humor just to get through their traffic and their strikes, are typical in possessing a very wry awareness of their heritage. We once asked a Roman chef why the classic *secondi* of his region—such as the delicious Roman dish of oxtails, *coda alla vaccinara*—were always prepared from what English disdainfully calls offal or variety meats. With a straight face, he told us it was because the politicians and the popes took all the good parts of the animals for themselves.

Whether that be true or no, it remains a fact that the cooks of this area perform wonders with the humblest and plainest ingredients. The next time you are in Rome, visit a very traditional Roman restaurant like Checchino dal 1887 and try a regional dish such as *rigatoni con la pajata*. Just don't ask what that delicious *pajata* is until you've finished the dish. (For those of you too impatient to wait for Rome, *pajata* is the duodenum of a milk-fed calf, cooked with the partly digested milk still in it, which is what makes it taste simultaneously so rich and so delicate.)

———————•———————

THE WINES OF CENTRAL ITALY

Central Italy is home to some of the best-known and least-known wines in the world, and sometimes they are the same wine: Chianti, for instance, which "everybody knows" is a mediocre red wine and always comes in a wicker flask (wrong on both counts); or "that charming little white wine" every vacationer in Rome or Florence recalls with such pleasure, but whose name—somehow—has escaped.

The wine situation in Central Italy is very different from that of the North. Both red and white wines are made in great abundance, but here the whites dominate both in the number of kinds made and in the quantity produced, though they do not often triumph over the reds in quality. The greatest difference between the Center and the North, however, lies not in what wines are made but how. In this region the custom of blending several different grape varieties—sometimes even blending white and red grapes to make a red wine, as in Chianti—has long held sway. With one or two important exceptions, this excludes the sort of single-grape varietal wine that was the rule in the North. Consequently, wines in the central provinces usually bear the name of the places they are made—Chianti, Orvieto, Frascati—rather than the grapes that make them. Or they are named with a combination of the two—Vernaccia di San Gimignano, for instance, where Vernaccia is the name of the grape variety, and San Gimignano the place the wine comes from.

Tuscany is unquestionably the most important wine zone in the Center of Italy. The hills surrounding Florence and running south to Siena, west almost to the sea, east to Arezzo and almost on into Umbria, produce great quantities of simple red and white wines, significant quantities of fine reds, and the tiniest handful of quality whites. This is Chianti land, in all its appellations:

- Chianti Classico, from the central zone of hills between Florence and Siena
- Chianti Montalbano from the area northwest of Florence
- Chianti Rufina, in the northeast of Tuscany
- Chianti Colli Fiorentini (the Florentine hills) from southeast of the city
- Chianti Colline Pisane (the hills of Pisa) from the area southwest of Florence, around Pisa
- Chianti Colli Senesi, the Sienese hills, directly south of the Classico zone and almost completely surrounding Siena
- Chianti Colli Aretini, from the hills around the town of Arezzo, east of Siena.

Chiantis differ markedly from one another, not only from zone to zone but even within the individual zones. This is because of the rugged character of the Tuscan countryside. That beautiful landscape of hills and valleys, sharp tors and gentle declivities, means for the winemaker a profusion of microclimates and soils. Each fold and wrinkle of the surface of the land affects the way the grapes grow and which of the several varieties that are blended in Chianti will thrive or suffer. That in turn determines the character of the wine those grapes make.

There is a more-or-less standard formula for Chianti. Its major component is the native Tuscan red grape Sangiovese, in proportions from 75 percent to 90 percent; plus the red grape Canaiolo nero in a range of between 5 and 10 percent, plus the white grapes Malvasia and/or Trebbiano, from a minimum of 5 to a maximum of 10 percent. For Chianti Classico—the wine made in the traditional heart of the Chianti zone and generally regarded along with Rufina as producing the Chianti with the greatest aging potential—the percentage of white grapes allowed in the blend is even smaller, between 2 and 5 percent. Finally, some winemakers add a spicing of up to 10 percent of nontraditional grape varieties (Cabernet sauvignon in particular is being widely adopted).

When you add to Chianti's diversity of climates and soils the variations that result from each maker's development of his own unique proportions for blending the different grapes, you wind up with a wine capable of many diverse incarnations. Chianti, in fact, can be everything from a young and fruity quaffing wine to an austere, full-bodied, and complex wine of great finesse. For people familiar with French wine, the situation is very similar to that of Bordeaux, where, in a few favored districts (the Médoc and Graves, St. Emilion and Pomerol), chateaux separated by only the width of a roadway can turn out wines of radically different styles and quality. Nobody in Chianti has yet produced a wine the stature of a Bordeaux First Growth, but some growers—Antinori, Frescobaldi, Selvapiana, and the related Carmignano winery, Villa di Capezzana—are clearly aiming for that class.

No distinction in Chianti is more important than that between plain Chianti and Chianti Riserva. In theory, every producer in every Chianti district could make a Riserva if he wished to. In fact, very few outside the Classico zone do (Rufina is the great exception). By law, a Riserva is aged minimally three years—at least part of that time in wood—before being marketed. A Riserva is the flagship of the Chianti-maker's fleet. It is usually the best wine he makes, the one on which the reputation of the house depends. It is fermented from the best grapes of the harvest from the best fields. Many of the smaller growers, with fewer resources to draw upon than the large houses, simply do not make a Riserva every year, but only when the harvest is good enough to warrant the distinction. Some larger houses follow this policy, too. A Riserva is always slightly higher in alcohol than a simple Chianti and is always, because of the time and expense of making it, more costly than a simple Chianti.

Riserva Chianti is made exactly as the finest wines are made anywhere: with first-rate materials, no gimmicks, and a lot of time—plus the best talents you can find in a winemaker, a lot of cooperation from the weather, and all the luck you can muster. In some years, like 1970, 1975, 1978, and 1979, Chianti makers hit the jackpot and wound up with a wine that just gets better year by year in the bottle. Most of the well-made 1970s, for instance, are drinking beautifully at this writing and will continue to do so for some years yet. The '75s still haven't finished growing, though they already taste wonderfully fruity and intense, with nice depth. And the '78s haven't yet emerged from their dormancy; they are still muffled, characterless at the moment, still a few years away from pleasurable drinking.

Producers of quality Chianti fall into two categories: large firms, usually family-owned, with roots in the Chiantigiana (as the heart of the Chianti zone in called) often going back centuries; and smaller, individual estates where the wine is made either very traditionally or very innovatively depending on the owner's personal vision. Among the established firms are such familiar and reputable names as Antinori, Brolio (the castle/estate of the Ricasoli family), Frescobaldi, Melini, Nozzole, Ruffino, Serristori, and Villa Banfi. A complete list of reliable estates would be far too long, but it would certainly include Avignonesi, Badia a Coltibuono, Boscarelli, Castellare, Castello di Volpaia, Chigi Saracini, Fossi, Monte Vertine, Selvapiana, and Spalletti.

Umbria produces a wine very similar to top-quality Chianti Classico from vineyards around the little town of Torgiano, between Perugia and Assisi. Its official name is Torgiano rosso (there is also a white variety), but you are most likely to see it in the United States under the brand name of its unquestionably best maker, Lungarotti, who calls it Rubesco. Ordinary Rubesco serves very well to accompany meat *secondi* of all sorts, while Rubesco Riserva mates very well with big roasts, game, and other strongly flavored dishes.

Even closer kin to Chianti is Vino Nobile di Montepulciano (not to be confused with Montepulciano d'Abruzzo, a much lesser wine). The wine is made from a similar blend of grapes and is treated in much the same way as Chianti, though many experts find that the site of the Montepulciano vineyards lends their best wines an elegance and breed superior to Chianti's. Others, however, question that distinction and regard Vino Nobile as simply another fine example of Riserva Chianti. Good makers include Avignonesi, Boscarelli, Fassati.

Brunello di Montalcino is yet one more close cousin of the Chiantis, but in its own austere and elegant way it is the family maverick. One of Tuscany's few varietal wines, it is made entirely from a special strain of Chianti's main grape, the Sangiovese, and cultivated only on the hills surrounding the medieval town of Montalcino in the province of Siena. Brunello—the local name for this subvariety of the Sangiovese—makes one of the world's longest-lived wines, a wine of tremendous complexity, authority, and beauty that perfectly accompanies richly flavored dishes, especially game. There are a number of good makers, in two distinct styles: the traditional (a wine hard and tannic in youth but mellowing beautifully and lasting long) and the modern (drinkable much sooner, but something of a question mark as regards longevity). The finest of the traditionalists are Barbi, Biondi-Santi, and Costanti. The moderns are spearheaded by Villa Banfi, Altesino, and Col d'Orcia, with strong support from Castelgiocondo. Il Poggione and Caparzo, which both make excellent Brunello, seem to hold a middle position between the two schools. Many Brunello houses use grapes from their younger vines to make a red wine called

Rosso di Montalcino. It receives less wood aging than Brunello and consequently is more accessible, ready to drink sooner, and much less expensive.

Another grape, somewhat more distantly related to the Sangiovese, lends its confusing name to one red wine and plays a major role in several others. Montepulciano d'Abruzzo is the grape and the wine—the latter a pleasant, fruity red to drink young and without ceremony. The connection with Montepulciano remains a mystery to experts. At present the grape variety is grown not at all in Montepulciano and only on a very small scale anywhere else in Tuscany, though it constitutes—as its name this time rightly indicates—the principal red grape of the Abruzzi and the Marches as well. Good brands to look for include:

- Casal Thaulero, Duchi di Castelluccio, and Illuminati in the Abruzzi, where the wine is called simply Montepulciano d'Abruzzo Rosso
- Fazi-Battaglia, Picenum, Tattà, Umani Ronchi, and Villa Pigna in the Marches, where the wine is usually called Rosso Conero or Rosso Piceno.

The white wines of central Italy are less easy to talk about because they are far more localized. Just about everyone who has visited Rome or Florence or Perugia has pleasant memories of a carafe of cool white wine sipped on a sunbaked terrace, and more often than not the name of that wine is as ethereal as its charm—was it Frascati? Orvieto? Verdicchio? Vernaccia? Galestro? Did it come from the Colli Albani? from Lake Trasimeno? Lago di Bolsena? San Gimignano? the Marches? the Abruzzi? The answer hardly matters, because most of these wines share the same characteristics. At their best, they are light-bodied and fresh tasting, with a delicate taste of white fruit (apples or pears, let us say) and enough alcohol and acidity to give them structure and make them feel lively on the palate. The Trebbiano grape goes into most of them, in percentages ranging from 20 to 100, and often too the Malvasia, which in the distant past made a sweet wine much prized in England: in one of Shakespeare's history plays, a pair of unfortunate young princes is drowned in a butt of Malmsey, i.e., Malvasia. Generally speaking, however, the white wines of central Italy are not recommended for such serious uses. Quintessentially, these are wines for drinking young—the younger the better—and without ceremony, before or with simple foods. They are created to be enjoyable, good quality, everyday wines, and they succeed admirably at exactly that.

There are literally hundreds of producers of these simple, pleasing wines from all the regions, and many of them appear—some regularly, others erratically—on the American market. Here is a small selection of recommendable brands, listed alphabetically by region:

REGION	WINE NAMES	BRAND NAMES
Abruzzi	*Trebbiano d'Abruzzo*	*Casal Thaulero; Duchi di Castel-luccio; Illuminati*
Lazio	*Castelli Romani, Colli Albani, Frascati, Marino*	*Fontana Candida, Gotto d'Oro, Principe Pallavicini, Villa Banfi*
Marche	*Verdicchio (from three locations: Castelli di Jesi, Matelica, Monta-nello)*	*Fazi-Battaglia, Garofoli, Villa Pigna*
Toscana	*Bianco del Chianti, Bianco della Lega, Galestro, Vernaccia*	*Antinori, Barbi, Badia a Colti-buono, Brolio, Frescobaldi, Guic-ciardini-Strozzi, Pietrafitta, della Quercia, Ruffino*
Umbria	*Colli del Trasimeno, Orvieto, Torgiano*	*Antinori (Castello della Sala), Bigi, Lungarotti (Torre di Giano), Petrurbani, Vaselli, Le Vellete*

In addition to these basic wines, a handful of special whites can also be found throughout the region. Lungarotti's Torre di Giano Riserva (Vigna il Pino), Brolio's Torricella, and Frescobaldi's Pomino (especially the Riserva from the Il Benefizio vineyard) all deserve particular remark, and are well worth whatever trouble it takes to seek them out. In addition, regional wine-makers are experimenting widely with new grape varieties—Chardonnay and Sauvignon blanc, for instance—and new blends. Some of the results are very promising, as at Antinori's Castello della Sala vineyards, Lungarotti's Umbrian plantings of Chardonnay, and Villa Banfi's extensive and ambitious Montal-cino vineyards, which have so far produced impressive bottlings of 100 percent varietal Chardonnay and Pinot grigio.

Tuscany preserves the old tradition of making Vin Santo, an unusual wine vinified from slightly dried Malvasia grapes and fermented and aged in a way that would destroy any other white wine. The fermentation, in partly filled and sealed small barrels, takes up to three years to complete because the barrels are stored not in the usual cool cellar but in an alternately freezing and baking attic, right under the roof. What emerges from the barrels after many years is amber in color, rich in aroma, and either austerely dry or lushly sweet or some improbably pleasing combination of the two. We are told that Vin Santo is an acquired taste, but we loved the wine from our first sip. There are few better desserts anywhere than a glass of Vin Santo and a few *biscotti di Prato*. All the major Chianti makers and most of the smaller Chianti estates produce some Vin Santo, and they usually pride themselves on it as the most authentically Tuscan of all their wines.

Finally, the last vineyard product to be mentioned from this area is—olive oil. All through central Italy, but especially in Tuscany and Umbria, the vineyards are interplanted with olive trees, which are a protected species. When one dies, another must be planted. When a new vineyard is set in, olive trees must be rooted in strict proportion to the number of vine stocks. The best produce of those trees is an extraordinary green, fruity nectar, obtained from the first, light pressing of the fruit. This extra-virgin olive oil is what transforms cold dishes and salads all through this part of Italy. Extra-virgin oil is only rarely used for cooking, but for a sheer unmediated olive-oil experience, it is superb. Many of the best makers, including a number of Chianti estates, have begun to export their extra-virgin oil to the United States.

———————◆———————

ANTIPASTI

In addition to the meat and seafood *antipasti* that central Italy shares with all the rest of the peninsula, the provinces of Lazio and Umbria and Tuscany also provide some distinctive dishes of their own. Principally these are based on bread and/or vegetables, reflecting accurately the somewhat spartan traditions of this ancient cuisine.

In Lazio and Umbria, fresh-baked bread joins the *antipasto* selection in the form of *focaccia*, a kind of flat bread flavored with relatively simple and usually dry toppings that range from unadorned coarse salt to onions and herbs. In Tuscany and Umbria and the Marches, slices from large round loaves are toasted and dressed in myriad ways to make their *antipasto* appearance as *crostini*.

Almost any vegetable, cooked or raw, has the potential to be used as an *antipasto* dish in central Italy, but the great majority of them are first given a light cooking and a dressing to counterpoint or complement their natural flavors. Artichokes are braised with white wine and mint, for example, and sweet, fleshy bell peppers are combined with a piquant marinara sauce. Some *antipasto* favorites amount to quite substantial dishes, almost lunches in themselves. One such is the popular Roman combination *fagioli con tonno*, a dish of white cannellini beans (cooked very simply with a little fresh sage and then cooled) that is presented to the diner strewn with chunks of tuna (the dark tuna packed in olive oil that all Italians relish), a drizzling of bright green extra-virgin olive oil, and a dusting of freshly ground black pepper.

These are honest foods, straightforward and direct. In this respect, the *antipasti* are a portrait in miniature of all the cooking of Rome and Florence and Siena and Arezzo and Perugia and Todi and Ancona and Sulmona. . . .

Focaccia with Salt

[FOCACCIA ALLA MODA TANA]

A *focaccia* is a disk of bread ranging anywhere from the thinness of a matzoh, as in this crisp example—our version of the speciality of the *trattoria* La Tana di Noiantri in Rome's Trastevere—to a huge cartwheel of a loaf 1 or 2 inches thick. To the simple pleasure of fresh-baked bread, *focaccia* adds some of the titillation of its southern cousin, the *pizza*, by virtue of the additional flavorings that are often brushed or sprinkled on as the *focaccia* bakes. This one, the very basic *focaccia*, goes nicely with before-dinner drinks. See the following recipe for a different sample of the breed.

---

1 recipe pizza dough (page 20)   2 teaspoons coarse sea salt or kosher
                                     salt

Make the dough and let it rise once. Punch down the dough and knead it briefly. Divide it into 4 pieces and shape each into a round. Let them sit on a floured board, covered with a damp towel, for another hour.

Preheat an oven lined with baking tiles to 500 degrees F, or as hot as possible.

Lightly flour a work surface and roll each round of dough to a thickness of ¼ inch. Let them rest 10 minutes to relax the gluten. Then, working with one piece at a time, alternately stretch the dough with your hands and roll it again to coax it out to a thickness of ⅛ inch or less. Prick the surface in a few places with a fork. Place the rounds directly on the hot oven tiles and sprinkle ½ teaspoon coarse salt over each (more or less as desired). Bake for 2 minutes. Then open the oven and, using the edge of a large spatula, bash each *focaccia* in several places to keep them from puffing up too much.

Bake 2 more minutes, or until the *focaccie* are crisp and lightly browned. Serve immediately.

WINE SUGGESTION
Romans would drink Frascati with this, but any light, dry white wine will taste fine.

Small Seasoned Focaccia
[FOCACCINE]

More common in countryside-restaurant bread baskets than the flaky-thin *focaccia* of the preceding recipe are strips cut from broad slabs of *focaccia* 1 to 2 inches thick and flavored with olive oil, salt, and often an herb or paper-thin slices of sweet onion. This recipe is for small round ones—dinner-plate size. They're good served on their own as an hors d'oeuvre with drinks, or as an accompaniment to a meat *antipasto* of *prosciutto*, *salame*, *mortadella*, etc.

(continued)

———◆———

1 recipe pizza dough (page 20)

FOR PLAIN FOCACCINE

3 teaspoons olive oil

3 teaspoons coarse sea salt or kosher salt

FOR HERB FOCACCINE

3 tablespoons olive oil

1 tablespoon minced oregano or sage

Prepare the dough, letting it rise once. Punch down the dough and knead it briefly. Divide it into 3 pieces and shape each into a round. Let them sit on a floured board, covered with a damp towel, for another hour.

Preheat an oven lined with baking tiles to 450 degrees F.

Lightly flour a work surface and roll each round of dough to a thickness of ¼ inch. Prick their surfaces in several places with a fork.

For plain focaccine:

Lay the dough rounds on the hot oven tiles, rapidly brush each one with 1 teaspoon of olive oil, and sprinkle on 1 teaspoon of coarse salt. Bake until the edges of the breads just begin to brown, 8 to 10 minutes. Check after 3 or 4 minutes, and if the dough is puffing up unevenly, bash it in several places with the edge of a large spatula. Serve at once.

For herb focaccine:

Warm the olive oil together with the sage or oregano. Place the rounds of dough on the hot oven tiles without seasoning them, and bake as above. As soon as the *focaccine* come out of the oven, brush them with the flavored olive oil, leaving a dry rim around the edges. Serve at once.

WINE SUGGESTION

As with focaccia, *just about any wine will go well with these* focaccine. *A light dry white like Frascati or Orvieto is an excellent choice.*

Garlic Bread with Tomato

[BRUSCHETTA CON POMODORO]

Toasted bread brushed with raw garlic and drizzled with olive oil has a different name in every dialect of Italy. It is the original of American garlic bread (usually an abomination), and it is wonderful when done right. Try making it when you can toast the bread over a charcoal or wood fire; it's a lesson in just how fine simple food can be. A homemade loaf of Tuscan bread or olive-oil bread, made according to the directions on page 21, is a good starting place for this recipe. Classic *bruschetta* is what you'd have if you stopped before adding the tomatoes and basil. The topping turns it from merely a tasty side order of bread to a charming little *antipasto*.

2 firm, fully ripe tomatoes
Salt
1 tablespoon minced fresh basil
4 slices of bread, ½ inch thick

1 garlic clove
¼ to ½ cup olive oil
Freshly ground black pepper

Drop the tomatoes into boiling water for 10 seconds, then drain and slip off their skins. Halve them and squeeze them gently over the sink to expel all their seeds (if they won't emerge, dip a finger into the channels in which the seeds grow and clear them out). Lightly salt the cut sides and stand them on a rack, cut side down, for 10 minutes to draw off additional moisture.

Blot the cut sides of the tomatoes with paper towels and then chop them into ⅛-inch cubes. Toss them with the minced basil, gently so as not to crush the tiny cubes.

Toast the bread slices in an oven, under a broiler, or over an open fire until they turn lightly golden. Halve the garlic clove and rub the cut side across the surface of the bread. Set each slice on an individual plate, pour 1 to 2 tablespoons olive oil over each, and then top with a tablespoon (or more, to taste) of the tomato. Salt and pepper the tomato and serve immediately.

WINE SUGGESTION
Any of the region's white wines will go well with bruschetta.

Chicken-Liver Crostini I

[CROSTINI DI FEGATINI E ACCIUGHE]

Crostini are the workhorses of Tuscan and Umbrian cooking; they appear as automatically alongside a glass of good wine as peanuts do in American cocktail lounges. This is a very flavorful and very easy preparation. The liver spread can be made entirely in advance, leaving only the toasting of the bread and the assembly for the last minute.

---

3 chicken livers (about ¼ pound)	Salt
1½ tablespoons olive oil	Freshly ground black pepper
1½ tablespoons butter	2 anchovy fillets
3 tablespoons dry red wine, sherry, or brandy	1 teaspoon drained and rinsed capers
¼ teaspoon marjoram	8 slices country-style bread

Clean the chicken livers and cut each into two or three pieces. Sauté them in the oil and butter until lightly browned. Turn heat to high and add the wine or brandy and the marjoram. Cook, stirring, until liquid evaporates. Off heat, salt lightly and pepper generously.

Put the contents of the pan into a blender or food processor. Add the anchovy and capers and blend into a nubbly purée. Return this mixture to the sauté pan and cook 5 minutes. Let cool and taste for salt. Can be done in advance up to this point.

Trim the crusts off the bread and toast the slices lightly on both sides under a broiler. Spread them thinly with the liver pâté.

WINE SUGGESTION

> *A light red wine such as a young Chianti (preferably one of the Sienese Chiantis) is ideal with this dish, but a crisp, dry white (Verdicchio, for instance) will also serve.*

Chicken-Liver Crostini II

[CROSTINI DI FEGATINI E MILZA]

Another version, this time richer-flavored and more complex in preparation. Here, too, the meat spread may be prepared entirely in advance—but not the day before, or it will lose some of its freshness and charm. Milza is one of the parts of a calf that our government thinks only cats should eat, so we substitute a small quantity of brain, which has much the same texture and flavor.

¼ pound chicken livers
¼ pound calf's brain
2 tablespoons olive oil
½ cup celery, finely chopped (1 stalk)
White part of 2 leeks, finely chopped
  (¾ to 1 cup)

¼ cup dry white wine
1 teaspoon drained and rinsed capers
8 slices country-style bread

Clean, trim, and cut the livers and brain into ½-inch pieces.

Heat the olive oil in a sauté pan. Add the chopped celery and leeks and cook gently, stirring often, for 10 minutes. Add the two meats, raise heat to medium, and sauté for 5 minutes, stirring, or until meats color lightly.

Raise heat further, pour in the wine, and cook until it evaporates. Lower heat, add the capers, and cook for 15 minutes. Stir often, and if the mixture shows a tendency to stick to the pan, add a few tablespoons of broth or water. (Do not let it get soupy, though.)

Pass the mixture through the medium blade of a food mill, or pulse it in a food processor until smooth. Return the purée to the pan and sauté over low heat until it thickens slightly.

Trim the crusts off the bread and toast the slices lightly on both sides under a broiler. Spread them not too thickly with the pâté.

WINE SUGGESTION
The same as for the preceding recipe.

Prosciutto and Cheese Crostini
[CROSTINI DI PROSCIUTTO E PROVATURA]

A nearly empty larder inspires Italian cooks rather than defeats them. This *antipasto* shows how they make a pleasing dish out of not quite enough of any single ingredient. *Provatura* is difficult to find in the United States, so we have adapted the recipe for young *provolone*. Young is crucial: Older *provolone* is much too sharp for this recipe and—even worse—does not melt well.

8 slices country-style bread
4 tablespoons butter
4 slices *prosciutto*

6 ounces young *provolone*, in ¼-inch
  slices

(continued)

Trim the crusts off the bread and toast the slices lightly on both sides in the broiler. Preheat the oven to 400 degrees F.

Lightly butter one side of each slice of bread. Lay them buttered sides up in a baking dish. On each, lay half a slice of *prosciutto* and distribute the cheese among the 8 pieces.

Melt 2 tablespoons of the butter and drizzle it over the tops. Set the dish in the oven and bake 8 to 10 minutes, or until the cheese softens.

WINE SUGGESTION

Follow the suggestions for the preceding crostini, *or try a young Chianti or other simple red wine.*

Fresh Favas with Pecorino
[FAVE E PECORINO]

Fave e pecorino constitutes the classic country *antipasto*, rustic and direct. The first time we encountered it, we thought we were seeing some sort of joke: a reasonably elegant Roman restaurant, crowded with well-dressed Italian television people (RAI offices were nearby), and suddenly the waiter plops a wooden crate full of beans on a nearby table. Imagine our surprise when those Roman sophisticates, instead of screaming in rage at his *brutta figura*, began enthusiastically eating their way through the boxful, aided by shards of *pecorino* and generous quantities of wine. That was one of the most forceful lessons we've ever received about the basic honesty of Italian cuisine. For this dish, it is essential that the beans be extremely fresh and crisp, not limp. The cheese should be a good grainy one, but not completely hard and dry. A *locatelli romano* would do quite well in place of a *pecorino*.

1¼ to 1½ **pounds fresh fava beans, in the shell**	½ **pound** *pecorino romano,* **in one chunk**

Wash and dry the beans. Heap them on a serving plate. Set the cheese on a cheese or marble board. Serve.

This is a dish eaten with fingers and a knife. Diners take bean pods onto their plates, strip them down, and pop the beans into their mouths, either in company with, or alternating with, slivers of the cheese, which they carve off the chunk with small sharp knives.

WINE SUGGESTION

A fresh young Chianti is what Romans drink with fave.

Antipasto Mushrooms
[FUNGHI DI NOIANTRI]

Mushrooms seem to have a talent for orchestrating other flavors and textures around themselves. Here they absorb a vivid tomato-based dressing perked up with wine vinegar and fragrant with herbs. Their preparation takes less than an hour and can be done several hours in advance. Either of the two *focaccia* recipes given earlier would go well with these mushrooms.

⅓ cup chopped onion
1 garlic clove, minced
½ cup olive oil
½ cup wine vinegar
2 cups drained, canned plum tomatoes
1 bay leaf
2 fresh basil leaves

¼ teaspoon oregano
1½ tablespoons chopped parsley
½ teaspoon salt
¼ teaspoon freshly ground black pepper
1 pound small, firm, white mushrooms

Sauté the onion and garlic in 3 tablespoons of the olive oil over medium heat for 5 minutes, until they are soft and translucent. Pour in the vinegar, raise the heat to high, and boil until the vinegar is reduced by half—about 3 minutes.

Roughly chop the tomatoes and add them to the pan, together with all the herbs and the salt and pepper. Simmer, uncovered, for 20 minutes, or until very thick.

Heat the remaining olive oil in a skillet. Add the mushrooms and toss continuously over high heat until they have taken up all the oil. Turn heat to low, salt lightly, and cook the mushrooms, stirring, until they begin to glisten with exuded juices. Turn heat back to high and continue cooking about 5 minutes, until done. Remove to a plate. If any mushroom juices are left in the pan, add them to the tomato sauce, further reducing the sauce, if necessary, to keep it very thick.

Stir the mushrooms into the sauce and simmer 5 minutes. Let cool to room temperature before serving.

WINE SUGGESTION
A fresh and fruity red wine goes well with these mushrooms; young Chianti—especially Chianti Rufina—or Montepulciano d'Abruzzo would be good choices.

Braised Artichokes with Parsley, Garlic, and Mint
[CARCIOFINI ALLA ROMANA]

The real *carciofi alla romana* preparation is for whole, large artichokes that in Italy are edible to a degree that American artichokes don't approach. Ours seem to have so much choke and so much external bristle and fiber that by the time they're adequately trimmed, they hardly resemble the ones so beautifully presented in Rome. Our compromise has been to preserve the Roman method of preparation but to use tiny artichokes, whose chokes are still tender and edible. Don't omit the mint; it makes the dish.

3 tablespoons lemon juice	1 garlic clove
1½ pounds small artichokes (10 to 14 to the pound)	½ teaspoon fresh mint
	⅜ teaspoon salt
2 tablespoons chopped parsley	⅓ cup olive oil

Stir the lemon juice into a bowl half full of cold water. Holding an artichoke with the top facing you, snap off the outermost few layers of leaves at the base. Continue until you reach the soft, pale green or yellow leaves. Slice off about the top half of the artichoke cone. With a vegetable peeler, pare away the green exterior of the artichoke bottom, leaving white flesh. Drop each finished artichoke into the bowl of water while preparing the rest.

When all the artichokes are prepared, drain and quarter them, and place them in a heavy-bottomed pot.

Chop the parsley, garlic, mint, and salt together. Stir them into the artichokes. Add the olive oil and about ½ cup water. Cover tightly, bring to a boil, reduce to a simmer, and cook very gently until the artichokes are nearly tender, about 25 minutes. At the end of this time, if the liquid has not been taken up, uncover the pot and raise heat to boil it away. If there is too much liquid to boil away within a minute or two, remove the artichokes to a serving dish, boil down the pan juices until nothing but seasoned oil remains, and pour that over the artichokes. Let cool somewhat before serving.

WINE SUGGESTION

Artichokes make a difficult companion to wine, but Romans would nevertheless drink a young, high-acid white wine like a Frascati or a Verdicchio with this dish.

Eggplant Nests
[NIDI DI MELANZANE]

In this cheerful presentation, small whole eggplants are hollowed out to make nests for a savory baked mixture of eggplant flesh, grated cheese, bread crumbs, parsley, and tomatoes. The nests are crowned with gleaming *mozzarella*, melted just enough to cling, and a crumble of crisped *pancetta* bits.

---

4 small eggplants, ¼ pound each.
2 tablespoons fine dry bread crumbs
2 tablespoons grated *pecorino ro-mano* cheese
2 tablespoons chopped parsley
⅓ cup drained canned tomatoes, chopped

2 tablespoons extra-virgin olive oil
¼ teaspoon salt
Freshly ground black pepper
3 ounces *pancetta*
½ pound *mozzarella*

Wash the eggplants. Drop them into boiling salted water, cook 10 minutes, then drain and spray them with cold water. Cut off the stems, then cut a lengthwise slice off each one, going about a quarter the depth of the eggplant. Hollow out the eggplants, leaving a wall at least ¼ inch thick all around. Reserve the pulp.

Preheat the oven to 350 degrees F. Oil 4 small gratin dishes. Mince the reserved eggplant pulp and mix it with the bread crumbs, cheese, parsley, tomatoes, olive oil, salt, and 5 or 6 grindings of black pepper. Salt the insides of the eggplant shells and fill them with this mixture. Set them in the gratin dishes and add a teaspoon of water to the bottom of each dish. Put them in the oven and bake 20 minutes.

While the eggplants are baking, chop the *pancetta* into very small dice and cut the *mozzarella* into 4 thick slices. When 20 minutes are up, remove the eggplant dishes, set a slice of *mozzarella* on top of each, strew the chopped *pancetta* over the top, and add another teaspoon of water to the dishes. Return to the oven and bake 20 more minutes.

Let the eggplants sit about 10 minutes before serving.

WINE SUGGESTION
A young red wine will go very well here; any simple Chianti or Monte-pulciano d'Abruzzo or Rosso Piceno will be fine.

Roasted Stuffed Tomatoes

[POMODORI RIPIENI]

This is a lovely summer *antipasto*, when the tomatoes are at their peak of ripe perfection. Prepare them in the morning while it is still cool so you don't have to turn on your oven during the heat of the day. They taste just as good cool—some people think better—as hot out of the oven.

4 large ripe tomatoes (½ pound each)	2 anchovy fillets
½ cup minced onion	1 cup fine dry bread crumbs
3 tablespoons plus 1 teaspoon olive oil	1 cup grated *parmigiano*
	½ teaspoon salt
6 fresh basil leaves	Freshly ground black pepper
2 teaspoons capers	

Preheat the oven to 350 degrees F. Cut a slice off the top of each tomato. Gently squeeze them upside down over a sink to remove seeds and liquid. Cut out the interior flesh, taking care not to pierce the shell, and chop the flesh.

In a small frying pan, sauté the onion until soft in 2 tablespoons of the olive oil.

Chop the basil, capers, and anchovy together. Mix them with the chopped tomato flesh, the onions and their sautéing oil, the bread crumbs, *parmigiano*, salt, and a generous quantity of pepper.

Fill the tomatoes with this mixture, set them in a buttered baking dish, and drizzle 1 teaspoon of oil over each. Bake for 20 to 25 minutes.

Can be eaten warm or at room temperature.

WINE SUGGESTION

A *crisp, well-chilled white wine—say, an Orvieto—makes a great companion to these tomatoes.*

Baked Peppers with Piquant Sauce

[PEPERONI ALLA MARINARA]

The intense vegetal sweetness of bell peppers, very simply baked in the oven, is enlivened by a piquant dressing—the type of moistener Italians call a *salsina*—here compounded of small amounts of anchovy and pickle, garlic and onion, butter and olive oil, wine and broth. You could serve these peppers atop slices of plain *bruschetta* or (to venture a northern touch) on top of grilled slabs of *polenta*. If you prepare the sauce at the same time the peppers are baking, the cooking time for this dish is little more than half an hour.

6 anchovy fillets	3 ounces dry white wine
2 tablespoons cornichons (about 6)	¾ cup broth (page 45)
1 garlic clove	¾ teaspoon oregano
3 tablespoons chopped onion	1½ pounds red or green bell peppers
1½ tablespoons olive oil	1 tablespoon chopped fresh basil
1½ tablespoons butter	

Mash the anchovy fillets with a fork. Very finely mince the cornichons, garlic, and onion together. Sauté the minced vegetables in the olive oil and butter for 2 minutes. Stir in the anchovy, wine, broth, and oregano. Cook, uncovered, over gentle heat for 25 minutes. There should be about ⅔ cup sauce. Turn off heat and set it aside until ready to proceed.

Preheat the oven to 350 degrees F. Wash the peppers, halve them, and remove all seeds and veins. Lay the halves on a sheet of oiled aluminum foil on a baking pan and bake them for 30 minutes.

Remove the peppers to a serving plate and arrange them with cavities up. Bring the anchovy sauce back to a simmer and pour it over the peppers. Sprinkle the chopped basil over all and serve at once.

WINE SUGGESTION

A bright, acid white wine is called for here: Verdicchio is probably the best bet.

Spiced Ricotta Spread

[RICOTTA PICCANTE]

Hors d'oeuvre spreads aren't very common in Italy, except as toppings for *crostini*. This one demonstrates the amazing versatility of *ricotta* as a base for seasonings. Most people won't be able to guess the ingredients. You could simply serve the spread with crackers, but we like the additional textural element of the raw endive.

1 small bunch arugula	½ tablespoon paprika
½ tablespoon tiny capers (nonpareils)	¼ teaspoon salt
½ pound *ricotta*	1 head Belgian endive
2 tablespoons olive oil	

(continued)

Wash and dry the arugula. Finely chop enough leaves to make ½ cup, loosely packed. (Reserve the rest for other uses.) Drain and rinse the capers.

Mix the *ricotta* in a bowl with the oil, paprika, salt, capers, and chopped arugula. Chill the mixture in the refrigerator for at least 1 hour.

When ready to serve, separate the endive leaves, washing and drying them if necessary. Place about 1 teaspoon of the *ricotta* mixture on the base of each endive leaf, arrange them attractively on a plate, and serve.

WINE SUGGESTION
By itself this dish is best served with a crisp white wine—Verdicchio, Frascati, Orvieto would all do.

Poached Whiting
[NASELLO LESSATO CON SALSINA]

One permanent fixture of a good Italian restaurant's *antipasto* table is a large, freshly poached fish. The species will vary according to season and locale, but a fish will always be there, at room temperature, ready to be served according to the diner's preferences: with a *salsina*—a little sauce, as in this recipe—or with olive oil and vinegar, or olive oil alone, or fresh mayonnaise, or lemon. This recipe is geared to small fish, to make individual portions, but for a larger fish you need only adjust the quantities and the cooking time to re-create perfectly the marine monarch of the *antipasti*.

———————◆———————

4 small whiting, ¼ pound each

FOR THE COURT BOUILLON

1 carrot	1 teaspoon coarse salt
1 celery stalk	6 peppercorns
½ cup chopped onion	4 cloves
1 tablespoon chopped parsley	½ cup lemon juice

FOR THE SAUCE

1 egg yolk	¾ teaspoon balsamic vinegar
⅛ teaspoon salt	1 tablespoon extra-virgin olive oil

Clean and rinse the whiting, leaving heads and tails intact.
Finely chop the carrot, celery, and onion. Strew them on the bottom of a

casserole just large enough to hold the fish comfortably. Add the parsley, salt, pepper, cloves, and lemon juice.

Lay the fish on this base and add enough cold water to just cover them. Cover and bring to a simmer over medium heat. Cook 6 minutes, regulating heat as necessary to prevent a hard boil, which would rip the delicate flesh of the fish. Remove the fish carefully to a plate and allow them to cool to room temperature.

While the fish are cooling, make the sauce. Beat the egg yolk briefly with the salt in a bowl, with a wire whisk or hand-held electric mixer. Beat in the balsamic vinegar. Slowly add the olive oil, beating to emulsify the mixture well. (If you want a milder, more mayonnaiselike sauce, simply go on adding olive oil; the egg yolk should take up to ¾ of a cup.)

When ready to serve, carefully skin the fish from heads to tails and lay them out on individual dishes. Garnish with lemon wedges, if desired. Serve, passing the sauce in a separate bowl.

WINE SUGGESTION

Dry white wine, of course, but one with some body: Torre di Giano, or an excellent white from the Chianti region, such as Badia a Coltibuono's.

PRIMI

The most important class of *primi* in the Center of Italy is unquestionably pasta, both fresh-made and dry. To be sure, there are soups—some great ones, in fact, like *ribollita*. And central Italians eat *risotto*, too; but far, far less of it than in the North. *Polenta* all but disappears, except for occasional, almost guest appearances in winter. And it's true that potato *gnocchi* become very popular in this part of Italy. But first and last, pasta is the *primo* of choice here.

It's next to impossible to be really systematic about the myriad preparations Italians have for pasta, but there are at least a couple of broad—very broad—classifications that a cook can keep in mind while choosing a *primo* to fit into a particular dinner. First, the obvious division between sauces based on seafood and sauces based on vegetables or meats. Second, the distinction between white pasta sauces and red sauces. Seafood sauces made *al bianco* almost invariably get that way from some combination of white wine, seafood broth, and/or olive oil. Consequently, they are usually light in texture and taste and comparatively liquid. White meat and vegetable sauces, on the other hand, generally result from using egg yolks in combination with cheese and either butter or oil. Consequently, they tend to be thick and clingy, with rather intense and concentrated flavors. Red sauces in both cases build on tomatoes, though the spices and auxiliary ingredients differ dramatically in the two categories. Seafood sauces will be cooked very quickly and brightly spiced, remaining, once again, comparatively liquid, while meat and vegetable sauces will be denser, with the meat or vegetable itself clearly dominating the spices or herbs. In planning a meal, the sort of sauce you choose depends finally on what you intend to serve before the *primo* or after it, and whether you want it to complement those dishes or contrast with them.

Bread Soup

[PAPPA MARITATA]

We begin with the simplest kind of soup, the sort known all over Italy only half jokingly as *acqua cotta*, cooked water. This recipe is adapted from a very ancient Tuscan one, researched and re-created by Donatella Cinelli, who is

a student of Sienese gastronomic traditions as well as the master cheese maker
at Fattoria dei Barbi, a Tuscan estate that, in addition to producing excellent
wine, also makes its own cheeses, *prosciutti*, *salami*, etc.

1 cup drained canned plum tomatoes	6 slices day-old country bread, 1 inch
½ celery stalk	thick
3 garlic cloves	2 eggs
5 cloves	¼ cup grated *parmigiano*
1½ teaspoons salt	½ cup chopped red onion
4 to 5 grindings pepper	Crushed red pepper
1½ tablespoons golden raisins	

Pass the tomatoes through the coarse blade of a food mill. Bring to the boil
10 cups of water with the celery, garlic, tomatoes, cloves, salt, and pepper.
Boil gently for 1 hour.

Remove and discard the celery stalk and the garlic. Return the soup to the
simmer, add the raisins, and cook 5 minutes. Then add the bread slices and
cook 3 minutes longer. Beat the eggs together in a small bowl and beat them
vigorously into the soup, breaking up the bread as you do so. Sprinkle with
the grated cheese, taste for salt, and serve at once.

Pass a bowl of the chopped red onion and another small bowl of crushed
red pepper at table.

WINE SUGGESTION
The wine of the region is the best companion to this simple yet exotic soup:
a young Rosso di Montalcino, by all means. Failing that, try a young
fruity Chianti—preferably Sienese (Boscarelli's would be fine).

Vegetable Soup
[MINESTRONE]

Minestrone is a generic name: It means a big, hearty soup. Every region has
its own version, featuring its own favorite vegetables and its own seasonal
abundance, but the structural principles remain constant. A *minestrone* always
contains one or more sorts of beans (kidney, baby lima, pinto, cranberry,
cannellini, etc.), one or more sorts of greens (savoy cabbage, spinach, Swiss
chard, escarole, beet greens, etc.), and one or more shapes of pasta (*tubetti*,
spaghetti, *fusilli*, *farfalline*, *stellette*, etc.). The more the merrier is also a

principle for all three of those categories. You can serve *minestrone* immediately, if necessary, but its flavor will deepen if the soup rests for several hours.

———————◆———————

¼ pound dried beans (about ½ cup)	2½ tablespoons chopped onion
Salt	2 basil leaves
1 celery stalk	¼ teaspoon dried thyme
¼ pound savoy cabbage	2 tablespoons olive oil
2 small boiling potatoes (about 6 ounces)	Freshly ground black pepper
	3 ounces imported Italian pasta
¼ cup drained canned plum tomatoes	

The night before, pick over the beans, rinse them, and let them soak in a large bowl of cold water.

Next day, drain the beans, put them into a large pot, and cover with 4 cups water. Add ½ teaspoon salt, bring to the boil, and simmer, covered, for 1 to 1½ hours, until the beans are nearly tender.

Wash and cut into bite-size pieces the celery, cabbage, and potato. Roughly chop the tomatoes. Chop the onion, basil, and thyme together. Heat the olive oil in a sauté pan and soften the onion mixture in it for 5 minutes. Add the celery, cabbage, potato, tomato, ¼ teaspoon salt, and several grindings of black pepper. Toss everything to coat it with the oil, then add ⅓ cup warm water. Cover and cook gently 20 minutes, until the vegetables are almost tender.

When the beans are ready, scoop out about a quarter of them and purée them through a food mill back into the pot. Add the vegetables from the sauté pan and all their juices. Bring the soup to a boil and stir in the pasta. Cook until the pasta is done, 10 to 12 minutes. Taste for seasoning.

WINE SUGGESTION
An unpretentious red wine from the Abruzzi or the Marches will make the best match with this hearty country soup.

Ribollita

This elaborate recipe may seem like a lot of trouble for a bean soup, but *ribollita* is no ordinary soup. If you can imagine a rustic aristocrat, this is it. Tuscan cooks will argue passionately in favor of their particular version of this peasant classic. Regrettably, one of its principal ingredients is not available in the United States—*cavolo nero*, or "black cabbage." Red cabbage doesn't work at all as a substitute. We've found the combination of Swiss chard and savoy cabbage to be the best approximation of the required flavor. The one truly essential ingredient is Tuscan extra-virgin olive oil, in generous quantity.

The soup can be eaten as soon as it is cooked—it smells so good fresh off the stove that the temptation is strong. However, the richness and subtlety that develop in the overnight rest and the "re-boiling" that gives the dish its name are well worth waiting for.

Making *ribollita* is a production number, unquestionably, so you might as well make a lot of it while you're about it. It keeps getting better for several days; how long it will continue to improve we can't say, because we've never had any left after the third day. This recipe will serve 8, with leftovers.

---

2 cups dried pinto beans
3 to 4 sage leaves (fresh or dried)
Salt
Freshly ground black pepper
½ cup extra-virgin olive oil, plus additional for serving
½ cup chopped onion
1 small *peperoncino rosso*
4 large plum tomatoes, peeled and quartered

1 teaspoon tomato paste
½ to ¾ pound Swiss chard, shredded
¼ of a savoy cabbage, shredded
4 carrots, sliced
4 small potatoes, sliced
3 celery stalks, sliced
¼ teaspoon dried thyme
1 large Bermuda onion

Two days before serving:

Pick over the beans and rinse well. Put them in a large pot, cover with ample cold water, and let them soak overnight.

One day before serving:

To the beans add the sage leaves, 1 tablespoon salt, ½ teaspoon black pepper, and additional water, if necessary, to cover the beans by at least 1½ inches. Bring to a boil and simmer for 1 hour, or until the beans are tender, adding more water as needed to keep the beans covered. Set the pot aside and cool.

Warm the olive oil in a very large soup pot. Add the chopped onion and the *peperoncino*. Sauté 8 to 10 minutes, or until the onion is golden, then add the tomatoes and the tomato paste. Simmer about 5 minutes longer, stirring occasionally to break up the tomato pieces. Remove the *peperoncino*.

Place a food mill fitted with the coarse blade over the soup pot and mill about three-quarters of the beans into the pot. Add the remaining whole beans and all their cooking liquid, all the sliced and shredded vegetables, a quart of cold water, the thyme, 1 tablespoon salt, and a generous amount of black pepper. Simmer, covered, for 2 hours.

(continued)

Remove the soup from the heat and let it cool uncovered. Then cover the pot and set it aside overnight.

On serving day:

Bring the soup back to a boil. Preheat the broiler, with broiler pan at its lowest setting. Slice large rounds of onion, thick or thin as desired. Fill 8 individual flameproof bowls with the soup. Float an onion slice in each bowl and pour on ½ tablespoon olive oil. Put the bowls under the broiler until the onion turns golden.

NOTE: You can also place at the bottom of each bowl a slice of bread that has been toasted and rubbed lightly with a cut garlic clove.

WINE SUGGESTION

This classic of country cooking takes beautifully to a red wine with body and a bit of a country burr of its own: a simple young Chianti in the bigger, old-fashioned style (for example, Antinori's Santa Cristina, Badia a Coltibuno, Fossi, Spalletti) or—perhaps even better—a Rosso di Montalcino from Fattoria dei Barbi or Col d'Orcia or Altesino.

Spaghetti with Summertime Sauce
[SPAGHETTI CON SALSA APPETITOSA]

This is a fine example of the many varieties of uncooked pasta sauces that one encounters all through central Italy in the warmest months. Usually they are made up in the morning and allowed to ripen at room temperature all day in covered bowls or large jars. Their ease of preparation gives little clue to their complex and sophisticated flavors.

———————————◆———————————

1 pound ripe tomatoes	3 tablespoons wine vinegar
2 tablespoons minced onion	Freshly ground black pepper
1½ tablespoons chopped parsley	1 pound imported Italian *spaghetti*
1½ tablespoons chopped fresh basil	⅓ cup olive oil
Salt	

Drop the tomatoes into boiling water for 10 seconds to loosen their skins; then drain, peel, seed, and chop them.

Mix the tomatoes, onion, parsley, and basil together in a bowl. Dissolve 1 teaspoon salt in 1 tablespoon of the vinegar and add it to the bowl, along with several grindings of black pepper. Mix well and transfer to an attractive serving bowl.

Bring 6 to 8 quarts of water to the boil; add 2 tablespoons salt and put in the pasta. When pasta is *al dente*, drain and place it in a warmed bowl. Toss it with the olive oil and the remaining 2 tablespoons vinegar. Serve immediately, allowing diners to spoon as much sauce as they like over their own portions.

NOTE: Substituting 3 or 4 tablespoons of chopped arugula for the parsley or basil produces a different but equally delicious sauce.

WINE SUGGESTION

Any simple, fruity red wine will do; young Chianti or Montepulciano d'Abruzzo would be fine. If the weather is really hot, a well-chilled light, dry white is also pleasing; try, for instance, a Frascati or Verdicchio or Trebbiano d'Abruzzo.

Summer Macaroni
[MACCHERONI ESTIVI]

An intriguing variant on the uncooked sauce theme: In this recipe, the *mozzarella* adds a new dimension to the dish. For complete success, you must keep your cubes of *mozzarella* small and hold the cheese at room temperature, so the warmth of the just-cooked pasta will be sufficient to soften it and release the best of its flavor. Grated cheese is not needed with this lovely sauce, though freshly ground pepper lends an extra lift.

2 pounds ripe plum tomatoes
¾ pound *mozzarella*
4 tablespoons chopped fresh basil
Salt
¼ teaspoon freshly ground black
  pepper

2 tablespoons wine vinegar
1 pound imported Italian macaroni
  (shells, *farfalle*, etc.)
6 tablespoons extra-virgin olive oil

Have all ingredients at room temperature. Drop tomatoes in boiling water for 10 seconds; drain and peel. Halve them and remove seeds, then cut them into bite-size pieces.

Cut the *mozzarella* into ½-inch cubes. Put the tomatoes into a serving bowl large enough to hold all the pasta. Add the basil, 2 teaspoons salt, pepper, and vinegar. Toss well and set aside while cooking pasta.

Bring 4 to 5 quarts of water to the boil; add 1 tablespoon salt and put in the pasta. When pasta is *al dente*, drain it very thoroughly, add it to the bowl with the tomato mixture, and toss well. Add the olive oil and toss again. Last, mix in the cubes of *mozzarella* and serve. Pass the pepper mill at table.

WINE SUGGESTION
Same as the preceding recipe.

Pasta with Beans
[PASTA E FAGIOLI]

The Roman version of this ubiquitous dish (see pages 84 and 260 for other versions). The inclusion of the pork skin gives the beans a greater succulence, just as it does in cassoulet, and is quite characteristic of Roman cooking. *Pasta e fagioli* takes a while to make: about 3 hours cooking plus the overnight soak for the beans, but most of that time is quiet simmering, not active work.

6 ounces dried cannellini (white beans)
3 ounces pork skin
2 cups broth (page 45)
½ cup basic central tomato sauce (page 32)
2 small garlic cloves, minced
1 tablespoon minced onion

1 tablespoon minced parsley
2 teaspoons salt
Freshly ground black pepper
¼ pound short, tubular imported Italian pasta, such as *pennette* or *tubettini*

The night before serving:
Pick over the beans and rinse them well. Place in a large bowl and cover them generously with water. Let them sit in the water until ready to use.

On serving day:
Bring a small pot of water to a boil, drop in the pork skin, and let it boil for 5 minutes. Drain it and cut it into short, thin strips.
Put the drained beans and the pork skin in a large pot. Add the broth and 2 cups cold water. Bring to a boil and simmer gently, covered, for 1 hour. Stir in tomato sauce, garlic, onion, parsley, salt, and pepper. Cover again and simmer 1½ hours. Stir in the pasta, cover, and cook until pasta is *al dente*. Serve with lots of freshly ground black pepper. Pass freshly grated cheese— *parmigiano* or *pecorino romano*—at table.

WINE SUGGESTION
A *simple red seems to work best with* pasta e fagioli, *but as with so many*

other dishes, Italians happily drink either white or red with it, apparently more governed by whim and weather than by any ironclad notion of enologic appropriateness.

183

Primi

Penne with Artichokes

[PENNE CON CARCIOFI]

This dish is adapted from a favorite *primo* of the Trattoria La Campana in Rome. The combination of artichokes and mint is *molto romano*, but if fresh mint is out of season, don't use dried; it won't work. Instead, try fresh thyme or oregano. Cooking time is just about 20 minutes, plus the time needed to trim the artichokes. If you get the size specified, you needn't remove the chokes. Any leftovers will make an excellent *frittata*.

½ lemon
1½ pounds small artichokes (10 to 14
  to the pound)
⅓ cup dry white wine
4 tablespoons olive oil
1 teaspoon chopped fresh mint
2 teaspoons chopped parsley

¼ teaspoon salt
1 pound imported *penne*
3 tablespoons butter
1 cup broth, optional (page 45)
2 tablespoons flour
¾ cup grated *parmigiano*

Prepare the artichokes. Squeeze the lemon into a bowl half full of cold water. Holding an artichoke with the top facing you, snap off the outermost few layers of leaves at the base. Continue until you reach the soft, pale green or yellow leaves. Slice off about the top half of the artichoke cone. With a vegetable peeler, pare away the green exterior of the artichoke bottom, leaving white flesh. Drop each finished artichoke into the bowl of water while preparing the rest. When all the artichokes are done, cut each one into sixths or eighths, leaving a bit of the base on each piece to hold it together. The pieces should be no more than ½ inch at their widest point.

Put the artichokes into a sauté pan with the wine, olive oil, and 1½ cups water. Cover and cook over medium high heat for 15 minutes, or until the artichokes are just tender. If the water has not been completely absorbed by that time, uncover, raise the heat, and boil it off.

Stir in the mint, parsley, and salt and sauté the artichokes in the oil remaining in the pan for 2 minutes. Turn off heat and set the pan aside until the pasta is nearly ready

Cook the *penne* in 4 to 5 quarts rapidly boiling salted water until *al dente*.

Put the butter in a large serving bowl and set it in the turned-off oven to warm. Bring the broth to a simmer, if you are using it.

When the pasta is almost done, reheat the artichokes. Sprinkle on the flour and sauté, stirring, for 1 minute. Then add the broth (alternatively, use 1 cup of the pasta cooking water) and stir thoroughly to obtain a uniform sauce, in consistency like a thin béchamel or velouté. Stir in the grated cheese.

Drain the pasta, toss it with the butter in the serving dish, and then mix in the artichoke sauce. Pass additional grated cheese and freshly ground black pepper at the table.

WINE SUGGESTION
Artichokes usually do not match well with wine, but this dish will partner happily with a crisp, acidic white such as Verdicchio.

Linguine with Clam Sauce
[LINGUINE ALLE VONGOLE]

This is the most fundamental white clam sauce for pasta, in its simplicity almost an *aglio e olio* (garlic and olive oil sauce) with clams. Don't be intimidated by the number of hot peppers called for; they're really a necessity to keep the dish lively and dancing on your palate. The most critical element of the recipe is to cook the clams very, very briefly—really just enough to warm them through.

36 small fresh clams, about 2 inches across the shells
8 garlic cloves
1 cup olive oil

4 *peperoncini rossi*
4 tablespoons chopped parsley
Salt
1 pound imported Italian *linguine*

Shuck the clams, saving their liquid. Cut each clam into 2 to 3 pieces (more if you are working with larger clams). Strain the clam liquid through a sieve lined with a dampened paper towel.

Peel the garlic cloves and crush them lightly with the flat of a heavy knife blade. Heat the olive oil together with the garlic, *peperoncini*, and parsley. Cook for 3 minutes at low heat, without letting the garlic color. Remove the *peperoncini* at this point if you wish. Raise heat to medium, add the clam liquid and ⅛ teaspoon salt, and simmer until the liquid is reduced by half. Set aside until pasta is done.

Bring 4 to 5 quarts of water to a boil. Add 1 tablespoon salt and the linguine and cook until *al dente*. When the pasta is about to come off the heat, add

the clams to the sauce and simmer together over medium heat for 1 minute.
Taste for salt.

Drain the pasta, place it in a heated serving bowl, and toss it thoroughly with the sauce. Serve at once.

WINE SUGGESTION

White wine, dry, crisp, and well chilled, is the natural companion of this dish. Frascati, Verdicchio, Orvieto, Trebbiano, Tuscan whites—all will serve well here.

Spaghetti with Tuna Sauce
[SPAGHETTI CON TONNO]

At first glance, this recipe may look uninteresting: What can you do with canned tuna, after all? In fact, the tuna, briefly cooked as it is, mingles flavors with the rest of the sauce in a way that produces quite a sophisticated dish.

1½ pounds plum tomatoes	Freshly ground black pepper
2 anchovy fillets	1 can (6½ ounces) imported Italian
2 garlic cloves	tuna packed in olive oil
6 tablespoons olive oil	1 pound imported Italian *spaghetti*
Salt	1 tablespoon chopped parsley

Drop the tomatoes into boiling water for 10 seconds, then drain, peel, seed, and dice them. Mince the anchovy fillets. Peel and halve the garlic cloves.

Sauté the garlic and anchovy in the olive oil over medium heat until the garlic is lightly golden. Discard the garlic. Add the tomatoes, a light sprinkling of salt, and a generous grinding of pepper. Stir well, cover, and cook gently for 10 minutes.

In a separate sauté pan, warm the tuna with all its oil, stirring to break up the pieces. Cook for 1 minute, then set aside until pasta is ready.

Bring 4 to 5 quarts of water to the boil; add 1 tablespoon of salt and put in the pasta. When it is nearly done, reheat the sauce and the tuna, combine them, and mix well. Drain the pasta, place it in a serving bowl, and toss it with the sauce. Sprinkle on the parsley and serve at once.

WINE SUGGESTION

Follow your own preference here. A crisp white, such as a Verdicchio, or an uncomplicated red—Montepulciano, young Chianti, etc.—would do equally well.

Tonnarelli with Prosciutto and Peas

[TONNARELLI CON PISELLI E PROSCIUTTO]

This dish is one of the workhorses of Italian cooking, appearing with local variations on menus the length and breadth of the peninsula. Most versions of it are vaguely northern in inspiration, using a generous amount of butter and cream. This authentically central version omits cream entirely and instead uses egg yolks as its liquid, which gives it a satisfying richness while at the same time keeping its sauce concentrated and clingy.

2 ounces *prosciutto*, in one piece	¾ cup broth (page 45)
4 medium mushrooms (about 2 ounces)	Salt
	Freshly ground black pepper
4 tablespoons butter	1 recipe basic egg pasta (page 24)
¼ cup chopped onion	2 egg yolks
4 ounces tiny frozen peas	Freshly grated *parmigiano*

Cut the *prosciutto* into ⅛-inch dice. Finely chop the mushrooms. Heat 2 tablespoons of the butter in a large sauté pan and sauté the onion over medium heat for 5 minutes. Add the peas, *prosciutto*, and mushrooms; stir together and cook 3 minutes. Add the broth and cook 3 minutes longer. Taste for seasoning.

Put the remaining 2 tablespoons butter into a large serving bowl and let it warm and soften in the turned-off oven. Bring a large pot of salted water to the boil.

Roll the pasta to the thinnest setting on the pasta machine and cut *tonnarelli* (the narrowest width) with it. Drop the *tonnarelli* into the boiling water and cook 1 minute after the water comes back to the boil. Drain and toss the pasta in the serving bowl with the butter.

Quickly stir the egg yolks into the hot sauce and dress the pasta with it. Pass *parmigiano* and the pepper mill at the table.

WINE SUGGESTION

This will take quite well to a medium-bodied red wine, say a Chianti Classico or a Rubesco.

Spaghetti alla Carbonara

Spaghetti alla carbonara has entered the pantheon of Italian cooking: It is regarded as one of the finest of pasta dishes all over the world. Naturally, there are many versions of the recipe, and many variations on its cooking technique. In our view, the crucial step is to toss the pasta with the oil and *pancetta* mixture *before* adding the egg and cheese mix. Otherwise, you wind up with scrambled eggs and pasta, which is not at all what this satiny sauce is meant to be. If you can't get *pancetta*, an equal quantity of bacon, blanched for a few minutes, will make a slightly different but still quite appetizing sauce. Working with everyday materials, this dish achieves a degree of elegance that makes it a perfect *primo* for an important dinner.

---

3 ounces *pancetta*	½ cup grated *parmigiano*
¼ cup chopped small white onion	½ cup grated *pecorino*
1 small *peperoncino rosso*	½ teaspoon salt
3 tablespoons butter	Freshly ground black pepper
3 tablespoons olive oil	1 tablespoon chopped parsley
4 eggs	1 pound imported Italian *spaghetti*

Finely dice the *pancetta* and sauté it gently with the onion and *peperoncino* in the butter and olive oil until *pancetta* is rendered and the onion soft, about 10 minutes. Discard *peperoncino*.

Beat the eggs in a bowl with the two cheeses, salt, several grindings of black pepper, and the parsley.

Bring 4 to 5 quarts of water to the boil; add 1 tablespoon salt and put in the pasta. When pasta is still slightly underdone, drain it and add it to the pan with the *pancetta*. Over low heat, toss thoroughly to coat the pasta with oil and butter. Off heat, stir in the egg-cheese mixture and toss vigorously. Serve at once.

WINE SUGGESTION

This dish likes either a full-bodied white or a not-too-tannic red. For the white, Lungarotti's Torre di Giano or Chardonnay, Villa Banfi's Chardonnay, Frescobaldi's Pomino, or Antinori's Castello della Sala would all be fine. For a soft red, many varieties will do: young Chianti, Montepulciano d'Abruzzo, Rosso Piceno, or even Vino Nobile.

Spaghetti with Amatriciana Sauce

[SPAGHETTI ALL'AMATRICIANA]

Another sauce that draws a lot of its flavor from *pancetta*, *amatriciana* is one of the most popular in Italy. It is easy to make, quick and flavorful, and it tastes just as good on fresh egg pasta as it does on *spaghetti* or *maccheroni*. *Pecorino romano*, rather than *parmigiano*, is the right cheese to serve: The *amatriciana* sauce prefers the sharper bite of the *romano* to the sweetness of the *parmigiano*.

1 pound plum tomatoes	3 tablespoons chopped onion
4 ounces *pancetta*	Salt
1 *peperoncino rosso*	1 pound imported *spaghetti*
6 tablespoons olive oil	Grated *pecorino romano*

Drop the tomatoes into boiling water for 10 seconds, then drain, peel, seed, and coarsely chop them. Dice the *pancetta* into ¼-inch cubes.

Sauté the *pancetta* and the *peperoncino* in the olive oil over moderate heat until most of the *pancetta* is rendered and the pieces begin to brown, about 10 minutes. Discard the *peperoncino*. Add the onion and sauté 5 minutes longer, or until onion is translucent. Add the tomatoes and 1 teaspoon of salt. Cover and cook, stirring occasionally, for 15 to 20 minutes, until sauce holds together well.

Bring 4 to 5 quarts of water to the boil; add 1 tablespoon of salt and put in the pasta. When it is *al dente*, drain it, place it in a serving bowl, and toss it with the hot sauce. Serve at once, passing grated *pecorino* at the table.

WINE SUGGESTION

Your best bet here is a relatively simple red wine, such as a young Chianti, though many Italians will take a dry white wine (Verdicchio, Frascati, Orvieto) with this dish, especially in summer.

Macaroni with Lamb Ragù

[MACCHERONI COL RAGÙ DI AGNELLO]

The name *ragù* signifies a long-cooked meat sauce. Far from being the norm in Italy, such sauces are reserved for the few occasions when the object is to

extract a maximum amount of flavor from a small amount of meat. This gently
simmered sauce does exactly that. What is unusual is the use of lamb in this way, since most Italian lamb is eaten quite young, long before the animal would grow anywhere near tough enough for Italians to think it needed long, moist cooking of this sort. The explanation is that this is a recipe from the Abruzzi, where lamb in all stages of maturity is far and away the commonest meat.

¾ pound boneless lamb	½ teaspoon salt
2 garlic cloves, chopped	½ cup dry white wine
½ teaspoon rosemary leaves, crushed	1½ cups drained canned plum to-
1 tablespoon chopped parsley	matoes
1 small *peperoncino rosso*	1 pound imported Italian short tu-
3 tablespoons olive oil	bular macaroni, e.g., *penne*

Trim all bits of fat and gristle off the lamb and cut it into ½-inch cubes.

In a casserole over a low flame, sauté the garlic, herbs, and pepper in the olive oil for 3 minutes, or until garlic is soft but not browned. Raise heat to medium-high, add the lamb, and stir frequently until it loses all its raw pink color.

Sprinkle on the salt, stir, and pour in the wine. Turn heat to high and cook, stirring, until wine is half evaporated. Place a food mill fitted with the medium blade over the pot and mill in the tomatoes. Bring the sauce to a simmer, turn heat low, cover, and let cook gently 1 to 1½ hours. Remove the hot pepper.

Bring 4 to 5 quarts of water to the boil; add 1 tablespoon salt and put in the pasta. When it is *al dente*, drain it, place it in a serving bowl, and toss it with the hot sauce.

WINE SUGGESTION

This sauce is fairly complex in itself and needs a red wine that will play up to it. A good choice would be one with a few years of bottle age: a four- or five-year-old Chianti Classico, say, or a similarly aged Vino Nobile, or a proprietary wine like Brusco dei Barbi.

Rigatoni with Prosciutto, Mushrooms, and Chicken Livers

[RIGATONI ALL'ITALIANA]

This meaty sauce develops great intensity in little more than half an hour of cooking time. We credit the *prosciutto* fat with harmonizing the powerful flavors of the other ingredients. *Prosciutto* fat can be obtained from the same people who sell you *prosciutto*; when trimming the hams, they frequently discard the extra fat, which is a real pity, since it gives a very distinctive taste to sauces.

⅔ cup chopped onion
2 ounces *prosciutto* fat
½ pound firm white mushrooms
4 slices lean *prosciutto* (about 2 ounces)
½ pound chicken livers
8 fresh basil leaves
12 tablespoons butter

1 cup dry red wine
2 cups drained canned plum tomatoes
Freshly ground black pepper
Salt
1 pound imported Italian *rigatoni*
½ cup freshly grated *parmigiano*

Finely chop the onion together with the *prosciutto* fat. Wash or wipe the mushrooms and slice them thin (the 3-millimeter blade on a food processor, or ⅛ to ¼ inch by hand). Cut the *prosciutto* into strips 1 inch by ¼ inch. Trim the chicken livers, removing any bits of fat or membrane, and cut each into pieces no larger than 1 inch. Chop the basil leaves.

Set a large, heavy-bottomed casserole over medium-low heat. Melt 4 tablespoons of the butter and sauté the onion and *prosciutto* fat in it until fat is rendered and onion translucent, about 5 minutes. Add the mushrooms and shredded *prosciutto* and continue to cook, stirring often, another 2 minutes. Then add the chicken livers and sauté, stirring, for 1 minute, or until they have lost their raw red color.

Raise heat, pour in the wine, and cook, stirring, until it completely evaporates. Set a food mill fitted with the medium blade over the casserole and mill in the tomatoes. Add several grindings of black pepper. Bring the sauce to a simmer and cook, covered, about 20 minutes, or until tomatoes have completely dissolved and sauce is slightly thickened. Taste for salt.

Bring 4 to 5 quarts of water to a boil; add 1 tablespoon salt and put in the pasta. When it is *al dente*, drain it and place it in a serving bowl. Toss it with the remaining 8 tablespoons of butter, cut into several pieces. Add the grated *parmigiano*, then the sauce, tossing after each. Sprinkle the chopped basil over the top and serve at once.

*The medley of flavors here requires a wine of equal harmony: A Vino
Nobile or Chianti Riserva, or even a Brunello from a lighter year, would
all be fine partners to the dish.*

Ravioli with Tomato Sauce
[RAVIOLI AL POMODORO]

Ravioli filled with *ricotta* are the most popular form of stuffed pasta in central
Italy. The success of this dish depends almost entirely on the freshness and
sweetness of the *ricotta*, so buy the best you can get, or make your own (page
29). You can also use partly firmed *raviggiolo* (page 28) instead of *ricotta*.
Ravioli, of course, are compatible with any number of other sauces, from
simple sage and butter to our lamb *ragù* or *amatriciana*. This recipe yields six
dozen *ravioli*, more than you will need for 4 people, but *ravioli* freeze very
well. To use them, do not thaw but drop them directly into boiling salted
water, and allow an extra 2 minutes' cooking time once they return to the
boil.

FOR THE FILLING

8 ounces *ricotta*	⅛ teaspoon salt
3 tablespoons grated *parmigiano*	Freshly ground black pepper
1 egg yolk	⅛ teaspoon freshly grated nutmeg

1 recipe basic egg pasta (page 24)	Freshly grated *parmigiano*
1 cup basic central tomato sauce (page 32)	

Mix all the filling ingredients. Divide the pasta into 4 pieces and roll them
out to the thinnest setting on a pasta machine.

Lay out one sheet of pasta on a lightly floured work surface and dot scant
teaspoonfuls of the filling on it at 2-inch intervals. Cover with another sheet
of pasta, smoothing out air pockets and pressing down to seal the dough around
the filling. Using a fluted pastry wheel or a plain knife, cut 2-inch square
ravioli. Repeat with the remaining sheets of dough. Set the *ravioli* to dry on
a floured board if not ready to cook at once.

When ready to serve, heat the tomato sauce. Bring 4 to 5 quarts of water
to a boil, add 1 tablespoon salt, and drop in the *ravioli*. Cook at a medium

boil for 2 to 3 minutes, until the pasta is tender when pierced with a fork. Drain and serve at once, allowing 12 *ravioli* per portion. Pass grated cheese at the table.

WINE SUGGESTION

Follow your own preferences here. A crisp white, such as a Verdicchio, or an uncomplicated red—Montepulciano, young Chianti, etc.—would do equally well.

Potato Gnocchi with Tomato Sauce
[GNOCCHI ALLA ROMANA]

In Rome, Thursday is *gnocchi* day. Every household makes or buys them for the family dinner, and the restaurant that doesn't offer them on Thursday may as well close for the day. This recipe makes far more delicate *gnocchi* than you are ever likely to get in a restaurant, because the lightest *gnocchi* paste requires minimal handling and immediate use. Other than that, *gnocchi* are not at all difficult to make. Airy, delicate *gnocchi* like these are probably the apotheosis of the potato. They may be treated in a variety of ways: In addition to dressing them with this basic tomato sauce, they may be tossed with *ragù*, or with a mixture of cheeses (*fontina* and *gorgonzola* is a popular version). They may also, after poaching, be lightly baked under a veil of butter and sage or butter and *parmigiano*, and so on.

1½ pounds baking potatoes
1 cup basic central tomato sauce
  (page 32)
2 egg yolks

1 teaspoon salt
1 cup flour

Boil the potatoes in their jackets in salted water until tender. Peel them immediately and pass them through the medium blade of a food mill into a large bowl.

Bring 4 to 5 quarts of salted water to a boil. Heat the tomato sauce to simmering.

Stir the egg yolks and the salt into the potatoes, then add the flour and mix to obtain a dough that is soft but not sticky. Add a few more tablespoons of flour if necessary, but try to handle the dough as little as possible.

Heavily flour a working surface and divide the dough into 4 to 6 pieces.

Take a piece of dough and roll it out lightly under your palms into a rope ½ inch in diameter. Cut 1-inch lengths and leave the pieces separated on the floured surface while you do the same with the rest of the dough. (You will probably need additional flour for the later pieces, because the dough gets sticky as it sits.)

Drop the *gnocchi* into the boiling water. In a minute or so, they will swell and rise to the surface. Cook them 2 minutes longer, then drain and serve with the sauce.

WINE SUGGESTION
   A *light white or red will do equally well here. Frascati or Tuscan white, or Montepulciano d'Abruzzo are all good choices.*

Gnocchi with Puréed Pepper Sauce
[GNOCCHI AL PEPERONE]

We first tasted this memorable sauce in the dining room of the Lungarottis' Hotel Tre Vaselle, in Torgiano in Umbria, where it was served on *frascarelli*, a local pasta somewhat like *spaetzle*. This adaptation makes an ideal dressing for very small pasta (*tubetti*, small shells, *farfellini*, etc.) as well as for *gnocchi*. Its texture is velvety, its flavor lush and pepper-sweet, and it is elegant as well—making it a fine candidate for a *primo* for a special occasion. It takes about 2 hours to prepare, but about three-quarters of that time is almost untended simmering. In fact, most of its preparation can be done in advance, leaving only reheating and assembly to be done while the *gnocchi* are cooking.

2 large red or yellow sweet peppers (about 1 pound)
1 celery stalk, thinly sliced (½ cup)
3 ounces onion, thinly sliced (1 cup)
3 tablespoons olive oil
1 small tomato (4 to 5 ounces), chopped
½ teaspoon salt
3 to 4 tablespoons *ricotta*
Freshly ground black pepper
Ingredients for 1 recipe of *gnocchi* (see preceding recipe)

Slice the peppers into thin strips (less than ¼ inch wide). Sauté them with the celery and onion in the olive oil over moderate heat for 10 minutes. Add the chopped tomato and the salt. Cover tightly and cook 1½ hours over the lowest possible heat, stirring from time to time. The vegetables should neither brown nor dry out.

Pass the entire contents of the pan through the medium blade of a food mill into a hot bowl. (The sauce may be done in advance to this point and reheated when ready to use.)

Soften the *ricotta*, either by putting it through a sieve or by mashing it thoroughly with a spoon, and stir it into the pepper purée. Add several grindings of black pepper.

Prepare and cook the *gnocchi* as described on page 193, drain and dress them with the sauce, and serve at once.

WINE SUGGESTION

A red wine of some complexity and substance is called for here. Rubesco would be ideal, or a Chianti Classico Riserva, or a Vino Nobile.

SECONDI

SECONDI

Central *secondi* follow the general lines of northern ones, though—with the big exception of *bistecca fiorentina*—the prime cuts of beef do not play a very big role. Fish, of course, are a staple of the regional diet, and chickens are very popular. Central Italians seem to share with peculiar intensity the consistent Italian preference for small animals over large: kid, baby lambs, tiny piglets, quail, and squab. There are lots of economic reasons for this—small animals require less feed, shorter periods of care, etc. (most such reasons make it a great mystery why veal is so much more costly than beef in the United States)—as well as perfectly good gastronomic ones, that is, that younger animals are more tender and delicate than their older relations. And, of course, like all Italians, central Italians are fond of organ meats. They regard liver, kidneys, sweetbreads, brains, tongue, and such as great delicacies. When beef does appear, it is most often in moist preparations, in braises and stews, rather than the American standard forms of roasting or broiling.

———————— ◆ ————————

Baked Striped Bass

[BRANZINO AL FORNO]

This simple method preserves beautifully the natural flavor of a fresh fish. Striped bass do not inhabit the Mediterranean, of course, but the treatment described here is an Italian standard that suits any nonoily fish except the strongest flavored. You can also use this same method to cook fillets of striped bass or scrod or sole; simply reduce the cooking time in accordance with the thickness of the fillets. Total preparation time for a whole fish is well under an hour.

———————— ◆ ————————

7 tablespoons olive oil
1 lemon, thinly sliced
1 striped bass, about 2 pounds, cleaned, scaled, and gilled
Salt

Freshly ground black pepper
2 small garlic cloves, sliced
2 tablespoons chopped parsley
⅓ cup dry white wine

Preheat the oven to 350 degrees F. Oil a baking dish with 1 tablespoon of the olive oil and lay a line of lemon slices down the center.

(continued)

Rinse the bass and pat dry. Salt and pepper its interior cavity and insert the garlic slices and parsley. Lay it in the baking dish on top of the lemon slices. Pour 3 tablespoons of olive oil over the fish. Salt and pepper it lightly, pour on the wine, and then the remaining 3 tablespoons oil.

Put the fish in the oven and cook for 40 minutes, basting every 10 minutes with the pan juices.

To serve, skin the fish and divide it into 4 portions in the kitchen. Pour a few tablespoons of the cooking juices from the pan over each portion.

WINE SUGGESTION

A substantial white wine is called for here: a really top-flight Orvieto or Frascati, or, better still, Torre di Giano or Pomino.

Braised Squid
[CALAMARI IN UMIDO]

Most Americans have encountered squid only as bait; Italians are smarter than that. If you've never eaten squid, or if you've eaten it only in California, where it is transformed into fried cardboard, you've got a treat in store. Don't be put off by squid's appearance, or even by having to clean it yourself if your fish store won't do it. It's easy and the dish is worth the trouble; in fact, it almost takes longer to describe than to do. Simply grasp the squid's body sac in one hand and the head and tentacles in the other and pull them apart gently but firmly, trying to remove all the contents of the sac. You may have to reach in with your index finger and detach the translucent, flat "spine." Cut off the tentacles just below the squid's eyes and push out the tiny "beak" at their center. Discard that and all the body contents. Under running water, peel away the mottled, loose skin of the body sac, then thoroughly rinse it and the tentacles inside and out. *Ecco! Calamari* ready for cooking. From this point on, the recipe requires only about half an hour. Serve it with plenty of fresh bread for soaking up the sauce.

2 pounds small squid	1 tablespoon chopped parsley
2 ounces Gaeta olives	½ cup olive oil
1 cup drained canned plum tomatoes	¼ teaspoon salt
2 garlic cloves	Freshly ground black pepper

Clean the squid and cut the bodies into ½-inch rings. Pit and halve the olives. Coarsely chop the tomatoes. Mince the garlic and parsley together.

Heat the olive oil in a large sauté pan and add the garlic and parsley. Sauté over moderate heat until the garlic starts to color. Turn the heat to medium-high, add the pieces of squid, and cook, stirring, for 1 minute.

Add the tomatoes, salt, and several grindings of pepper. Cook, covered, for 15 minutes, regulating the heat to maintain a high simmer. Add the olives and cook for 1 to 2 minutes. Serve at once.

WINE SUGGESTION
Best companion to this dish is a simple, dry white wine. Verdicchio is an excellent choice.

Deep-Fried Salt Cod
[BACCALÀ FRITTI]

Baccalà—salted and air-dried codfish—is an institution in Italy, where it is prepared in dozens of ways. It always plays an important part of the main meal on the great fast days such as Christmas Eve and Good Friday, and it was for years a staple of the cooking of Italian Jews—so much so that this particular fried preparation still remains the specialty of several of the best restaurants of what was once the Roman ghetto. Good baccalà is widely available in the United States, in fish stores and delicatessens in Italian neighborhoods. The light batter given here is a versatile one, which can be used for frying other fish, squid, zucchini or zucchini blossoms, eggplant slices, or meats. Italians love deep-fried foods; assorted platters of fish or flesh or vegetables—*fritti misti di pesce o di carne o all'Italiana*—are specialities of many restaurants. Obviously, you can substitute fresh cod for *baccalà* in this recipe; the effect will be moister and looser-textured, but you'll lose the particular "cured" quality that only *baccalà* has.

1½ pounds *baccalà*	1 teaspoon olive oil
¾ cup flour	3 to 4 cups oil for frying
⅛ teaspoon salt	1 egg white

Three days before serving:
Cover the *baccalà* with ample cold water and let it soak, changing the water twice a day.

On serving day:
Put the *baccalà* in a pot with fresh water to cover. Bring it to a boil, then

immediately drain the fish. Remove any remaining bones or bits of skin and cut it into 8 pieces, working along the natural separations of the flesh.

Put 1 cup of water in a broad shallow bowl. Gradually beat in the flour, using a fork or whisk, to make a light batter. Stir in the salt and olive oil.

Pour cooking oil into a 10-inch skillet or heavy-bottomed pot, to a depth of 1 inch. Heat the oil to just below the smoking point (360 to 375 degrees F). When the oil is ready, beat the egg white into stiff peaks and fold it into the batter. Dip the pieces of fish and fry them until golden, which will take about 3 minutes to a side if the pieces are 1½ to 2 inches thick.

WINE SUGGESTION

Crisp, dry white wine, well-chilled: Frascati, Orvieto, Trebbiano, Verdicchio—all are excellent with baccalà.

Fricasséed Chicken

[POLLO IN FRICASSEA]

This chicken cooks in a moist medium that eventually, with the addition of egg yolks, becomes its velvety sauce. Those who are experienced with fricassées will find the technique odd, because the chicken is not browned first in the cooking fat but is introduced directly into an already thickened liquid. Uncanonical it may be, but it makes for a very tender and toothsome bird. Total cooking time is just about 1¼ hours.

1 chicken, about 3 pounds, cut into serving pieces	1½ tablespoons olive oil
1 carrot	2 tablespoons flour
1 celery stalk	1 cup broth (page 45)
1 small onion	Salt
Several sprigs of fresh parsley	Freshly ground black pepper
1½ tablespoons butter	2 egg yolks
	Juice of ½ lemon

Rinse and dry the chicken. Pull off any loose pieces of fat. Cut the carrot and the celery stalk in half lengthwise, then crosswise. Cut the onion into quarters or thick slices. Rinse and dry the parsley.

Melt the butter with the oil in a large sauté pan over medium heat. As soon as the butter foam subsides, stir in the flour and cook, stirring, for 3 minutes, until the flour is lightly browned. Add the broth, a few tablespoons at a time, stirring constantly to avoid lumps.

As soon as the sauce comes to a simmer, add the pieces of carrot, onion, celery, and parsley. Lower the heat, cover the pan, and cook, stirring occasionally, until the vegetables are half-tender, about 15 minutes.

Add the chicken pieces to the pan. Salt and pepper them lightly, then cover and continue to simmer, turning the pieces occasionally, until the chicken is done—30 to 40 minutes. The sauce should remain quite thick throughout the cooking, but if it appears to be drying too much, add a tablespoon or two of broth or hot water.

Beat the egg yolks together with the lemon juice in a small bowl. When the chicken is done, transfer the pieces to a serving plate and keep warm. Remove and discard the vegetables from the sauce and boil down the sauce briefly if there is more than about 1 cup of liquid in the pan. Then slowly pour the egg yolk mixture into the liquid, stirring vigorously to obtain a smooth cream. Taste for salt, pour the sauce over the chicken, and serve at once.

WINE SUGGESTION
This dish needs a good, full-bodied white wine such as a Pomino or a Torre di Giano.

Chicken with Peppers
[POLLO ALLA ROMANA]

This dish is very pretty to look at and just as good to eat, with its cheery red peppers and sauce and its lively, straightforward flavors. A pleasant variant, if you aren't preceding this dish with a pasta course, is to add 1½ pounds parboiled potatoes to the sauce along with the peppers. Total cooking time is 45 minutes to 1 hour.

1 chicken, about 3 pounds, cut into serving pieces
4 large red or green bell peppers (1½ pounds)
2 garlic cloves
⅓ cup olive oil
½ cup dry white wine
2 cups drained canned plum tomatoes
Salt
Freshly ground black pepper

Rinse the chicken pieces and pat them dry with paper towels. Wash the peppers, halve and seed them, and cut them into 1½-inch squares.

In a heavy-bottomed casserole, sauté the garlic in the olive oil for 2 minutes. Add the chicken pieces and brown them well on all sides. Pour on the wine and cook over high heat until it evaporates, about 5 minutes, stirring and turning the chicken several times, and scraping up browned bits from the bottom of the pan.

Coarsely chop the tomatoes and add them to the pan, along with salt and pepper to taste. Simmer for 15 minutes. Add the peppers (and the potatoes, if you are using them), stir, cover, and cook gently until the peppers are tender but not mushy (15 to 30 minutes, depending on the freshness of the peppers). Stir from time to time.

At the end of the cooking time, if the sauce is too thin, transfer the pieces of chicken and peppers to a serving dish, keep them warm, and reduce the sauce rapidly over high heat. Pour the sauce over the chicken and serve at once.

WINE SUGGESTION

Follow your preferences here. A crisp white, such as a Verdicchio, or an uncomplicated red—Montepulciano, young Chianti, etc.—would do equally well.

Braised Chicken

[POLASTRELLO IN PADELLA]

A very different way to treat chicken from the preceding recipe: *prosciutto* and *peperoncino* give this preparation an authority and depth quite unlike the lively sweetness of the other. This is a red-wine dish, and no mistake about it. About 45 minutes from start to finish.

1 chicken, about 3 pounds, cut into serving pieces	Freshly ground black pepper
2 pounds ripe plum tomatoes	½ cup dry white wine
2 ounces *prosciutto*	1 *peperoncino rosso*
4 tablespoons olive oil	1 tablespoon fresh oregano (or ½ tablespoon dried)
2 garlic cloves	2 tablespoons chopped fresh basil
Salt	

Rinse the chicken pieces and pat them dry. Drop the tomatoes into boiling water for 10 seconds, then drain, peel, seed, and roughly chop them. Dice the *prosciutto*.

Heat the olive oil in a large sauté pan and sauté the whole garlic cloves and diced *prosciutto* for 1 minute. Raise heat to medium and add the chicken pieces. Salt and pepper them lightly and brown them on both sides.

Raise heat to high. Pour on the wine and let it evaporate, stirring constantly to keep chicken pieces from sticking to pan. When the wine is almost entirely gone, add the chopped tomatoes, the basil, oregano, and the *peperoncino*. Cook over medium heat for 20 minutes, turning the chicken pieces from time to time.

When the chicken is tender, remove it to a hot serving dish and keep it warm. Reduce the sauce until it is quite thick, spoon it over the chicken, and serve at once.

WINE SUGGESTION

Best match with this dish would be a dry, fruity red wine such as Montepulciano d'Abruzzo or Rosso Piceno.

Spit-Roasted Squabs

[PICCIONI ARROSTI]

If you own a countertop rotisserie, this is the time to use it: It cooks these birds to perfection. Lacking that, put them in a 350-degree-F oven for 30 to 40 minutes, turning and basting them every 5 or 10 minutes. And don't, if you can possibly help it, omit the grappa; it lends a wonderful aroma to the whole preparation.

4 squabs, ¾ pound each	Freshly ground black pepper
12 large fresh sage leaves	12 thin slices bacon
2 teaspoons fresh thyme	2 tablespoons Chianti or other
4 ounces *prosciutto*	dry red wine
4 tablespoons butter	2 tablespoons Tuscan grappa (or sub-
Salt	stitute cognac)

Preheat a countertop rotisserie. Rinse and dry the squabs.

Chop together the sage and thyme. Set aside about a third of the herbs. Add the *prosciutto* to the remainder and continue chopping until the *prosciutto* is well minced.

Fill the body cavity of each squab with one-quarter of the herb mixture and 1 teaspoon of the butter. Thread them onto the rotisserie spit, head to tail. Sprinkle them with salt and pepper and the remaining chopped herbs, then cover them with the bacon slices, tie securely with string, and place them on the rotisserie.

Melt the remaining 3 tablespoons butter and stir in the Chianti and grappa.

Periodically baste the birds with this mixture as they cook. Total roasting time will be about 1 hour.

WINE SUGGESTION
An excellent Chianti, such as a Classico Riserva, is the perfect complement to these squabs.

Veal Scallops with Prosciutto, Chicken Liver, and Anchovies

[SCALOPPINE ALLA PERUGINA]

Umbrian cooking tends to be the most elaborate of the central Italian cuisines (perhaps because only Umbria, in the Center, has any significant supply of truffles), and this is a particularly rich preparation for a cut of meat that is normally treated with great simplicity almost everywhere in Italy. This dish takes less than half an hour to prepare.

1 pound veal cutlets	2 teaspoons capers
Salt	Peel of ½ lemon
Freshly ground black pepper	2 garlic cloves
2 ounces *prosciutto*	4 tablespoons olive oil
1 chicken liver	Juice of ½ lemon
3 anchovy fillets	4 fresh sage leaves

Pound the veal cutlets thin. Cut them as nearly as possible into 4-inch squares, pat them dry with paper towels, and salt and pepper them lightly.

Mince together the *prosciutto*, chicken liver, anchovies, capers, lemon peel, and garlic. Put the mixture into a large sauté pan, add the olive oil, lemon juice, and sage leaves. Sauté over moderate heat until sizzling. Add the veal pieces and cook, covered, for 8 to 10 minutes, turning several times. Lower heat as necessary to keep the cooking gentle.

Remove veal to a serving dish and keep warm. Add 4 tablespoons of water to the pan, scrape up the browned bits from the bottom, and reduce the liquid over high heat to a dense sauce. Pour this over the veal and serve at once.

WINE SUGGESTION
Rubesco makes a perfect companion to this dish. Failing that, try Vino Nobile.

Beef Stew with Onions

[STRACOTTO ALLA FIORENTINA]

There are hundreds of ways to do *stracotto*, which only means "extra-long cooked." Most of them are fine, but not too different from the way the French or Germans or Belgians or even Americans might approach the situation: By one means or another, you wind up with something like pot roast. This Florentine version, however, produces a dish that doesn't resemble a run-of-the-mill pot roast at all. Yes, that second quantity listed is correct. Onion fans will love this.

½ cup plus 3 tablespoons olive oil
3 pounds onions, finely chopped
1 carrot, finely chopped
1 celery stalk, finely chopped
2 tablespoons chopped fresh basil leaves
1 tablespoon salt

½ cup dry red wine
1 cup drained canned plum tomatoes, chopped
3 garlic cloves
3 pounds chuck fillet or bottom round
Salt
Freshly ground black pepper

Warm ½ cup of the olive oil in a heavy-bottomed deep pot. Add the onions, carrot, celery, basil, and 1 teaspoon of the salt. Cook uncovered over medium heat for 30 minutes, stirring often. Add the wine and tomatoes, cover, and cook 15 minutes.

Sliver the garlic cloves. Make small slits all over the meat and insert the garlic slivers. Salt and pepper the meat lightly.

In a casserole large enough to hold all the ingredients, warm the remaining 3 tablespoons olive oil, add the meat, and slowly brown it on all sides. (This will take about 20 minutes.)

Add the vegetables and all their juices to the meat. Cover and continue cooking over gentle heat for 2 to 3 hours, stirring occasionally, until the meat is very tender. If the sauce seems too dry, add small amounts of broth or water. Remove the meat to a serving platter and keep warm. Purée the vegetable mixture through a food mill fitted with the fine blade. Pour some of this sauce over the meat. Put the rest into a gravy boat or bowl and pass at table.

WINE SUGGESTION
A good red wine with some depth is called for here: Chianti Riserva (Classico or Rufina), Rubesco Riserva, even a Brunello.

Perugian Beef Rolls

[INVOLTINI ALLA PERUGINA]

Another example of the characteristic Umbrian merging of many ingredients into a surprising and pleasing harmony. Wrapping these elegantly filled beef rolls in caul fat—rather than tying them with string—adds the final touch of richness to the dish. For a discussion of caul fat, see pages 35–36.

½ pound caul fat
2 slices stale bread, crusts removed, cut into cubes (¾ cup)
½ cup milk
4 ounces lean pork
4 ounces boneless, skinless chicken breast
2 ounces *prosciutto*
1 garlic clove
1 tablespoon grated *parmigiano*

⅛ teaspoon freshly grated nutmeg
¼ teaspoon salt
5 grindings of black pepper
¼ teaspoon dried marjoram
1 egg yolk
4 pieces of beef round (about ¾ pound) sliced thin and pounded
¼ cup olive oil
½ cup dry white wine

Soak the caul fat in cold water for 1 hour to soften it. Soak the cubes of bread in the milk until soft. Cut the pork, chicken, and *prosciutto* into medium-sized pieces. Quarter the garlic.

In a food processor, pulse the pork, half the *prosciutto*, and the garlic until well chopped. Add the chicken and pulse it, too. Transfer the meats to a bowl and mix in the soaked bread, grated cheese, nutmeg, salt, pepper, marjoram, and egg yolk.

Divide the filling into 4 portions. Spread a portion of filling on each beef slice, and roll them up into neat packets, tucking in the ends.

Drain the caul fat. Spread it out carefully on a board and cut off 4 pieces large enough to envelop the *involtini*. Roll them up, tucking the ends in.

Cut the remaining *prosciutto* into julienne strips. Warm the olive oil in a pan with the *prosciutto* for 2 minutes. Add the *involtini* and brown them on all sides. Then add the white wine, cover, and cook over low heat for about 1 hour, turning the *involtini* often and basting them if necessary with a little water.

WINE SUGGESTION
This dish will respond well to an excellent red wine: Chianti Classico Riserva, Vino Nobile, Rubesco Riserva, Brunello.

Lamb Sauté with Wine and Vinegar
[ABBACCHIO ALLA ROMANA]

In Rome this dish is cooked with tiny, unweaned lambs. Their flesh is pale and rich, and the dish is unforgettable. Here, alas, our babiest lambs are half grown. Nevertheless, the preparation remains unusual and delicious—well worth making, if only to taste how well this combination of lamb, anchovy, and vinegar works. This is probably is a very old element in Italian cooking: The ancient Romans had a sauce called *garum* made from fish that they too used with fowl and meats. About 1 hour preparation time.

3 pounds boneless shoulder of lamb	¼ cup dry red wine
4 garlic cloves	1 tablespoon fresh rosemary leaves
3 tablespoons olive oil	3 anchovy fillets
Salt	¼ cup red wine vinegar
Freshly ground black pepper	

Cut the lamb into 3-inch chunks, removing as much fat as possible. Dry the pieces with paper towels. Slice 1 garlic clove lengthwise into 2 or 3 pieces.

In a large pan, sauté the garlic pieces in the oil until they are brown, then press them to release their juices and discard them. Brown the lamb on all sides in the pan, in several batches if necessary to prevent crowding. Lightly salt and pepper them as they brown. When all the lamb is brown, return earlier batches to the pan, raise heat, add the wine, and cook, stirring, for 3 minutes, scraping up any browned bits from the bottom of the pan.

Cover, lower heat to a simmer, and cook for 20 minutes, or until the lamb is beginning to get tender. (Too much cooking at this point may cause the lamb to toughen later on.) Defat the sauce if desired. The dish can be prepared up to this point several hours in advance.

When ready to proceed, put the remaining garlic cloves, rosemary, and anchovy fillets into a blender and process them into a paste, adding a little of the vinegar if necessary for moisture. Once the mixture is homogeneous, blend in the remaining vinegar.

Bring the lamb and its defatted juices back to a simmer and stir in the seasoning mixture. Cook at medium-high heat, uncovered and stirring often, for 7 to 10 minutes, until the vinegar is reduced to about a third and the sauce is thickened slightly. Serve at once.

WINE SUGGESTION
A complex red wine works best with this dish, though some diners enjoy

a full-bodied white (Torre di Giano, Pomino) with it. First choice should be a Chianti Classico Riserva of good vintage, or a well-aged Vino Nobile.

Crown Roast of Pork

[ARISTA]

Depending on whom you listen to, *arista* either means simply "roasted" (*arrosto*) or is Greek for "the best"—an exclamation attributed to a visiting Orthodox bishop who tasted this dish in Florence centuries ago. What *arista* means to a cook is a brilliantly spiced and herbed loin of pork, just as fragrant and delicious cold as hot, and cooked so the flavors of the condiments totally pervade the meat. We've given a festive touch to our version by turning it into a crown roast. The whole loin, trimmed, curved, and tied into a circle, makes a striking presentation for an important dinner. This handsome piece of meat needs at least 8 people to do it justice. Any butcher should be willing to prepare the cut. A precise cooking weight is less important than an appropriate number of chops for the number of diners. For a smaller number of diners, half the quantity of seasonings can be used on a straight loin roast. To help the seasonings penetrate the meat, we use a food processor to turn them into a paste. Lacking that piece of equipment, you can make the paste in a mortar, or simply rub the ingredients separately into the meat. Note that in Italy, *arista* is commonly served warm or at room temperature rather than piping hot. Sliced very thin and at room temperature, it often appears as an *antipasto* or light luncheon dish as well. Total preparation time is 6 hours plus, but only a small fraction of that is working time: "Marinating" and slow roasting make up the bulk of it.

15 medium-size garlic cloves	2 tablespoons salt
4 tablespoons dried rosemary	2 tablespoons olive oil
1½ tablespoons freshly ground black pepper	1 crown roast of pork, approximately 6 pounds

Begin preparations at least 6 hours before serving. Mince the garlic in the food processor. Add the rosemary, pepper, and salt. Process everything to an even crumble. With the machine running, slowly pour in the olive oil. Process to a paste, stopping to scrape down the sides of the bowl as necessary.

Rub this paste into all the surfaces of the meat and let it sit at least 2 hours at room temperature.

Preheat the oven to 375 degrees F. Roast the meat in an open roasting pan for approximately 3 hours, or until its interior temperature is 170 to 185 degrees (depending on how moist you prefer pork). Take the roast out of the oven and let it sit on a carving board at least 30 minutes before serving.

To carve, simply cut between the rib bones and separate an individual chop for each diner.

WINE SUGGESTION

Arista will match well with the best red wine in your cellar. Choose among Brunello, Vino Nobile, Rubesco, Chianti Classico Riserva. Surprisingly, a top-quality, full-bodied white wine will also partner pleasingly with it: Try, for instance, Lungarotti's Torre di Giano Riserva, Brolio's Torricella, or especially Frescobaldi's Pomino Riserva Il Benefizio.

Roast Suckling Pig
[MAIALINO ARROSTO]

Italians love to spit-roast small, whole animals. In the case of pigs, they extend the range from the smallest, as in this recipe, to 45 or 50 pounders, as in Lazio's beloved *porchetta*. The latter is a bit impractical for the home cook, so we've adapted this more modest preparation for oven roasting. Gentle, low-temperature cooking keeps the piglet tender, while the basting both keeps the flesh moist and gives the skin a pleasing color and texture.

1 piglet, about 7 pounds	1 tablespoon olive oil
3 cloves	2 bay leaves
¼ teaspoon coriander seeds	1 tablespoon rosemary leaves
3 garlic cloves	12 basil leaves
½ teaspoon salt	12 sage leaves
⅛ teaspoon freshly grated nutmeg	3 tablespoons lard
Several grindings of pepper	½ cup dry red wine

Preheat the oven to 325 degrees F. Wash the pig inside and out and pat it dry with paper towels.

Crush the cloves and coriander seeds in a mortar. Put the garlic through a press and mix it together with the salt, nutmeg, pepper, coriander, cloves, and olive oil. Rub this mixture all over the inside of the pig. Strew on the bay leaves, rosemary, basil, and sage leaves. Sew up the pig's body cavity, place it on a rack in a large roasting pan, and rub its skin all over with the lard.

Put the pig in the oven. After 15 to 20 minutes, baste with the red wine.

Continue roasting for a total of 3 hours, basting at approximately 20-minute intervals with the pan drippings (or water or more wine if the pan is too dry). The pig's skin should turn a deep rich brown.

Remove the pan from the oven and let the pig rest for 5 minutes, then serve.

WINE SUGGESTION

Choose among Brunello, Vino Nobile, Rubesco, Chianti Classico Riserva. If you wish a white wine (some people prefer it with this dish), try Lungarotti's Torre di Giano Riserva, or Brolio's Torricella, or Frescobaldi's Pomino Riserva Il Benefizio.

Roast Leg of Boar

[CINGHIALE ARROSTO]

Boar is always a special-occasion dish, the acme of game. There's something about even the name that calls to mind the essence of wildness. Even with ranch-raised game, which is 99 percent of what is available here in the United States, the dense, lean, muscular flesh of boar demands slow, moist cooking and long marinating. This recipe allows almost a week for a classic dry marinade to do its work. You can prepare the shank end of a fresh ham this same way: Cut the marinating time to 3 days and adjust the cooking time according to weight. It will give a less gamy but more juicy dish—and fresh ham does have the virtue of being more readily available than boar. Total preparation and cooking time is about 4 hours.

———————

1 tablespoon peppercorns	1 leg of boar, about 7 pounds, bone
12 juniper berries	in
1 tablespoon rosemary	3 tablespoons olive oil
3 garlic cloves	½ cup dry red wine
	Broth (page 45)

Grind together the peppercorns, juniper berries, and rosemary. Smear them all over the boar. Cover and let it marinate in the refrigerator 5 to 6 days, turning the leg over once a day.

The morning of cooking day, cut the garlic into slivers, make little cuts all over the boar, and insert the garlic.

Preheat the oven to 325 degrees F. Set the meat on a rack and drizzle the olive oil over it. Put the pan in the oven. After 30 minutes, baste with the red wine. Continue to baste at intervals with broth, about ½ cup at a time. Allow 30 minutes per pound cooking time: 3½ hours total for this 7-pound leg. When it is done, remove it from the oven and allow it to sit for 10 minutes before serving. If you wish, you may deglaze the roasting pan with a little wine or water and prepare what Italians call a *salsina*, just a small quantity of sauce, to serve alongside the boar. Carve as you would a leg of lamb.

WINE SUGGESTION

Serve Riserva bottlings of your best red wines here: Brunello, Vino Nobile, Rubesco, Chianti Classico.

Sausages with Rape

[SALSICCIE CON RAPE]

This is a spicy, down-home dish, with a palate-tingling counterpoint between the warmth of the sausages and the vegetable bitterness of the rape. Great winter food! Be sure to accompany this dish with fresh bread. Leftovers, if any, can be chopped and used to fill *calzone*, which are almost as popular in the Abruzzi (where this recipe comes from) as they are farther south. Total preparation time is about half an hour.

1½ pounds broccoli rape	2 garlic cloves
1 recipe spicy sausage (page 37), or 2 pounds commercial Italian-style hot sausage	5 tablespoons olive oil
	Salt

Wash and trim the rape. Snap off and set apart the tender blossoms and roughly chop the remainder. Cut the sausage into 2-inch segments. Peel and lightly crush the garlic cloves with the flat of a heavy knife blade.

Warm the olive oil in a pan with the garlic; when the garlic colors, press it against the bottom of the pan and discard it. Add the sausage pieces and sauté 8 to 10 minutes, turning and piercing them in several places with a fork from time to time.

Add the rape, reserving the blossoms. Salt lightly and cook, covered, for 5 minutes, adding a little hot water if rape seems to be drying out. Then add the blossoms and cook for 3 minutes longer, or until they are tender. Serve at once.

(continued)

WINE SUGGESTION

Serve a hearty, country-style red wine with this dish: Montepulciano d'Abruzzo, or, if you want something with more complexity, a Rosso di Montalcino.

Braised Oxtails

[CODA ALLA VACCINARA PICCANTE]

No other meat is quite like oxtail: It has a richness of flavor and texture that rewards slow cooking, as in this classic Roman recipe. The final cooking aromas of this dish, for instance, will drive otherwise quite temperate people mad with hunger and impatience. The late addition of the celery lightens and brightens the dish, cuts the lushness of the oxtails back to size, and provides a pleasing textural contrast as well. The little red pepper will disappear completely into the sauce, where you will taste it as a small, genial warmth. Slightly more than 4 hours' total cooking time.

---

2 oxtails, about 3 pounds, cut up	Freshly ground black pepper
4 garlic cloves	½ cup dry white wine
⅓ cup olive oil	2 cups drained canned plum toma-
1 *peperoncino rosso*	toes
Salt	1 pound celery (6 to 8 large stalks)

Bring 3 quarts of water to a boil in a large pot. Drop in the oxtails and parboil for 30 minutes. Drain and pat them dry.

Slice each garlic clove into 2 to 3 pieces. Brown them in the olive oil along with the *peperoncino*. When the garlic is golden, press the pieces firmly against the bottom of the pan and then remove them, but leave the *peperoncino* in.

Add the pieces of oxtail. Salt and pepper them lightly and stir them around to coat them with the oil. Then raise heat, add the white wine, and boil until the wine is almost entirely evaporated.

Mill the tomatoes through the coarse blade of a food mill into the pan. Stir and cook at a low simmer, partly covered, for 3 hours. If the sauce thickens too much, add a little of the oxtails' parboiling water, or plain hot water.

Meanwhile, wash and trim the celery and cut it into 2-inch pieces. After the oxtails have cooked for 3 hours, or when the meat is just beginning to separate from the bone, stir in the celery and a light sprinkling of salt, and cook, covered, for another 30 minutes. Serve at once.

A slightly acid red wine partners well with this dish. Young Chianti, especially from the Classico zone or from the Pisan or Aretine hills, would make an excellent choice.

Braised Beef Tripe

[TRIPPA ALLE MARCHE]

This is a very comforting dish, the kind of food that can persuade you that, despite all the counterindications, you may make it to the end of the week after all. If you can't get a *prosciutto* bone (every *prosciutto* has at least one, and the shopkeeper has to do something with it) use a bone from a fresh ham. This dish takes about 4 hours from start to finish.

2 pounds tripe	2 tablespoons chopped parsley
2 ounces pork skin	½ teaspoon dried marjoram
3 ounces lard	Peel of 1 lemon
⅔ cup chopped onion	1 *prosciutto* bone
1 garlic clove, chopped	1 teaspoon salt
⅔ cup chopped celery	1 tablespoon tomato paste
⅔ cup chopped carrot	Freshly grated *parmigiano*

Bring a large pot of lightly salted water to a boil. Add the tripe and simmer for 1 hour. Drop the pork skin into boiling water and boil for 1 minute, then drain and cut into strips 2 inches by ¼ inch.

Melt the lard in a large casserole. Add the onion, garlic, celery, carrot, parsley, marjoram, and lemon peel. Sauté over low heat until the vegetables are soft, about 10 minutes.

When the tripe is done, cut it into strips 2 to 3 inches long by ½ inch wide. Add it to the casserole along with the pork skin, the *prosciutto* bone, the salt, and the tomato paste dissolved in 1 cup of hot water. Bring to a boil, reduce to a simmer, cover, and cook 2½ hours, stirring often and adding more hot water if necessary.

Serve with abundant *parmigiano*.

WINE SUGGESTION
Your choice, really; white or red will both do well. Nothing too fancy, though. A decent Orvieto or Frascati, or young Chianti Classico or Rosso di Montalcino, are the sorts of wine you want.

Mozzarella Soufflés

[SOUFFLÉS DI MOZZARELLA]

This recipe is a cosmopolitan Roman transformation of the traditional Italian *sformato* (a molded half-mousse, half-soufflé, usually vegetable). It makes an excellent light *secondo* or luncheon dish. About 15 minutes' preparation time, 20 minutes' baking.

———————◆———————

6 egg whites	2 tablespoons flour
1 cup heavy cream	Salt
8 ounces *mozzarella*	Freshly ground black pepper
4 tablespoons butter	½ cup grated *parmigiano*

Bring the egg whites and the cream to room temperature. Cut the *mozzarella* into ½-inch dice. Preheat the oven to 375 degrees F. Generously butter four 1½-cup individual soufflé dishes.

Melt 2 tablespoons of the butter in a medium-size heavy-bottomed saucepan. Stir in the flour and cook over low heat, stirring constantly, for 2 minutes, without letting the flour brown.

Turn off heat and add the cream, a few tablespoons at a time, stirring constantly. The sauce will seize up at first, but will eventually smooth out into a thick cream. Lightly salt and pepper it and stir in the *mozzarella* and *parmigiano*.

Whip the egg whites until stiff but not dry. Fold them into the cheese mixture. Divide it among the four dishes. Bake 20 minutes, or until the soufflés are well puffed and golden-brown on top. Serve immediately.

WINE SUGGESTION
This dish will match happily with any not-too-complex wine, red or white. Orvieto would be a nice choice for a white, and almost any young, dry red will do well.

———————◆———————

CONTORNI

I n the Center, vegetables begin to assume more importance in the meal, appearing in any and all the courses as the seasons allow and appetite dictates. Vegetable preparations tend to be, for the most part, simple. By far the most popular methods are steaming or boiling, just as anywhere else in the world. Greens and beans and asparagus, beets and carrots and potatoes, cauliflower and peas and zucchini are so treated, then drained and dressed either with oil—occasionally with butter—or with fresh lemon juice, and served either hot or at room temperature. Some vegetables are deep-fried: artichokes, for instance, and zucchini, and zucchini flowers. Some are grilled: onions, bell pepper, eggplant, zucchini. And some are roasted: peppers, potatoes, artichokes. When they are handled more elaborately, it is usually by combining them with tomato, or with onion, or with herbs, or with some medley of all three.

———————◆———————

Country-Style Artichokes
[CARCIOFI ALLA PAESANA]

With the tender artichokes of Italy, this dish takes hardly any more time than to slice the artichokes into their sauté pan. Ours, unfortunately, require some preliminary trimming and paring, though at the size recommended, the chokes are edible. It's worth the effort, however, for this excellent vegetable dish. The touch of tomato mellows the artichokes interestingly and makes them a good companion to simply cooked meats and fish.

———————◆———————

3 tablespoons lemon juice
1½ pounds small artichokes (10 to 14 to the pound)
2 tablespoons olive oil
3 garlic cloves, halved

1 *peperoncino rosso*
¼ teaspoon dried marjoram
Salt
Freshly ground black pepper
1 teaspoon tomato paste

Stir the lemon juice into a bowl half full of cold water. Holding an artichoke with the top facing you, snap off the outermost few layers of leaves at the base. Continue until you reach the soft, pale green or yellow leaves. Slice off about the top half of the artichoke cone. With a vegetable peeler, pare away the green exterior of the artichoke bottom, leaving white flesh. Drop each finished artichoke into the bowl of water while preparing the rest.

When all the artichokes are prepared, drain and slice them lengthwise into ½-inch pieces, then dry them in a towel.

Heat the olive oil in a sauté pan and add the garlic and *peperoncino*. Sauté until garlic is golden, then crush each piece lightly into the oil with a fork and remove it. Also remove the hot pepper.

Add the artichoke pieces and the marjoram and sauté 3 minutes. Salt and pepper lightly, and add the tomato paste dissolved in ¼ cup water. Cover and cook 10 minutes. Stir in another ¼ cup water and cook another 10 minutes.

WINE SUGGESTION
Follow the wine indicated for your secondo.

Deep-Fried Artichokes
[CARCIOFI FRITTI]

Whole large artichokes, deep-fried until they look like copper sculptures, are a speciality of restaurants in the Jewish quarter of Rome. They are surprisingly tender, and their flavor is concentrated by the quick, high-temperature cooking. Regrettably, the variety of artichoke that responds well to this treatment doesn't seem to grow in America, so this adaptation for small artichokes, with tender edible chokes, is designed to give the genuine taste, if not the genuine appearance, of the Roman dish.

2 lemons	Oil for deep-frying
1 pound small artichokes (10 to 14 to the pound)	Salt
	Freshly ground black pepper

Squeeze half a lemon into a bowl half full of cold water. Holding an artichoke with the top facing you, snap off the outermost few layers of leaves at the base. Continue until you reach the soft, pale green or yellow leaves. Slice off about the top half of the artichoke cone. With a vegetable peeler, pare away the green exterior of the artichoke bottom, leaving white flesh. Drop each finished artichoke into the bowl of water while preparing the rest.

When all the artichokes are prepared, drain and quarter them, making sure that every piece has a bit of the bottom to anchor the leaves. Then dry them very thoroughly in a towel.

Preheat frying oil to 375 degrees F. Place a platter lined with paper towels in the turned-off oven. Fry the artichokes a few at a time until golden brown and crisp. Drain them on the paper towels and sprinkle with salt and pepper. Serve with lemon wedges.

WINE SUGGESTION

Deep-frying considerably ameliorates artichokes' usual hostility to wine. A dry, acid white wine, well-chilled—something like Verdicchio or a top-flight Frascati—is an excellent accompaniment to this dish. If your se-condo is strongly flavored, however, follow its lead.

Green Beans Sautéed with Tomato
[FAGIOLINI A CORALLO]

This method of preparing green beans is usually reserved in Italy for the broader, flatter variety that we sometimes call Roman or Italian beans, but we have found it works very well with all sorts of green and wax beans. In fact, it is especially good as a flavor-restorer for older, tougher, end-of-the-season beans. About 45 minutes' total preparation time.

¾ to 1 pound green beans	2 tablespoons olive oil
5 plum tomatoes (about 10 ounces)	Salt
¼ cup finely chopped onion	Freshly ground black pepper

Snap tips off beans; rinse and drain them. Drop the tomatoes into boiling water for 10 seconds, then drain and peel them. Coarsely chop them.

Cook the chopped onion in the olive oil in a broad sauté pan until soft, about 5 minutes. Add the green beans and cook over moderate heat, stirring often, for 5 minutes.

Add the cut-up tomatoes. Salt and pepper everything moderately, mix well, cover, and cook gently for 30 minutes, or until the beans are tender. Stir often and add tablespoonfuls of hot water if the beans seem to be frying.

Serve in a hot vegetable dish.

WINE SUGGESTION

Go with the wine suggested for your secondo.

Green Beans with Fennel
[FAGIOLINI ALLA FIORENTINA]

The fennel seed adds a lively and unusual note to this simple preparation. It needs just about half an hour from start to finish.

¾ to 1 pound green beans	3 tablespoons olive oil
Salt	Salt
¼ teaspoon fennel seeds	Freshly ground black pepper
¼ cup thinly sliced onion	2 teaspoons tomato paste

Snap tips off beans; rinse and drain them. Drop them into boiling salted water, and when the water returns to a boil, cook uncovered until not quite tender, 8 to 12 minutes, depending on the age and freshness of the beans. Then drain them.

Grind the fennel seeds to powder in a mortar or blender. Cook the sliced onion in the olive oil in a broad sauté pan until soft, about 5 minutes. Add the drained beans, salt and pepper, and the powdered fennel. Sauté, stirring, over moderate heat for 2 to 3 minutes.

Dilute the tomato paste in ¼ cup hot water and add it to the beans. Stir again, cover the pan, and cook over low heat for about 10 minutes, or until beans are tender. If necessary to keep beans from drying out, add a tablespoon or two of hot water.

WINE SUGGESTION
Follow the suggestion for your secondo.

Fresh Shell Beans
[FAGIOLI ALLA TOSCANA]

Tuscans are notorious in Italy for their love of beans, so much so that they are known as *mangiafagioli*—bean eaters—and "Fagioli" must be the most common nickname for young boys in Florence. This is the basic bean preparation that Tuscans consume by the kilo, sprinkled with black pepper and their exquisite olive oil.

2 pounds fresh cranberry beans (about 3 cups, shelled)	6 to 8 fresh sage leaves
½ cup olive oil	Salt
4 whole garlic cloves	Freshly ground black pepper
	Extra-virgin olive oil

Preheat the oven to 300 degrees F.

Shell and pick over the beans. Rinse and drain them, and put them into a heavy-bottomed ovenproof pot. Add the oil, garlic, and sage, then water to cover. Bring to a simmer on top of the stove, then put them into the oven for 1 hour, or until the beans are tender and the liquid entirely absorbed.

Check from time to time, and if it looks as if the water will not be absorbed at the end of the hour, remove the cover for the last 15 minutes. Conversely, if it looks as if the water will be gone before the beans are done, add a little hot water.

When the beans are finished, drain them and put them into a serving dish. Dress generously with salt, pepper, and extra-virgin olive oil before serving.

WINE SUGGESTION

If you're just having a dish of beans, bread, and oil—and why not?— pour yourself a glass of a fruity young Chianti as well. Otherwise, follow the suggestion for your secondo.

Sautéed Escarole

[SCAROLE SALTATE]

For this sautéed escarole dish, try to select heads of escarole with bright yellow hearts—the paler and larger the better. The amount of olive oil can be reduced, if desired, but the charm of the dish is really in the oil. Remember: Olive oil is good for you. The optional nutmeg, raisin, and pignoli show just how far north in Italy the Saracens—or Saracen cooking, at any rate—once penetrated. Spinach is also good done this way.

———————————◆———————————

2 small or 1 large head escarole (about 1¾ pounds)
½ cup olive oil
1 garlic clove, minced
Salt

Freshly ground black pepper
Freshly grated nutmeg, optional
1 tablespoon pignoli, optional
1 tablespoon raisins, optional

Trim the bases of the escarole heads. Separate the leaves and wash them very carefully, ripping off any blackened leaf tips. Put the leaves in a large pot and pour on boiling water to cover. Cover the pot and bring it to a boil. Lower heat and simmer 7 to 10 minutes, until the thickest stems are almost tender.

Drain and rinse the escarole in cold water. Allow to cool until touchable, then squeeze gently to remove excess liquid. Roughly chop.

(continued)

In a large sauté pan, warm the olive oil. Add the garlic and the escarole, salt and pepper to taste, and a grating of nutmeg, if desired. If you wish a more southern, slightly Saracen accent, you can at this point also add the pignoli and the raisins. Sauté, stirring, for 5 to 10 minutes, until the escarole is well imbued with the oil and seasonings.

Serve hot, warm, or at room temperature, garnishing with lemon wedges.

WINE SUGGESTION
Follow the choices indicated for your secondo.

Sautéed Tuscan Mushrooms
[FUNGHI IN PADELLA]

In Tuscany and all throughout central Italy, preparations like this one are used to emphasize the succulence of fresh *funghi porcini*. Until the happy day when *porcini* are common on the American market, we'll have to content ourselves with using a small amount of the concentrated dry ones to produce an approximation of their flavor in less authoritative mushrooms. Treated this way, *cremosini* come very, very close to the texture and flavor of fresh *porcini*, and that is a treat indeed. This method also works very well with *shiitake*, or ordinary cultivated mushrooms. Incidentally, it's worth knowing that *porcini* are often eaten as *secondi* rather than as *contorni*.

½ ounce dried *porcini*	½ teaspoon chopped fresh thyme
¾ to 1 pound *cremosini* mushrooms	½ teaspoon chopped fresh mint
6 tablespoons olive oil	1½ teaspoons tomato paste
2 garlic cloves	Salt
½ teaspoon chopped fresh basil	Freshly ground black pepper

Put the dried mushrooms in a bowl and pour 1 cup of boiling water over them. Let them sit for 30 minutes. Then drain them, reserving the water. Rinse them thoroughly, coarsely chop them, and rinse again to remove all traces of grit. Lay a dampened paper towel in a small sieve and strain the mushroom soaking liquid through it.

Clean and trim the fresh *cremosini*. Separate the stems and caps, and cut both into thin strips.

Warm the olive oil in a broad sauté pan. Soften the garlic in the oil with the basil, thyme, and mint. Add the sliced *cremosini* and brown them gently.

Then add the chopped dried mushrooms. Salt and pepper lightly, stir well, and cook gently, covered, for 15 minutes. As the pan juices cook off, add a few tablespoons of the mushroom soaking liquid to keep the mixture moist.

Dilute the tomato paste in ¼ cup of the mushroom soaking liquid, stir it into the pan, and cook uncovered for 5 to 6 minutes. Serve at once in a warmed vegetable dish.

WINE SUGGESTION
A young red wine, preferably Tuscan: Chianti, Vino Nobile, Rosso di Brunello.

Roasted Potatoes with Bay Leaves
[PATATE AL ALLORO]

This recipe amounts to a Tuscan variant on the Roman rosemary potatoes. We first tasted these at Badia a Coltibuono, deep in the heart of Chianti country.

———◆———

1½ pounds small boiling potatoes
¼ cup olive oil

Bay leaves equal in number to the potatoes

Scrub the potatoes. Boil them in their jackets in lightly salted water until half cooked, 12 to 15 minutes. Drain and spray them with cold water to stop the cooking.

Preheat the oven to 400 degrees F. Peel and halve the potatoes. Cut a thin slit in the center of each half potato and insert half a bay leaf. Put them in a bowl, pour on the olive oil, and toss to coat. Transfer the potatoes to a lightly oiled pan (or to the roasting pan, if you are roasting a piece of meat). Bake 30 minutes, turning the potatoes once or twice during the cooking.

Serve hot.

WINE SUGGESTION
Follow the wine indicated for your secondo.

Roasted Rosemary Potatoes

[PATATE AL FORNO]

This is the favorite way of preparing potatoes in Rome. Order a roasted meat, and the odds are it will arrive garnished with these potatoes, even if you've already had a pasta course. Italians just don't see them (which we think of as two starches) as occupying the same ecological niche. The rosemary lends a lot of its scent and some of its taste to the potatoes.

1½ pounds small boiling potatoes   1 tablespoon rosemary leaves
¼ cup olive oil

Scrub the potatoes. Boil them in their jackets in lightly salted water until half cooked, 12 to 15 minutes. Drain and spray them with cold water to stop the cooking.

Preheat the oven to 400 degrees F. Peel and quarter the potatoes. Toss them delicately in a bowl with the olive oil and rosemary, until all surfaces are evenly coated. Put them in a lightly oiled pan (or in the roasting pan, if you are roasting a piece of meat). Bake 30 minutes, turning the potatoes once or twice during the cooking. Serve hot.

WINE SUGGESTION
Follow the wine indicated for your secondo.

Braised Zucchini

[ZUCCHINI IN TEGAME]

This is the style of cooking Italians mean by *casalinga*, home style: just a few ingredients and an uncomplicated technique, producing a distinctive and instantly pleasing taste. This braise needs just about 45 minutes.

---

1 pound small zucchini (about 4)   Salt
3 tablespoons chopped onion   Freshly ground black pepper
2 tablespoons olive oil   1 tablespoon chopped parsley
⅓ cup chopped plum tomato

Scrub and trim the zucchini. Cut them into 1½ inch lengths, then slice each piece lengthwise into thirds.

Sauté the onion in the olive oil until soft and lightly golden, about 8 minutes. Stir in the chopped tomato and cook, covered, for 10 minutes. Add the zucchini and salt and pepper to taste. Stir, cover the pan, and continue cooking over moderate heat until the zucchini are tender, 20 to 25 minutes. Just before serving, stir in the parsley.

WINE SUGGESTION
Follow the choice indicated for your secondo.

Zucchini Tartlets
[SFORMATINI DI ZUCCHINI]

An attractive serving presentation for these plump, little unmolded vegetable custards is to arrange them in a ring around the edge of the meat platter, possibly alternating with roasted potatoes with bay leaves (page 219). An herbed, spit-roasted chicken with these vegetable garnishes is a classic Tuscan Sunday *secondo*.

1 pound small zucchini	2 tablespoons minced onion
1½ cups broth (page 45)	1 tablespoon olive oil
6 tablespoons butter	1 egg
4 tablespoons flour	3 tablespoons grated *parmigiano*
Salt	Butter and bread crumbs for molds

Scrub and trim the zucchini. Drop them into boiling salted water and cook until almost tender, 5 to 10 minutes, depending on size. Drain and spray them with cold water to stop the cooking.

Make a *vellutata*: Bring the broth to a simmer. Melt 3 tablespoons of the butter in a medium-size pot and stir in the flour. Cook over low heat, stirring, for 2 minutes. Off heat, add the broth, a few tablespoons at a time, stirring vigorously to smooth the sauce after each addition of broth. When all the broth has been incorporated, return the pot to the stove and simmer, stirring, for 4 to 5 minutes, or until sauce has thickened somewhat. Taste for salt.

Preheat the oven to 400 degrees F. Cut the zucchini into ¼-inch dice. Soften the minced onion in the olive oil and the remaining 3 tablespoons butter. Add the zucchini and sauté, stirring, for 2 minutes. Salt and pepper lightly.

(continued)

Stir the egg and cheese into the *vellutata*. Add the entire contents of the zucchini pan to the *vellutata*.

Bring a kettle of water to a boil. Generously butter eight ¼-cup custard cups and coat with bread crumbs. Divide the zucchini mixture among them. Set them on a rack in a roasting pan and pour on boiling water to come halfway up the cups. Bake for about 1 hour, or until a knife blade inserted into the center comes out clean and the edges are browned and shrinking a little from the sides of the cups.

Unmold and serve, 2 to a person.

WINE SUGGESTION
Follow the choice indicated for your secondo.

As in the North, most desserts in the Center build on a base of fruits and nuts rather than on the taste of sugar. The recipes that follow are typical: pastries, relatively hearty rather than elegant; simple cookies—*biscotti*; puddings—*budini*—based on fresh, sweet *ricotta*.

Any of these desserts may be followed by a glass of Vin Santo, either dry or sweet, but only simple cookies like *biscotti di Prato* or *noccioletti* are ever served along with Vin Santo. And, yes, they are dunked. The combination is simple, and simply ambrosial.

Winter Fruit Compote
[MACEDONIA INVERNALE]

Macedonia made with fresh seasonal fruits is without doubt the most popular summer dessert in the cities of central Italy. This winter version takes advantage of the concentrated flavors of dried fruit to bring a little sunshine into the chilly months. It takes just about half an hour to make, and should be made up in advance.

¾ **pound dried fruit, approximately**
  (e.g., 4 figs, 6 pitted prunes, 4 peach
  halves, 8 apricot halves)
1 **lemon**
2 **oranges**

1 **large apple**
1 **large pear**
2 **bananas**
¼ **cup sugar**

Steam the dried fruits over boiling water until softened, 10 to 20 minutes depending on how firm they are.

Grate the peel of the lemon and half the peel of 1 orange. Put them in a large bowl and squeeze in the juice of the lemon.

Peel and remove all the white pith from the oranges. Cut them into ½-inch slices and then cut each slice into quarters, reserving their juice. Remove any pits, then add the oranges and their juice to the bowl.

Peel, core, and cut into bite-size pieces the apple and the pear. Add them to the bowl, stirring to coat them with lemon juice to prevent discoloration. Slice in the bananas and stir.

Cut the dried fruits into bite-size pieces and add them to the bowl. Sprinkle on the sugar and mix gently but thoroughly. Cover and refrigerate for 1 hour or more before serving.

Ricotta and Strawberry Parfait
[BUDINO DI RICOTTA CON FRAGOLE]

Italians use *ricotta* in many ways, but perhaps love it best in desserts, where its gentle taste and softness really shine. Try this simple recipe with your own homemade *ricotta* (page 29) to see just how much real freshness can contribute to the success of a dish. This preparation requires little more time to make than it takes to hull strawberries.

———————◆———————

1 pound *ricotta*
1 egg yolk
3 tablespoons amaretto liqueur
4 teaspoons granulated sugar

1 pint fresh strawberries
Juice of ½ lemon
1 ounce slivered almonds

Put the *ricotta* in a bowl and beat it with a spoon until smooth. Add the egg yolk, amaretto, and sugar. Mix well and chill until ready to serve.

Hull the strawberries, rinse them briefly, drain, and pat them dry. Halve them if large and toss them in a bowl with the lemon juice. Chill until ready to serve.

Distribute the strawberries in 4 individual dishes. Scoop the *ricotta* mixture over the top and sprinkle on the slivered almonds.

Deep-Fried Ricotta
[BOMBE DI RICOTTA]

Some restaurants in Rome are so proud of their skill at deep-frying that they even deep-fry dessert. This recipe is our approximation (they wouldn't part with the secret) of a luscious speciality of Piperno's. The crisp, golden exterior conceals a heart of melting white *ricotta*, speckled with equally melting bits of bitter chocolate. *Da morire*, the Italians would say—it's to die for.

———————◆———————

3 pair amaretti cookies
¼ cup semisweet chocolate morsels
1 pound *ricotta*
2 eggs

Oil for deep-frying
1 cup fine dry bread crumbs
Flour

Crush the amaretti cookies into a powder. Chop the semisweet chocolate morsels. Thoroughly mix together the powdered amaretti, chocolate, *ricotta*, and 1 egg.

Heat the oil in a deep-fryer to 340 degrees F. Beat the remaining egg in a small bowl and spread the bread crumbs on a plate.

Flour your hands well and shape the *ricotta* mixture into balls about 2 inches in diameter. Roll them in the beaten egg and then in the bread crumbs. Fry until golden, drain on paper towels, and serve at once.

Hazelnut Macaroons

[BRUTTI MA BUONI]

The whole difference between French and Italian attitudes toward food is summed up in the name of these delicious cookies. The French would call them something elegant like *noisettes de beauté* or something fanciful like *coeur léger*. Italians call them Ugly but Good—even though they're not particularly ugly. You may draw what moral you please from this. The recipe makes about 36 cookies, which keep very well in a tightly covered tin.

2 cups shelled hazelnuts
½ cup granulated sugar

Pinch of ground cinnamon
4 egg whites

Preheat the oven to 350 degrees F. Spread the hazelnuts on a baking sheet and toast them in the oven for 10 minutes. Reduce oven heat to 275 degrees. While the nuts are still warm, rub them together in a dish towel to get off as much of the brown skins as possible.

Grate the nuts into light fluffy particles, then mix them with the sugar and cinnamon in a good-size pot.

Beat the egg whites into stiff peaks. Fold them into the nut mixture. Put the pot over low heat and cook, stirring frequently, about 20 minutes, or until the mixture has dried out somewhat.

(continued)

Drop the mixture by teaspoonfuls onto a buttered baking sheet, leaving the shapes irregular. Bake at 275 degrees for 1 hour. Transfer to a rack and let cool completely.

WINE SUGGESTION
It's not orthodox, but these are nevertheless very good with Vin Santo.

Hazelnut Cookies
[NOCCIOLETTI]

Italians dote on hazelnuts, and who will blame them? These cookies taste deeply of the toasted nuts, and they're simplicity itself to make. You don't have to be fanatical about getting every flake of brown skin off the nuts, but the more you can remove the better, because there's a bitterness in the skin that "muddies" the clarity of the nut flavor. This recipe makes about 2 dozen *noccioletti*.

½ cup shelled hazelnuts
¼ pound softened butter
½ cup confectioners' sugar

1½ tablespoons honey
1 cup flour

Preheat the oven to 350 degrees F. Spread the hazelnuts on a baking sheet and toast them in the oven for 10 minutes. Wrap them in a dish towel and rub them together briskly to get off as much of the brown skins as possible. Then grind the nuts until coarse, or pulse them in a food processor, leaving them somewhat nubbly.

Cream the butter with ⅓ cup of the confectioners' sugar. Beat in the honey, then the flour and the nuts, to make a homogeneous dough.

Flour your hands and roll bits of dough into hazelnut-size balls. Place them on a greased baking sheet 1 inch apart. Bake at 350 degrees for 20 to 25 minutes, or until firm. Let them cool for about 10 minutes, then roll them in the remaining confectioners' sugar.

WINE SUGGESTION
These cookies taste very fine with Vin Santo.

Biscotti di Prato

From Florence south to Siena, throughout the width and breadth and depth of the Chianti-growing zone, these crunchy almond bars are all but the official biscuit. A double baking dries them out and concentrates their nutty sweetness—which is released by dipping them into a glass of Vin Santo, the luscious Tuscan dessert wine. That combination is a classic marriage, but *biscotti* are also quite amenable to being dunked into a cup of *espresso*. Quantities given below will make about 6 dozen *biscotti*, which will keep indefinitely in a tin.

4 ounces blanched almonds	¼ teaspoon salt
2½ cups flour	¼ teaspoon baking soda
2 cups granulated sugar	3 eggs

Preheat the oven to 350 degrees F. Spread the almonds on a baking sheet and toast them in the oven until lightly golden. Cool them. Coarsely chop half of them, leaving the rest whole. Butter two large baking sheets.

Mix flour, sugar, salt, and baking soda together. Beat in the eggs and then the whole and chopped almonds, to obtain a firm dough. Knead the dough briefly, then divide it into 4 pieces. On a lightly floured work surface, roll each piece under your hands into a cylinder 15 inches long and about 1½ inches in diameter. Place two rolls, well separated, on each baking sheet and put them in the oven for 15 to 20 minutes, until very lightly browned and firm to the touch.

With a spatula, carefully transfer the rolls to a cutting board and slice each one diagonally into cookies about ½ inch thick. Set wire racks on the baking sheets and lay out the *biscotti* on them. Return them to the oven for 20 to 30 minutes, or until the *biscotti* are very firm and crisp.

Let the *biscotti* cool on the racks, then transfer them to a tin for keeping.

WINE SUGGESTION
These are the orthodox—almost the compulsory—accompaniment to Vin Santo.

Rocciata

An Umbrian specialty somewhat like a strudel, packaged up in small logs. It's called *rocciata*—rocky—because all the chopped fruits and nuts make it look like a small-scale topographical map of some pretty rugged terrain. It is not, however, the least bit difficult to eat. About 45 minutes' preparation and assembly, 30 to 45 minutes' baking.

FOR THE PASTRY

1⅓ cups flour
⅛ teaspoon salt
4 tablespoons granulated sugar

4 tablespoons light olive oil
5 to 6 tablespoons cold water

FOR THE FILLING

4 ounces dried figs (about 4 large)
3 ounces pitted prunes (about 8 medium)
3 ounces golden raisins
4 ounces shelled nuts (hazelnuts, almonds, walnuts, pignoli)

1 large apple
1 tablespoon light olive oil
4 tablespoons Marsala
½ cup granulated sugar

Confectioners' sugar

Make the pastry:

In an electric mixer or food processor, mix together the flour, salt, and sugar. With the machine running, add the oil and water and mix to obtain a soft dough. Flour it and let it rest (in the flour bin is a good place) for at least 30 minutes.

Make the filling:

Steam figs and raisins over boiling water for 5 minutes (also prunes, if they are not the soft variety). Coarsely chop the figs, prunes, and nuts. Peel, core, and coarsely chop the apple.

Put all the fruits and nuts into a large bowl. Add the oil, Marsala, and granulated sugar. Mix well.

Assemble and bake:

Preheat the oven to 375 degrees F. Divide the pastry into 8 pieces. Roll each piece very thin, into a circle about 8 inches in diameter. Spread about ½ cup of the filling over the entire surface of the dough (leaving edges free) and roll the pastry into a log shape, tucking in the ends.

Place the *rociate* on an oiled baking sheet and bake 30 to 40 minutes. They will brown only lightly. Cool on a rack. Sprinkle with confectioners' sugar before serving.

WINE SUGGESTION
> *Tuscans might object to serving their Vin Santo with an Umbrian dessert, but no one else will. Also fine with* rocciata *is Asti Spumante.*

Apple Tart
[CROSTATA DI FRUTTA]

Most Italian pastry making is based on *pasta frolla*, but recipes for that extremely tender sweet dough don't necessarily translate well with American flours. This amenable version of *pasta frolla* is our adaptation of the traditional recipe. It gives results that look and taste very much like the made-in-Italy original. The fruit in a *crostata* is most commonly apple, but other fruits can and do take their turns in season. Remember, the *pasta frolla* needs at least 1 hour in the refrigerator to firm, and can sit there for a day or two if necessary.

———————————♦———————————

FOR THE *PASTA FROLLA*

1¼ cups flour
¼ cup granulated sugar
¼ teaspoon salt
¼ teaspoon finely minced lemon rind

3 ounces butter, cut into several small pieces
2 to 3 tablespoons milk

FOR THE FILLING

1 pound apples
¼ cup rum

2 tablespoons granulated sugar

FOR THE GLAZE

½ cup apricot jam

1 tablespoon sugar

To make the pastry, blend the flour, sugar, salt, and lemon rind. Cut in the butter, mixing to the consistency of coarse meal. Add the milk, a tablespoon at a time, mixing only until the dough holds its shape. Gather it into a ball, wrap it in wax paper, and refrigerate for at least 1 hour.

For the filling, peel, core, and thinly slice the apples. Toss them well with the rum and sugar, and let them sit for at least 30 minutes.

Preheat the oven to 375 degrees F. Roll the dough to a thickness of ⅛ inch. Line a 9-inch pie plate with it, trimming it with enough margin to double the pastry back inside the walls of the plate. Press the doubled pastry together to thin it somewhat and raise the edges.

Arrange the apple slices in an attractive pattern over the dough and pour on any juices left in the bowl. Gather up the remaining pastry, roll it out again, and cut lattice strips to decorate the top of the *crostata*.

Strain the apricot jam into a small, heavy-bottomed pot. Stir in the sugar. Bring to a simmer and cook 3 to 4 minutes. While this glaze is still warm, paint a coat of it over the exposed surfaces of apple. Place the *crostata* in the oven and bake 50 minutes.

Jam Tart
[CROSTATA DI MARMELLATA]

The other most popular version of *crostata*, just as Italian as the preceding apple tart.

FOR THE *PASTA FROLLA*

1¼ cups flour	3 ounces butter, cut into several small
¼ cup granulated sugar	pieces
¼ teaspoon salt	2 to 3 tablespoons milk
¼ teaspoon finely minced lemon rind	

FOR THE FILLING

1 jar (12 ounces) orange marmalade	1 egg

To make the pastry, blend the flour, sugar, salt, and lemon rind. Cut in the butter, mixing to the consistency of coarse meal. Add the milk, a tablespoon at a time, mixing only until the dough holds its shape. Gather it into a ball, wrap it in wax paper, and refrigerate for at least 1 hour.

Preheat the oven to 375 degrees F. Roll the dough to a thickness of ⅛ inch. Line a 9-inch pie plate with it, trimming it with enough margin to double the pastry back inside the walls of the plate. Press the doubled pastry together to thin it somewhat and raise the edges.

Spread the marmalade evenly over the dough. Gather up the remaining pastry, roll it out again, and cut lattice strips to decorate the top of the *crostata*. Beat the egg in a bowl with 1 tablespoon of water and paint the dough with two coats of it. Place the *crostata* in the oven and bake 40 minutes.

THE SOUTH

THE SOUTHERN ITALIAN MENU

ANTIPASTI

Pork Bread • Stuffed Bread
Rice and Vegetable Salad
Roasted Peppers and Anchovies
Zucchini with Basil • Marinated Zucchini
Eggplant with Tomatoes, Capers, and Olives
Caponata • Stuffed Peppers
Grilled Mozzarella with Anchovy Sauce
Mozzarella in Carozza • Quick Mozzarella Torte
Miniature Calzone

PRIMI

Pizza Margherita • Puglia-Style Pizza
Spaghetti with an Uncooked Sauce
Quadrucci with Basil-Tomato Sauce
Macaroni with Ricotta and Tomato Sauce
Linguine with Light Tomato Sauce
Spaghetti with Eggplant and Peppers • Pasta with Beans
Tubetti with Broccoli • Shells with Cauliflower Sauce
Linguine with Shrimp
Spaghettini with Mixed Seafood • Tommaso's Capellini
Pasta with Fresh Sardines
Ziti with Prosciutto • Rigatoni with Ham Sauce
Rigatoni with Ricotta and Sausage • Neapolitan Cannelloni
Baked Macaroni with Peppers • Baked Ziti

SECONDI

Stuffed Swordfish Rolls • Baked Swordfish Steaks
Neapolitan Salt Cod • Mussels in Spicy Red Sauce

Sicilian Fish Stew
Sautéed Chicken with Basil and Tomatoes • Chicken with Capers
Rabbit in Sweet-Sour Sauce
Palermo-Style Breaded Veal Chops • Veal Marsala
Veal Scallops Stuffed with Artichokes
Veal Scallops with Prosciutto and Mozzarella
Stuffed Veal Roll
Beef in Ragù • Stuffed Beef Roll
Stuffed Pork Chops • Stuffed Pork Rolls
Vegetables Baked with Tomato and Cheeses
Eggplant Baked with Mozzarella

CONTORNI

Baked Artichokes
Asparagus in Tomato Sauce
Al Cirillo's Beans • Broccoli in White Wine
Carrots in Marsala • Deep-Fried Eggplant
Potato Salad with Hot-Pepper Oil
Boiled Potatoes with Herb Dressing
Baked, Sliced Potatoes and Tomatoes • Baked Peppers
Pepper Stew • Sautéed Zucchini
Cianfotta

DOLCI

Strawberries in Orange Juice
Zabaglione • Coffee Custard
Chocolate Pudding
Mount Vesuvius
Neapolitan Almond Cookies • Cinnamon-Anise Biscuits
Sweet Biscuit Rings
Pastiera Napoletana • Ricotta Cake

The South of Italy—the southern half of the Abruzzi, Campania, Calabria, Basilicata, Molise, Puglia, Sicily—is a land both poorer and richer than the other two sections: poorer in resources, and richer in invention. Vegetables and olive oil and fish are the trinity that rules the kitchen, and durum-wheat pasta, made without eggs, is the hard-working servant-of-all-tasks that supports them. The sun and the sea and the harsh hills dictate the culinary style. Meat dishes are few, and except for special occasions, small. Finfish, shellfish, mollusks—almost everything that lives in the sea is harvested and relished in its season. Vegetables, too, bulk large on the tables, in every role from *antipasto* through *contorno* to *secondo*. The tomato grows especially well in the warm southern sun, and is ubiquitous in the cooking of the region, as are garlic and fragrant herbs. The style of this area compares to the rest of Italy as does Provençal cooking to the rest of France. The two areas share the same love of aromatic herbs, the same joy in reflecting the brightness and warmth of the sun in their cooking.

The style of southern Italian cooking is totally misrepresented—travestied, in fact—by thick, overcooked tomato sauces reeking of garlic salt and stale oregano and other abominations. All too many Americans, alas, think of that as the essence of Neapolitan or Sicilian, Calabrese or Barese cooking. Nothing could be further from the truth. Southern cooks may have the deftest, most delicate touch in all Italy. The flavors of the South are light, bright, and vivid, not heavy and strong. The cooking of the South can be described as a *cucina dei poveri*, but it is also a cuisine that has a longer history than almost any in Europe. The city of Sybaris, which became for the ancient Romans a byword for luxury and self-indulgence, and especially for indulgence in the pleasures of the table—the same place that gave us our word *sybarite*—was a Greek city, founded well before 500 B.C. in southern Italy, the land the Greeks knew as Oenotria, the land of wine. It may be difficult for the casual tourist traveling through the beautiful but bare hills of the South to believe that these regions and Sicily were once the richest farmlands of the Mediterranean, for centuries the fertile breadbasket of the Roman Empire. Even before that, Sicily was a center of high culture when Rome was still a mud village, and Naples—Napoli, Nea Polis, Greek for New City—a world capital, as the world then was.

The glory days are gone, of course, and now the South figures in the Italian mind as *il problema del mezzogiorno* and in the American mind as the home of the Mafia and the meatball hero. Neither stereotype touches the truth, least of all about a cuisine of remarkable subtlety and sophistication. If any cooks in Italy have mastered the art of making a little go a long way, and making that little both healthful and delicious, they are the family cooks of southern Italy.

Antipasti throughout the South consist almost exclusively of vegetables and seafood. The exceptions? A little *coppa*, some *prosciutto*, local *salami*. The rule? Seafood salads, or poached fish dressed with olive oil and lemon and served at room temperature; or mussels in a hot peppery brine; or shellfish lightly steamed in a bath of white wine, olive oil, minced garlic, and parsley; or marinated sardines or anchovies or small whole octopi; or zucchini or eggplant or peppers in any of a dozen dressings; or a dish of olives; or a roasted pepper, or real *mozzarella* in any of its many forms—as *ovalini di bufala*, small eggs of the delicate cheese, drizzled with olive oil and a crackling of black pepper, or slices from the larger globes and logs, accompanied by firm salad tomatoes, or grilled, or deep-fried *in carrozza*.

Southern *primi* play with paradoxes. They offer incredible variety within very narrow limits. Egg pasta virtually disappears from the menu here, except for occasional uses in *lasagne* or a few other stuffed pasta dishes. *Risotto*, too, plays a very minor role here. Warm breads, on the other hand, play major roles in many different guises: *pizza* and *pizzella* and *calzone* appear with an array of toppings and fillings, from the familiar tomato and *mozzarella* to simple broccoli to a whole fantasy of ingredients, as in the *pizza dei quattro stagioni*, with a different topping on each quadrant and each of a different color to represent the seasons for which the dish is named.

But the real stars among the *primi* are *stelle, orzi, semi di melone, spaghetti, linguine, vermicelli, capellini, fusilli, penne, rigatoni, ziti, zitone, tubetti, farfalle, radiatore, onde, occhi di lupo,* and any of a thousand other fanciful names for the various shapes that hard, extruded pasta adopts here. Their sauces vary even more imaginatively, from the tasty and simple—any of a half a dozen different cheeses and freshly ground black pepper—to the wildly complex. The fillings of a festive *lasagne*, for instance, will include tomato and béchamel, cheese and *prosciutto*, olives and eggs, sausages and eggplant. Nowhere else in the world do water and flour wear so many different shapes and bear so many different flavors on their backs as here.

(If the prose begins to sound a little rapturous in this section, it's because one of us is of Neapolitan descent, and memories of the sight and scent and taste of dishes like these touch deep chords. One of us believes that if he had to choose a single cuisine to eat for the rest of his life, this would be the one, because of its subtlety, variety, and sheer goodness. We are talking real food here.)

Most southern *secondi* are very simply, almost minimally, cooked. Southern cooks treat fish especially with great respect, leaving its natural flavors intact as much as possible. Very small fish tend to be fried whole, and very large ones may be poached or roasted whole, but almost all medium-size fish end up on the grill, along with slices—what we would call steaks rather than fillets—from the large ones. Most are washed in brine and patted dry before being set on the fire, and sometimes a whole fish will be "breaded" with coarse salt, a method that, when properly handled, seals in the fish's juices and natural flavors and produces a seafood dish of incomparable flavor and delicacy. (When poorly executed, the fish becomes merely salty.) Sometimes a steak or fillet or a butterflied fish is brushed with lemon juice and pepper before grilling. Rarely are the seasonings or preparations more elaborate than that.

Meat *secondi* more often than not are accompanied by a sauce, even if it is only a spoonful or two of the meat's own pan juices scraped up with a splash of wine. The unspoken assumption, the product of centuries of gradual impoverishment of the land, is that the fish are tender and flavorful enough to stand alone, but the meats need all the help they can get. This is certainly no longer everywhere true: In restaurants, at least, the meat tastes as good and is as tender as anywhere in Italy, but old attitudes die hard, and the most traditional meat dishes of the region all call for slow, moist cooking. Thin scallops of veal are the only real exception.

Southern *contorni* stand among the real glories of this cuisine, and will also be one of the greatest sources of disappointment for the American cook who has tasted the dishes in Italy and tries to reproduce them at home. Some varieties—the tiny artichokes with no spurs or fibers and with completely edible chokes, for instance, or those enormous, glossy sweet red peppers—simply are not grown in this country; or if they are, they don't find their way to market with any regularity. We do have vegetables with the same names as those that Italians do such wonders with, but the sad fact is that ours don't taste the same as theirs. In fact, many of ours don't taste at all. This is the single greatest obstacle to cooking authentically Italian dishes in this country. If you have access to a farmer's market, by all means patronize it to buy the freshest produce you can get in its proper season. If you have a real grocery store near you, befriend the produce man. Adopt him. Fawn on him. Ply him with your best wines. A real greengrocer is a treasure beyond price, and the closest thing you will ever discover to a secret ingredient in Italian cooking.

As with desserts all over Italy, the *dolci* of this region do not taste terribly sweet—nor, contrary to popular opinion, are they usually drenched with rum or liqueurs. Southern Italy, in fact, does not indulge much in spirits of any sort: It is not really grappa country, and the climate just doesn't suit brandy consumption. *Amari*—that is to say, digestive bitters—are often offered, particularly if the dinner is an important or festive one. A Sicilian brand, Averna, is the most popular in Italy and is pretty widely available here. Most Americans will find it an acquired taste, but it is one worth the effort of acquiring. A small glass of an *amaro* like Averna after a large dinner does seem to promote digestion, and it leaves a pleasing, warm, clean taste in the mouth. For real masochists, Fernet-Branca is the bitterest, most scouring of the *amari*. Such drinks are always taken after coffee (the espresso of Naples is reputed to be the best in Italy), which of course is always taken after the simple dessert, unless the dessert is biscuits or dry cookies.

THE WINES OF SOUTHERN ITALY

The story of southern Italian wines is very quickly told, at least as far as the American market is concerned: A handful of great reds, a smaller handful of great whites, and a whole armful of pleasant quaffing wines, mostly white, with names ranging from the unfortunate—Asprino—to the poetic—Lacryma Christi (the tears of Christ).

Many bottles of these simple, everyday wines appear briefly on the American market and disappear as quickly as they came, depending on the vagaries of European supplier, American importer and distibutor, and local market conditions. Only a few names have managed to maintain a steady enough presence here to justify describing as widely available. Here are some of the best of those few.

- Castel del Monte, from Puglia. Red, white, and rosé. The red shows good character and a bit of spine, the white is drinkable and forgettable, and the rosé is charming. Rivera is the best and most widely distributed brand.
- Cirò, from Calabria. Both red and white, the latter at best fresh, fruity, and pleasing, the red capable of some body and depth. Librandi is the maker you're most likely to see in the United States.
- Corvo, from Sicily. A brand-named wine available in both white and red, made by Duca di Salaparuta. Both the red and the white are pleasant,

drinkable, and inexpensive wines, good with *antipasti, primi,* and simple

secondi.

- Lacryma Christi, from Campania, on or near Mount Vesuvius. Red, rosé, and white, with the white made dry, semisweet, or sweet, and sometimes sparkling, so read the labels carefully. The red can be very fine. Many decent makers, but the best is unquestionably Mastroberardino.
- Regaleali, from Sicily. Made by Conte Tasca d'Almerita in red, white, and rosé, all rather fuller and more intensely flavorful than most southern wines. Not aperitif wines but good dinner wines; they will stand up well to the most strongly flavored or elaborate dishes.

Two white wines from the South deserve special attention. In our opinion the best white wine of the South and without question one of the top two or three white wines in all Italy is Mastroberardino's Fiano di Avellino, a medium-bodied, straw-colored wine of amazing complexity and charm. It takes bottle aging much better than all but a few other Italian white wines. We recently drank a ten-year-old Fiano that not only was still alive and supple but also had developed considerable depth and intensity during its aging. In most vintages, ten years' aging would definitely be pushing the outer limit, but, for a palate that relishes the taste of mature wines (as opposed to preferring them young and fruity), there is no reason that a bottle of Fiano shouldn't have greater interest at five or six years of age than when it was first bottled. That Fiano responds well to aging is hardly surprising: The variety has been cultivated in the same high hills about thirty miles east of Naples for more than two thousand years.

Right behind Fiano in quality and interest is Mastroberardino's other great white wine, Greco di Tufo, made from a grape first introduced to the area by the Greeks, as its name implies. Fuller in the mouth and more immediately accessible than Fiano, Greco makes a wonderful accompaniment to all sorts of fish, shellfish, and white-meat dishes. It doesn't seem to develop in the bottle for as long as Fiano does, even though it seems a bit fuller-bodied. Greco is best to drink when it is between three and five years of age.

In fine red wines, the South provides a greater choice. From Sicily comes Rosso del Conte, a special reserve of Conte Tasca d'Almerita's red Regaleali, a wine of long life and great polish. Like most of the wines to be mentioned now, this red matches well with strongly flavored meats, especially roasts, and with fine cheese. From Puglia we get Il Falcone, a special reserve of the Rivera Castel del Monte and a rich, full wine best drunk when eight to ten years old. Salice Salentino is another fine Pugliese red in a completely different style, fuller, rounder—fleshier almost—with a pleasing little bitter sting in the finish.

Basilicata gives us Aglianico del Vulture, a noble red wine of rich aroma and flavor. Aglianico is the name of the grape: It means Hellenic, i.e., Greek. This is another ancient grape, cultivated in these parts for two and a half millennia. Vulture is the name of the extinct volcano on whose slopes the grapes are grown, and, yes, it does mean vulture, but that says nothing at all about this fine wine. D'Angelo is far and away the best maker of Aglianico, and the firm's wines are usually very inexpensive for their quality.

All these wines can readily stand comparison with the first-rate northern reds, but there is one southern red capable of challenging the very top place. That is Taurasi, also vinified from the Aglianico grape, cultivated this time in Campania in the same area as Fiano and Greco, and made once again by Mastroberardino. At between ten and twenty years of age, the Riserva of this wine, which is made only in very fine harvests, provides an extraordinary wine experience.

Finally, we need to say a word or two about Marsala, the best-known and least-understood wine of the South. Real Marsala is a fine, sherry-like, fortified wine. Like sherry it comes in several grades of sweetness and dryness, and as with sherry one drinks the dry as an aperitif and the sweet with or as dessert. Marsalas flavored with coffee or chocolate or bananas or figs or anything at all are not real wines; they are chemical cocktails, and you drink them at peril to your stomach and taste buds. If you have any in your house, throw them out now and promise never to buy them again.

Here are the three grades of Marsala to know about: *Fine* (pronounced fee-nay)—dry or sweet, light amber color, brief barrel aging; *Superiore*—the prestige grade, dry or sweet, long-aged and long-lived; *Vergine*—light amber gold color, lightly fortified, long-aged, and fully dry. Marsala Vergine makes a first-class aperitif, though some dry Superiore (which is the most popular grade in Italy and much more widely available here than Vergine) is almost as good. Rallo and Pellegrino are the best makers: They produce Marsala in every grade and style.

The South also produces small quantities of excellent Passito, a sweet desert wine of great concentration, made from semi-dried grapes. Those from the island of Pantelleria, fermented from Moscato grapes, and from the Lipari islands, fermented from Malvasia, are particularly fine.

———————◆———————

ANTIPASTI

Southern Italians are fond of vegetable and seafood *antipasti*. Those two categories between them account for all but a tiny fraction of the *antipasti* prepared and consumed in the region.

The seafood *antipasti* share a broad similarity of treatment, no matter what their ingredients. Shellfish of all sorts will be quickly steamed open in a pan containing a light film of olive oil and white wine, a small mincing of garlic and parsley, and a generous grinding of pepper. So prepared, they are served immediately, with lots of fresh bread to mop up their broth. When mussels are at their plumpest and tastiest, they are served as *cozze in pepata*; scrubbed clean and debearded, they are coaxed open by being repeatedly showered with a hot, heavily peppered brine, a cupful or so of which accompanies each portion. (There is even a special gadget for holding them during this operation, a broad, perforated spatula that looks much like a chestnut roaster.)

Squid and octopi—whole if tiny, cut up if larger—are gently poached until tender in an aromatic broth, then drained and dressed with olive oil and a hint of garlic, lemon juice, and black pepper (and occasionally a mince of crisp celery or bell pepper, or a handful of cut-up black olives) and served at room temperature. These simple treatments are easily replicable in the United States. Needless to say, the fresher your seafood the better they will taste, but frozen squid, octopi, and shrimps are not necessarily a disaster. Such creatures—the crustaceans generally, in fact—take reasonably well to freezing. And as for special implements, like the spatula described above for *cozze in pepata*; just improvise. You can get the same job done with an ordinary sieve.

The vegetable *antipasti* are more various in their modes of preparation, but they are alike in that all but the most heavily vinegared may also be served as *contorni*. Many are elaborate dishes in themselves, which can also serve as *secondi*—eggplant parmigiano, for instance. The simpler presentations are usually roasting or grilling and then dressing with a light, fragrant olive oil and pinches of fresh oregano or marjoram.

Steaming or boiling also plays a role in creating these vegetable *antipasti*. A simple favorite, for instance, that can appear in a southern meal as *antipasto* or *contorno* or sometimes even as *secondo* is *insalatone*. The name means simply a big salad, but it is applied almost always to a dish of boiled or steamed vegetables that rarely includes any of the conventional leafy salad greens. It is instead composed of such things as green beans and/or shell beans, carrots, onions, new potatoes, and zucchini, served slightly warm or at room temperature, and all lightly salted and peppered and dressed with top-quality olive oil and a small amount of fresh lemon juice.

Pork Bread

[PANE CON CICCIOLI]

This loaf makes a fine rustic treat for picnics, snacks, hors d'oeuvre, etc. You can use almost any variety of meats: leftover roast pork, partly rendered sausage meat or thick-sliced bacon, *salami*, chunks from the end of a *prosciutto*, pork cracklings (which would be a pretty accurate translation of *ciccioli*).

½ recipe olive-oil bread dough (page 20)

1½ ounces lean *pancetta*

1½ ounces baked ham

¼ cup grated *pecorino romano*

10 peppercorns, crushed

Make the dough, letting it rise once. Cut the *pancetta* and ham into ¼-inch dice. Rub 2 to 3 tablespoons of flour into a lintless dish towel and set the towel on a baking sheet.

Punch down the dough, add all the other ingredients, and knead them into the dough. Roll the dough under your hands into a thick cylinder 16 to 18 inches long. Curve it around into a ring and press the ends together. Set the ring on the floured towel and fold the ends of the towel loosely over it. Put the covered loaf on its baking sheet in a warm place to rise for 1 hour.

Preheat an oven lined with baking tiles to 400 degrees F. Have a water-filled sprayer handy. Turn the loaf upside down onto the tiles and spray the oven liberally with water. Spray twice more in the next 15 minutes.

After the bread has baked 15 minutes, turn the oven down to 375 degrees. Continue baking for 25 minutes longer, or until a knuckle thumped on the bottom of the loaf produces a hollow sound. Cool the bread on a rack.

WINE SUGGESTION

A *light red wine—Cirò, for instance—would taste best with this, but really almost anything, red or white, will do.*

Stuffed Bread

[PANE RIPIENO]

A sort of *antipasto* salad inside a loaf of bread, this attractive preparation serves well as either an *antipasto* by itself or as a component of a larger, mixed *antipasto* tray. It also makes a good cocktail canapé and delicious picnic food.

A double recipe of olive-oil bread dough (page 20), baked into a long loaf according to the directions on page 21, will be about the right size to hold the filling. Remember, the loaf must be filled the day before it is to be eaten.

½ pound *mozzarella*	1 tin (2 ounces) anchovies
6 ripe plum tomatoes	1 large oblong loaf of bread
1 large green pepper	Salt
4 scallions	Freshly ground black pepper
2 ounces oil-cured black olives	

Cube the *mozzarella*. Drop the tomatoes into boiling water for 10 seconds, then drain, peel, seed, and chop them. Wash, core, and chop the pepper. Mince the scallions. Pit and quarter the olives. Drain and chop the anchovies, reserving their oil.

Cut the loaf of bread in half lengthwise and pull out the insides. Break the crumb into walnut-size chunks and mix them together with all the prepared vegetables, the *mozzarella*, the anchovies, and their oil. Taste and add generous amounts of salt and pepper.

Fill the hollowed-out loaf with this mixture. Put the halves back together and wrap tightly in aluminum foil. Refrigerate overnight. Serve cold, cut into 1-inch slices. The slices may be skewered with decorative toothpicks, either for appearance or for security, if the bread halves show any sign of separating.

WINE SUGGESTION
Crisp, well-chilled white is wanted here. Cirò, Corvo, Castel del Monte —any of these will do well.

Rice and Vegetable Salad
[INSALATA DI RISO]

This lively mélange is perfect for summer eating, as an *antipasto*, a lunch, or a picnic dish. Lots of small steps but no real difficulties to the preparation.

1 small eggplant	1 small cucumber
1 green pepper	Juice of 1 lemon
1 medium zucchini	4 chopped basil leaves
1 cup long-grain rice	½ teaspoon oregano
½ cup olive oil	Salt
2 small tomatoes	Freshly ground black pepper

(continued)

Wash and dry the eggplant but do not peel it. Cut it into 1-inch chunks, salt them generously, and let them sit in a colander in the sink for half an hour.

Turn a gas stove burner to its highest flame. Set the pepper directly on the grate. As the skin blackens in the flame, turn the pepper with tongs until its entire surface is black. Then drop it into a brown paper bag, close the bag, and leave it there for at least 5 minutes. Under a thin stream of running water, scrape away all the blackened skin of the pepper with a paring knife. Then cut it open, remove all seeds and membrane, blot it dry with paper towels, and cut it into strips ½ inch wide by 2 inches long.

Scrub the zucchini, cut it into 2-inch lengths, drop them into boiling water, and cook until just tender, 10 to 15 minutes. Drain the pieces, run cold water over them to stop the cooking, and when cool enough to handle, cut them into ½-inch strips.

Drop the rice into a large quantity of boiling salted water and cook rapidly, uncovered, until barely tender, 12 to 15 minutes. Drain in a sieve and spray with cold water.

Blot the liquid from the eggplant pieces and sauté them in ¼ cup of the olive oil until soft—about 10 minutes.

Wash and dry the tomatoes and cucumber. Cut the tomatoes into eighths and the cucumber into ¼-inch slices.

In a large serving bowl, gently mix together the rice, pepper, zucchini, eggplant, tomato, and cucumber. Add the lemon juice, chopped basil, oregano, and the remaining ¼ cup olive oil. Salt and pepper to taste.

WINE SUGGESTION
Well-chilled, lightly acid white wine is called for here. Choose among Cirò, Corvo, Castel del Monte, even Lacryma Christi.

Roasted Peppers and Anchovies
[PEPERONI ARROSTI CON ACCIUGHE]

In size and sculptural contours, the sweet peppers grown in southern Italy make our boxy American bell peppers look like wax toys. However, by using only firm, glossy, green (or better, red) peppers and letting them steep in olive oil for no more than a day before serving, you can make a version of this utterly simple *antipasto* that will be worlds away from the limp and listless version you may know of from cans—or restaurants. If you can find crisp fresh pimentos, you'll get an even closer approximation to the Italian flavor. It's also worth knowing that a slice of *bruschetta* doesn't go badly at all with or under these peppers.

---

2 large red or green bell peppers	Freshly ground black pepper
2 salt-packed whole anchovies	½ cup extra-virgin olive oil
Salt	

Turn a gas stove burner to its highest flame. Set a pepper directly onto the grate. As the skin blackens in the flame, turn the pepper with tongs until its entire surface is black. Then drop it into a brown paper bag and close the bag. Roast the second pepper in the same way, put it into the bag, and leave them there for at least 5 minutes.

Under a thin stream of running water, scrape away all the blackened skin of each pepper with a paring knife. Then cut the peppers in half, remove all seeds and membrane, and blot them dry with paper towels.

Also under running water, skin and fillet the anchovies. Pat the fillets dry with paper towels.

Set the pepper halves on individual serving dishes and salt and pepper to taste. Top each with an anchovy fillet. Drizzle 2 tablespoons of olive oil over each pepper.

WINE SUGGESTION

White wine is wanted here, and almost any of the southern varieties will do very well.

Zucchini with Basil

[ZUCCHINI AL FUNGHETTO]

Al funghetto means mushroom-style, which ought to inform you that this manner of first quick-frying a vegetable to seal it, then sautéing it briefly with an aromatic herb, is a popular way to handle mushrooms, too. Eggplants—small ones especially—also respond well to this treatment.

¾ pound medium zucchini	Olive oil
Salt	1 tablespoon chopped fresh basil

(continued)

Scrub the zucchini and cut them into ½-inch disks. Salt them generously and place them in a colander. Let them drain, over the sink, for 1 hour. Dry each slice with paper towels or a lint-free cloth, pressing moderately to get out as much liquid as possible.

Pour olive oil into a small heavy skillet to a depth of ½ inch and heat it to 350 degrees F. Fry the zucchini slices a few at a time until golden, then remove them to a dish.

Drain off all but 1 to 2 tablespoons of the oil. Return the zucchini to the pan together with the basil. Mix well and let them simmer together over low heat for about 2 minutes, stirring occasionally. Serve hot, warm, or at room temperature.

WINE SUGGESTION

A white wine with a bit of body goes well with these zucchini. Try a still Lacryma Christi or Castel del Monte.

Marinated Zucchini

[ZUCCHINI MARINATI]

This preparation must be made entirely in advance, since the zucchini must ripen for a week in their marinade. It requires a fair amount of time, but each step is simple and most of the time is waiting, so you can easily prepare it while doing other chores in the kitchen. It keeps well in the refrigerator for a couple of weeks, but should be brought to room temperature before serving. This treatment is also excellent with small eggplants.

1½ pounds small zucchini (9 to 10)	1 cup white vinegar
Salt	8 juniper berries
Freshly ground black pepper	8 peppercorns
Olive oil	1 bay leaf
6 large fresh basil leaves	

Wash the zucchini, scrubbing with a vegetable brush if necessary. Slice them lengthwise into ¼-inch boards.

Salt the pieces heavily and pepper them lightly on both sides; let them stand on end in a colander for 2 hours.

Sterilize a quart jar by boiling it in water to cover for 10 minutes. Leave it in the hot water until ready to fill.

Remove the zucchini slices from the colander and dry them with paper towels or a lint-free cloth, pressing them gently to get out as much liquid as possible.

Pour olive oil into a small heavy skillet to a depth of ½ inch. Heat the oil to 350 degrees F. Fry the zucchini slices a few at a time, until they are just golden, and drain them on paper towels.

Remove the jar from the sterilizing pot, drain it briefly, then put in the zucchini slices. Add the basil leaves.

Measure 1 cup of the frying oil and put it into an enamel or glass pot with the vinegar, juniper berries, peppercorns, and bay leaf. Cover the pot and bring this marinade to a boil, then let it cool. Pour the marinade over the zucchini and close the jar tightly. Check the jar regularly for the next day or two: If the zucchini absorb so much of the liquid that they are no longer fully covered, add enough equal parts of olive oil and vinegar to keep them submerged. They will be ready to eat after a week in the marinade.

WINE SUGGESTION
The vinegar marinade will make problems for most wines. Best bet is a dry, acid white wine, well-chilled; try Cirò or Corvo.

Eggplant with Tomatoes, Capers, and Olives
[MELANZANE AL FUNGHETTO]

This is a more elaborate version of the cooking method of the preceding recipe. The simpler version is most often used when the vegetables are at their flavorful best. This present treatment really brightens up older or end-of-the-season vegetables. It is also used to give variety to a mixed vegetable *antipasto* tray. It adapts very well to mushrooms, zucchini, even peppers. (Naturally, omit the salting and draining with mushrooms or peppers.)

1 pound small eggplants	8 oil-cured or Gaeta olives
1 teaspoon salt	1 garlic clove
3 ripe plum tomatoes	Olive oil for frying
1 tablespoon tiny capers	

Peel the eggplants, taking care to remove all the green pith. Cut them into ½-inch disks. Toss them with the salt in a colander and let them drain into the sink for 1 hour.

(continued)

Drop the plum tomatoes into boiling water for 10 seconds, then drain them and slip off their skins. Roughly chop them. Rinse and drain the capers. Pit the olives, halving them if they are very large. Sliver the garlic clove.

Dry each piece of eggplant with paper towels, pressing moderately hard to get out as much moisture as possible.

Pour olive oil into a small heavy skillet to a depth of ½ inch. Heat the oil to 350 degrees F. Fry the eggplant slices, a few at a time, until they are nicely golden, and remove them to a dish.

When all the eggplant is fried, take 2 tablespoons of the frying oil and put it into a bigger skillet. Add the slivered garlic and the tomatoes and cook over moderate heat for 10 minutes, stirring often, until the tomatoes are well softened.

Add the eggplant slices, capers, and olives. Mix well and cook for 5 minutes, stirring occasionally.

Serve hot, warm, or at room temperature.

WINE SUGGESTION
A well-chilled white wine, such as Lacryma Christi or Corvo, would be the most common accompaniment to dishes like this in Italy, but they also respond well to a simple red wine such as Cirò or Castel del Monte.

Caponata

Caponata must be the official Sicilian *antipasto*. The most elaborate—and one of the most delicious—of the vegetable *antipasti*, it is a complete vegetable garden in one dish. This recipe yields about 2 quarts of *caponata*. That sounds like a lot, but you will eat a lot, and the remainders keep well (refrigerated).

2 medium eggplants	5 tablespoons wine vinegar
1 tablespoon salt	1 tablespoon sugar
6 plum tomatoes	¼ cup drained tiny capers
1 large green pepper	¼ teaspoon freshly ground
1 large onion	black pepper
5 celery stalks	1 tablespoon pignoli
¾ to 1 cup olive oil	½ cup olives

Peel the eggplants, taking care to remove all the green pith. Cut them into 1-inch cubes. Toss them with 2 teaspoons of the salt in a colander and let them drain into the sink for 1 hour.

Drop the plum tomatoes into boiling water for 10 seconds, then drain them and slip off their skins. Roughly chop them. Wash and halve the pepper; remove seeds and membrane and cut the halves into 1-inch squares. Coarsely chop the onion and celery.

Dry each piece of eggplant with paper towels, pressing moderately hard to get out as much moisture as possible. Sauté them in the olive oil for 10 minutes, stirring often, then drain with a slotted spoon and transfer to a plate.

Add a little more oil to the pan, if necessary, and sauté the peppers for 5 minutes; remove to the plate. Put the onion and celery in the pan, cover, and simmer gently until the celery is tender, about 15 minutes. Add the tomatoes, cover again, and cook 10 minutes.

Meanwhile, mix the vinegar, sugar, capers, remaining teaspoon of salt, and the pepper together in a small pot. Simmer, covered, for 1 minute; set aside.

Return eggplant and peppers to sauté pan. Add the vinegar mixture, the pignoli, and the olives. Stir all together well and simmer, covered, for 10 minutes. Let cool before serving.

WINE SUGGESTION

A *full-bodied white wine is excellent with this dish. Try Regaleali or even Greco di Tufo.*

Stuffed Peppers

[PEPERONI IMBOTTITI]

This dish provides solid food with a bright, vivid taste: an oven-roasted pepper half, filled with rice flavored with fennel and rape, served warm. It makes an excellent midwinter *antipasto*, and it can also serve very nicely as a meatless *secondo* or light lunch.

4 medium bell peppers, red or green	1 tablespoon olive oil
1 pound broccoli rape	½ cup arborio rice
1 fennel bulb (about ½ pound)	1½ cups broth (page 45)
1 tablespoon butter	

Wash and halve the peppers lengthwise, removing all the core, seeds, and fibrous ribs. Wash and trim the broccoli rape and the fennel. Quarter the fennel bulb. Bring a large quantity of salted water to the boil. Add the rape and fennel and boil slowly for 15 minutes.

(continued)

Drain the vegetables and pass them through the medium blade of a food mill. Set the purée aside.

Melt the butter and oil in a heavy-bottomed pot. Add the rice, stirring to coat all the grains with the fat. Sauté 1 to 2 minutes. Reduce heat to medium-low and start adding broth, a ladleful at a time. Stir often and add more broth only as the rice begins to dry out. Cook for 35 to 45 minutes, or until the rice has absorbed all its liquid.

Stir the vegetable purée into the rice and cook for another 5 minutes. Off heat, allow the rice mixture to sit, covered, for 30 minutes.

While the rice is cooking, preheat the oven to 425 degrees F. Roast the pepper halves on a lightly oiled pan or cookie sheet for 20 to 30 minutes. Remove from oven. Taste the rice mixture for salt and pepper. Correct seasoning and divide the mixture evenly among the pepper halves. Serve warm.

WINE SUGGESTION
A white wine with some body is called for here: Lacryma Christi will do, but Regaleali or even Greco di Tufo will do better.

Grilled Mozzarella with Anchovy Sauce
[MOZZARELLA AI FERRI]

This is an almost magical dish. Slices of *mozzarella* are laid on a very hot griddle. They don't just melt and run, as you might expect, but instead form a thin crisp golden crust, within which the cheese is liquid and luscious. Success requires a very hot griddle and fairly dry *mozzarella*. If you have a fresh moist one, let it sit unwrapped in the refrigerator on paper towels for a day or two to dry out. This same treatment is also excellent with *scamorza*, a much firmer and a more strongly flavored cheese. Either cheese, prepared this way, can also be served as a *secondo*.

1 pound *mozzarella*	6 anchovy fillets, roughly chopped
4 tablespoons butter	3 teaspoons milk

Several hours before cooking, cut the *mozzarella* into ½-inch-thick slices and lay them on a rack or paper towels to drain.

Make the anchovy sauce. Melt the butter in a small saucepan over low heat. Add the anchovy pieces, stirring and breaking them up with a fork until they completely dissolve. Gradually stir in the milk and mix to form a smooth cream. Set sauce aside until needed. Stir to recombine ingredients before serving, if necessary.

Heat a griddle to very hot—so that a flick of water on the surface will instantly form tiny balls that skitter across the hot surface before vaporizing. Lightly oil the griddle if it is not thoroughly seasoned.

Lay 1 slice of *mozzarella* on the griddle. If the heat is right, the cheese should "oil up" immediately, but not liquefy. In about 1½ minutes, when the edges begin to brown, carefully turn the slice with a spatula. The bottom should be golden. Cook until golden on the other side, about another minute.

Cook the remaining slices in the same manner, transferring them to a warming oven as they are done. When all are ready, serve at once with the anchovy sauce on the side.

WINE SUGGESTION
   A *full-bodied white wine makes an ideal accompaniment to this dish. Regaleali or Greco di Tufo are good choices.*

Mozzarella in Carozza

A classic southern *antipasto* that occasionally also doubles as a *secondo, mozzarella in carozza*—literally, in a carriage—amounts to the apotheosis of French toast. It is often accompanied by the same anchovy sauce used in the preceding recipe for grilled *mozzarella*.

8 slices firm fresh sandwich bread	2 eggs
¾ pound *mozzarella*	¼ cup milk
Oil for deep-frying	Salt
¼ cup flour	Freshly ground black pepper

Trim crusts off bread. Cut the *mozzarella* into 4 slices about ⅜ inch thick and slightly smaller than the bread slices. Center each piece of *mozzarella* between 2 pieces of bread and press hard on the sandwich. Really flatten the bread; it will fluff up again in the frying.

Pour ½ inch of frying oil into a skillet and heat it to 360 degrees F. Put the flour in a small shallow bowl and ¼ inch of water in another. In a third, beat the eggs together with the milk and a sprinkle of salt and pepper.

Taking each sandwich in turn, dip the edges first in the flour, then in the water, so that a thin paste forms, which will keep the *mozzarella* from oozing out during the frying. Then lay the sandwich in the bowl of beaten egg and soak it thoroughly on each side, as for French toast. Drain it briefly and transfer it to the hot oil. Fry 2 to 3 minutes on each side, until golden brown. Drain on paper towels and serve as soon as all are cooked.

WINE SUGGESTION
Red or white will do well here, but if you use an anchovy sauce, the nod should go to a good white like Regaleali or Lacryma Christi, or even Greco di Tufo.

Quick Mozzarella Torte
[TORTINO DI MOZZARELLA]

This easy dish consists of much the same ingredients as *mozzarella in carozza*, but the preparation is almost totally undemanding. This makes it a good *antipasto* for a meal whose other components require a great deal of attention.

8 slices Italian-style bread, ½ inch thick	1 to 2 tablespoons butter
1 egg yolk	½ pound *mozzarella*
½ cup milk	1 teaspoon fennel seeds
8 anchovy fillets	3 tablespoons freshly grated *parmigiano*

Preheat the oven to 400 degrees F. Trim crusts off bread. Put egg yolk, milk, and anchovy fillets into a blender and blend until smooth. (Alternatively, mash the anchovy and egg yolk in a bowl, then beat in the milk with a wire whisk.)

Generously butter a shallow baking dish just large enough to hold the slices of bread in one layer. Arrange them in the pan and moisten each slice with 1½ tablespoons of the milk mixture, trying not to let it spill over onto the bottom of the pan. (If the bread is reluctant to take up the liquid, pierce it in several places with a fork to hasten absorption.)

Cut the *mozzarella* into ¼-inch slices and lay them evenly over the bread. Sprinkle on the fennel seeds and then the *parmigiano*. Place the dish in the oven and bake uncovered for 20 minutes, until cheese is bubbly and just starting to brown on top. Let sit for 5 minutes before serving.

WINE SUGGESTION
Same suggestions as for preceding recipe.

Miniature Calzone
[CALCIONI MOLISANI]

These baby *calzone* contain a delicious filling of *prosciutto* and two different cheeses. Use them by themselves as canapés or *antipasti*, or mix them with other warm *antipasti*. If you have trouble finding *scamorza*, you may substitute young *provolone* or young *pecorino* or smoked *mozzarella*.

FOR THE PASTRY

1½ cups flour	1 egg
¼ teaspoon salt	2 tablespoons lemon juice
4 tablespoons vegetable shortening	

FOR THE FILLING

2 ounces *prosciutto*	1 tablespoon chopped parsley
2 ounces *scamorza*	¼ teaspoon salt
8 ounces *ricotta*	½ teaspoon freshly ground
1 egg yolk	black pepper

Oil for deep-frying

To make the pastry, blend the flour and salt in a bowl. Cut in the shortening, mixing to the consistency of coarse meal. Beat the egg together with the lemon juice and add it, mixing only until the dough holds its shape. The dough can be wrapped in wax paper and refrigerated until ready to use. Bring it back to room temperature before proceeding.

Cut the *prosciutto* and *scamorza* into small dice. Mix them with the remaining filling ingredients. Heat deep-frying oil to 360 to 375 degrees F.

Roll the dough on a lightly floured surface to a thickness of ⅛ inch. Cut it into 2-inch rounds. Center about a teaspoon of filling on one round of dough, moisten the rim with a finger dipped in water, and top with another round. Press down firmly to seal the pouch. Drape a clean dish towel over the finished *calcioni* while you prepare the rest.

Fry them a few at a time, regulating the heat to maintain a constant temperature, for 3 to 5 minutes, until golden. Drain on paper towels.

WINE SUGGESTION

A white wine such as Lacryma Christi or a light red such as Cirò or Castel del Monte will make fine partners to these calcioni.

PRIMI

Southern Italian *primi* constitute an entire wardrobe of dressings for dry, durum-wheat pasta. All that the land and sea afford go to clothe that hardworking monarch of the kitchen. The honors for most frequent use are just about evenly divided between vegetables and seafood, with meats a very distant third.

The heir apparent—or at least the pretender to the throne—is *pizza*, in all its guises and with all its relations (the *calzone* clan). Between these two, you can account for about 90 percent of all southern *primi*.

———————◆———————

Pizza Margherita

The classic *pizza margherita*, for which this is the recipe, is the concentrated essence of what humanity needs to survive and be happy: fresh bread, a little tomato, some good cheese, a scent of oregano. If you think *pizza* is that gloppy mass served up by Pizza Hut, the restraint of Neapolitan *pizza* will amaze you. Each pie is an individual portion—a small (about dinner-plate size), thin, crispy, crusty disk of simple bread, the merest smear of a very light and fresh tomato sauce, a gauzy veil of *mozzarella* (sometimes even just a few spots of it), a pinch of oregano (mostly for the perfume), and if you want to be extravagant, an anchovy fillet or two: that's all. There are lots of variations, of course, and you can heap onto a *pizza* just about anything the structure will bear. But Italians are likely to be more restrained than Americans about that. A thin slice or two of *prosciutto* is just about the only meat that ever goes on a pizza in Italy. Most toppings are vegetal and lightly applied: mushrooms, pitted olives, roasted peppers, artichokes—things of that sort. Even seafood occurs more often as a *pizza* topping than sausage or *salami* or their kin. But once you've learned the basic techniques, you can please yourself.

There are a few tricks to making good *pizza*. Cooking on the stone is most important, and well worth the small expense it involves. See the discussion of oven tiles on page 19. If you use tiles or a stone for *pizza*, you'll also need a baker's peel, the large wooden spatula that bakers use to take items in and out of the oven. There is only one trick to know about its use. Spread it with a small amount of cornmeal before you place the *pizza* on it. The cornmeal acts like tiny ball-bearings to keep the *pizza* from sticking to the peel. Even

with the cornmeal, don't dawdle at this point, especially if your dough is very
moist. To put your *pizza* in the oven, place the leading edge of the peel right
on the stone just about where you want the far edge of your *pizza* to sit. Hold
the peel at a shallow angle—between 15 and 30 degrees—and in one sharp,
smooth motion simply yank the peel out from under the *pizza*. There's really
nothing to it, though almost everybody ruins at least one *pizza* as the price of
admission to the ancient guild of *pizzaiuoli*.

1 recipe pizza dough (page 20)   ½ to ¾ cup basic southern
¾ pound *mozzarella*   tomato sauce (page 31)
Cornmeal   Oregano

Make the dough as directed and let it rise once. Preheat an oven lined with
baking tiles to its hottest setting—500 degrees F is best, but 450 degrees will
do if your oven goes only that high.

Punch down the dough, divide it into 4 equal pieces, and form them into
flattened rounds. Set them on a floured work surface, cover with a towel, and
let them sit for at least 10 minutes to relax the gluten.

Coarsely grate or shred the *mozzarella*. Spread 1 tablespoon of cornmeal
onto a *pizza* peel. Have all ingredients nearby so you can work fast once the
dough is on the peel.

Prepare 1 *pizza* at a time. Take a piece of dough and alternately roll it out
with a rolling pin and stretch it between your hands to obtain a circle 8 to 9
inches in diameter and no thicker than ⅛ inch. Set it on the cornmeal-covered
peel and quickly spread on 2 tablespoons of the tomato sauce, then ½ cup
(loosely packed) of the *mozzarella*. Sprinkle a pinch of oregano over the top
and quickly slide the *pizza* into the hot oven, leaving room for the other *pizze*.

Prepare the remaining three *pizze* in the same way. Bake until the crusts
are lightly golden, about 5 minutes at 500 degrees, a little longer at lower
temperatures. Remove with a large spatula to individual plates and serve.

WINE SUGGESTION
Pizza *loves all wine, though white is by far the commonest quaff with it.
Lacryma Christi would make a good choice. Pizza* wine in the United
States tends to mean junk, just as franchise pizza *means glop; in Italy,
pizza is a real food, and it deserves—and gets—a real wine.*

Puglia-Style Pizza
[PIZZA PUGLIESE]

Here is a sauceless variant, quite different in style and very tasty. Young *provolone*, coarsely grated or thinly sliced, can be pleasingly substituted for up to half the *mozzarella*.

1 recipe pizza dough (page 20)	Olive oil
6 ounces *mozzarella*	Oregano
2 ounces boiled ham	Cornmeal
3 ounces very thinly sliced onion	

Prepare the *pizza* dough and divide it into 4 pieces as directed in the preceding recipe. Preheat an oven lined with *pizza* tiles to 500 degrees F. Coarsely grate or shred the *mozzarella*. Sliver the ham.

Roll and stretch a piece of dough into a round 8 to 9 inches in diameter. Distribute one quarter of the *mozzarella* over it. Separate the onion slices into rings and strew one quarter of them over the *mozzarella*. Top with one quarter of the slivered ham. Drizzle 1 to 2 teaspoons of olive oil over the top and sprinkle on a pinch of oregano.

Bake the *pizze* about 5 minutes at 500 degrees, up to 10 minutes at lower temperatures, or until their edges are puffed and golden and their centers bubbly.

WINE SUGGESTION
This delightfully cheesy dish very much appreciates a simple red wine. Corvo, Lacryma Christi, or Regaleali would all be good choices.

Spaghetti with an Uncooked Sauce
[SPAGHETTI CON SALSA CRUDA]

This is one more version of the popular raw sauces; we give two other variations on pages 180 and 181. Fully ripe plum tomatoes and fresh basil are vital to the success of this quintessential hot-weather dish. The vibrant flavors of this lively sauce seem to marry best with thin pastas like *spaghetti*, *spaghettini*, and *capellini*.

1½ pounds very ripe plum tomatoes
¼ pound Gaeta olives
1 garlic clove
8 large basil leaves

½ teaspoon plus 1 tablespoon salt
¼ teaspoon freshly ground
  black pepper
½ cup olive oil
1 pound imported Italian *spaghetti*

Drop tomatoes into boiling water for 10 seconds, then drain, peel, and seed them. Cut them into strips about ½ inch by 1½ inches. Pit and halve the olives. Mince the garlic. Chop the basil leaves.

Mix the tomatoes, olives, garlic, basil, ½ teaspoon salt, pepper, and olive oil together in a large serving bowl. Let them sit for at least 1 hour at room temperature.

Bring 4 to 5 quarts of water to the boil; add 1 tablespoon of salt and the *spaghetti*. Cook until *al dente*. Drain thoroughly and add the pasta to the sauce bowl. Toss well and serve.

WINE SUGGESTION

Reasonably light white wines, well chilled, will match very well with this dish: Castel del Monte, Cirò, Corvo, Lacryma Christi—nothing heavier than those.

Quadrucci with Basil-Tomato Sauce
[QUADRUCCI CON BASILICO E POMODORO]

Here is a simple variant of the basic southern sauce, used for one of the rare occasions when fresh egg pasta appears in this part of the world. It's a light and zesty summer dish, to be made when basil is at its peak of flavor and abundance. *Quadrucci* are simple squares of fresh pasta, and while you could substitute *fettucine* or any other shape, remember that it's an Italian article of faith that certain pasta shapes go best with certain sauces.

———◆———

1 recipe basic egg pasta (page 24)
1 packed cup fresh basil leaves

½ recipe basic southern tomato sauce
  (page 31)
1 tablespoon salt

Roll the pasta to the thinnest setting on the pasta machine. Cut it with a fluted pastry wheel into 1-inch squares.

(continued)

Wash and dry the basil. Set aside a few sprigs of the smallest leaves for garnish; roughly chop the rest. Bring the tomato sauce to a simmer, add the chopped basil, and cook gently, partly covered, for 5 minutes.

Bring 4 to 5 quarts of water to a boil. Add the salt, then the *quadrucci*. Cook 1 to 2 minutes, or until *al dente*. Drain the pasta, toss with the sauce, garnish with the reserved sprigs of basil, and serve at once.

WINE SUGGESTION

This dish wants a simple, cold white wine: Cirò or Lacryma Christi are both good choices.

Macaroni with Ricotta and Tomato Sauce
[MACCHERONI CON SALSA DI RICOTTA]

Another variant on the basic southern sauce, also extremely simple but quite different in effect from either the plain sauce or the basil-scented sauce of the preceding recipe. This one—to the Italian sense of the fitness of pasta shapes—calls for short tubular *maccheroni*.

½ pound *ricotta*
½ recipe basic southern tomato sauce (page 31)

1 tablespoon salt
1 pound imported Italian *maccheroni*

Let the *ricotta* come to room temperature. Heat the tomato sauce until simmering.

Bring 4 to 5 quarts water to a boil. Add the salt, then the *maccheroni*. Cook until *al dente*. Drain the pasta and place it in a warmed serving bowl. Toss with the sauce, then with the *ricotta*.

WINE SUGGESTION

Choose an unpretentious red wine, such as Corvo or Castel del Monte.

Linguine with Light Tomato Sauce
[LINGUINE CON FILETTO AL POMODORO]

Here is another very simple tomato sauce for pasta, one that uses less tomato, in larger chunks, and considerably more olive oil than our basic southern sauce. This is not, despite appearances, an oily-tasting sauce; it is light and fresh-tasting. Made this way, it often becomes the base to which other ingredients—especially whole shellfish—are added for the briefest possible cooking. (See page 264 for a version using shrimp.) The sauce takes less than 15 minutes from start to finish.

1½ pounds ripe plum tomatoes	2 tablespoons chopped parsley
¾ cup olive oil	Salt
1 garlic clove	1 pound imported Italian *linguine*

Drop the tomatoes into boiling water for 10 seconds, then drain and peel them. Cut each one in 3 or 4 pieces and squeeze them gently by handfuls to remove some of the liquid. (If using canned tomatoes, halve them and set them in a sieve to drain off as much liquid as possible.)

Heat the olive oil in a large sauté pan. Halve the garlic clove and sauté the pieces until lightly golden, then press and discard them. Add the tomato pieces and simmer them for about 10 minutes. They should not fully dissolve into a purée. Stir in the parsley and ½ teaspoon of salt; turn off heat.

Cook the *linguine* in 4 to 5 quarts of rapidly boiling salted water until *al dente*. Drain, dress with the sauce, and serve at once.

WINE SUGGESTION

A very simple red or a light white, like Corvo or Castel del Monte, is called for.

Spaghetti with Eggplant and Peppers
[SPAGHETTI ALLA SIRACUSANA]

This is a pretty dish and a zesty one, a Sicilian standard with the characteristic southern lightness of touch. About 15 minutes' preparation time, and less than 30 minutes of cooking.

(continued)

½ pound small eggplants
2 large red or yellow bell peppers
   (about ¾ pound)
1 cup canned plum tomatoes, with
   their juice
4 basil leaves
2 teaspoons tiny capers
5 tablespoons olive oil

2 large garlic cloves, unpeeled
2 anchovy fillets, chopped
Salt
Freshly ground black pepper
1 pound imported Italian *spaghetti*
⅔ cup freshly grated *pecorino romano*
   (about ¼ pound)

Peel the eggplants and cut them into ½-inch dice. Rinse and halve the peppers, remove seeds and membranes, then cut crosswise into ⅜-inch-wide strips. Roughly chop the tomatoes. Shred the basil leaves. Rinse and drain the capers.

In a large sauté pan, warm the olive oil. Add the eggplant, anchovies, and garlic. Sauté over moderate heat, stirring occasionally, for 8 to 10 minutes, or until eggplant is soft. Then add the peppers, tomatoes, capers, and basil. Stir well, bring to a simmer, cover, and cook over medium heat, stirring occasionally, for 12 to 15 minutes, until peppers are tender.

Discard garlic cloves. Taste for seasoning and add salt, if necessary, and a generous amount of freshly ground black pepper.

Bring 4 to 5 quarts of water to a boil, add 1 tablespoon salt and then the *spaghetti*. Cook until *al dente*, then drain and place the *spaghetti* in a warmed serving bowl. Add the hot sauce and toss to coat thoroughly. Add half the cheese and toss again. Serve at once, passing the remaining cheese at the table.

WINE SUGGESTION
*An uncomplicated red is what we want here; Corvo, Castel del Monte,
or Lacryma Christi are all good candidates.*

Pasta with Beans

[PASTA E FAGIOLI]

This is the southern version of this pan-Italian favorite (see pages 84 and 182 for the northern and central variants). In Campania, the pasta for this homey, comforting dish is always a miscellaneous lot of broken pieces. Several different shapes will be in there—ends of *linguine* and *spaghetti*, small shells and butterflies, *orecchiette* and *tubettini*—but there will always be some *fusilli*, the corkscrew pasta beloved of Neapolitans. Without *fusilli*, Neapolitans swear, *pasta e fagioli* just doesn't taste right.

½ pound dried red kidney beans
1 pint broth, optional (page 45)
½ pound fresh plum tomatoes
1 garlic clove
2 tablespoons olive oil
1 small *peperoncino rosso*
½ teaspoon oregano

½ teaspoon salt
Freshly ground black pepper
6 ounces imported Italian pasta
Additional olive oil, optional
Grated *pecorino romano*, optional
Crushed red pepper

Pick over and rinse the beans and put them in a large pot with water to cover by 2 inches. Bring to a boil, boil 2 minutes, then turn off heat and let the beans sit in the water for 1 hour. Alternatively, soak the beans overnight in water to cover generously.

Drain the beans, put them back in the pot, and add 3 pints of fresh water (or 2 pints water and 1 pint broth). Bring to a boil, reduce to a simmer, and let the beans cook, covered, while you do the next steps.

Drop the tomatoes into boiling water for 10 seconds, then drain, peel, seed, and chop them. Halve the garlic cloves lengthwise and sauté them with the *peperoncino* in the olive oil for 2 to 3 minutes. Add the tomatoes, the oregano, salt, and several grindings of pepper. Cook gently, covered, for 10 minutes.

Remove the *peperoncino*, then add the sauce to the bean pot. Cook until the beans are almost tender—which may range from 1 to 2 hours in all, depending on how dry the beans were to start. (The recipe may be done ahead to this point.) Then add the pasta and continue cooking until the pasta is tender, adding a few tablespoons of hot water, if necessary, to keep the sauce from getting too thick.

Taste for seasoning and add salt, pepper, and, if desired, a lacing of olive oil. Let the beans sit off heat for 5 minutes, then serve, passing the grated cheese and crushed red pepper.

WINE SUGGESTION
Red or white wines do almost equally well here, with a slight edge going to red. In either color, Lacryma Christi is a logical choice.

Tubetti with Broccoli
[TUBETTI CON BROCCOLI]

This recipe comes from Puglia, where it is always served with generous amounts of freshly grated *pecorino romano*. Indeed, the piquancy of the *pecorino* is absolutely essential to the success of the dish. *Parmigiano* does not work as a substitute; it's too sweet.

2 pounds broccoli
1 cup olive oil
2 garlic cloves, sliced lengthwise into
   3 pieces each
1 tablespoon minced onion
1 small *peperoncino rosso*

4 anchovy fillets, chopped
1½ tablespoons salt
1 pound imported Italian *tubetti*
Freshly grated *pecorino romano*
Freshly ground black pepper

Cut off all thick stems of the broccoli. Separate and save only the florets, the tiny stems, and any small fresh leaves. Wash and drain them.

Warm ¾ cup of the olive oil in a sauté pan. Add the garlic, onion, and red pepper. Over a low flame, sauté until the garlic begins to turn golden, then discard it. Add the chopped anchovy and continue to cook, stirring, until the anchovy dissolves. Turn off heat and keep the mixture warm.

Bring 6 quarts of water to a boil, add the salt, and then the broccoli. Cook 4 to 5 minutes, until broccoli is done but still firm. Remove broccoli with a slotted spoon and keep warm.

In the same water, cook the pasta until *al dente*. Drain it and toss it with the remaining ¼ cup olive oil. Mix in the broccoli, then add the garlic-onion-anchovy oil mixture. Toss well. Serve immediately, with generous amounts of *pecorino romano* and freshly ground black pepper.

WINE SUGGESTION
   White Castel del Monte is the first and best choice. Cirò or Corvo will also serve.

Shells with Cauliflower Sauce

[MACCHERONI CON CAVOLFIORE]

This dish displays the telltale signs of Saracen influence—the tasty trinity of anchovies, raisins, and pine nuts that pop up so often in Italian cooking. The way tomato paste is used here—to provide a gentle but pervasive tomato accent—is typical of the way that much-abused-in-America substance is treated in Italy. Shells or a similar-shaped macaroni are important to the dish, since they act as tiny catch-basins for the succulent nubbly sauce.

1 cauliflower (about 1½ pounds)	2 ounces pignoli
2 ounces golden raisins	1 tablespoon salt
6 tablespoons olive oil	1 pound imported Italian *conchiglie*
1 cup chopped onion	1 cup grated *pecorino romano*
2 tablespoons tomato paste dissolved in 1 cup water	2 tablespoons chopped fresh basil or parsley, or a combination of both
6 anchovy fillets	

Divide the cauliflower into florets. Wash them, drop them into 3 to 4 quarts boiling salted water, and cook 7 minutes. Drain and refresh them under cold water. Divide them further into pieces about 1 inch in diameter.

Soak the raisins for 15 minutes in hot water, then drain them.

Heat 3 tablespoons of the olive oil in a large skillet. Add the chopped onion and sauté gently until soft and translucent but not browned. Add the dissolved tomato paste, cover, and cook gently for 15 minutes.

Put the remaining 3 tablespoons oil and the anchovies in a small pan. Cook over a low flame, stirring, until the anchovies completely dissolve.

Add the cauliflower pieces to the onion-tomato sauce. Simmer, covered, for 5 minutes. Then add the anchovy oil, pignoli, and raisins, and cook another 5 to 10 minutes, until the cauliflower is tender but not falling apart.

Bring 4 to 5 quarts of water to a boil, add the salt, and then the pasta. Cook until *al dente*, drain, and place in a warmed serving bowl. Toss with the sauce, then sprinkle the grated cheese and chopped fresh herbs on top.

WINE SUGGESTION

This is a white-wine dish, and it wants one with some fruit and body. Regaleali or Lacryma Christi would be excellent choices.

Linguine with Shrimp
[LINGUINE CON GAMBERI]

This recipe illustrates the way the *filetto al pomodoro* sauce described on page 259 can be used with seafood. This is probably one of the simplest, most bare-bones cooking techniques in the southern repertoire for combining seafood with pasta. Small whole clams and mussels, either shucked or in their shells (well scrubbed and debearded), sea scallops, cleaned and cut-up squid, small pieces of fish—any of these can be treated in this same manner.

½ pound small shrimp (about 2 dozen)	2 tablespoons chopped parsley
1½ pounds ripe plum tomatoes	Salt
¾ cup olive oil	1 pound imported Italian *linguine*
1 garlic clove	

Shell, rinse, and pat dry the shrimp.

Follow the instructions for making *filetto al pomodoro* on page 259. Two minutes before the sauce is finished, add the shrimp to it, and stir them in thoroughly. Cook, stirring, until they lose their translucency and for no more than 1 minute beyond that.

Bring 4 to 5 quarts of water to a boil, add a tablespoon of salt, and cook the *linguine* until *al dente*. Drain, dress with the sauce, and serve.

WINE SUGGESTION

A white wine serves best here: Lacryma Christi, Regaleali, even Greco di Tufo would all be excellent.

Spaghettini with Mixed Seafood
[SPAGHETTINI AL FRUTTA DI MARE]

Southern Italians are almost unanimous in believing that seafood sauces require extremely thin *pasta lunga*, that is, long, *spaghetti*-shaped pasta. In Italy, this recipe would be made with *scampi* or with clawless Mediterranean lobster. Rock lobster tails are a good facsimile of both in flavor and texture. The technique of finishing a pasta in its sauce is a useful trick to know; it concentrates the sauce and at the same time more deeply imbues the pasta with the basic flavor of the dish.

16 mussels
⅓ cup white wine
2 large rock lobster tails (1 pound)
3 garlic cloves, halved
1 *peperoncino rosso*
⅓ cup olive oil

1 cup basic southern tomato sauce
  (page 31)
3 tablespoons chopped parsley
Salt
Freshly ground black pepper
1 pound imported Italian *spaghettini*

Scrub the mussels well. Place them in a large pot with the white wine and steam over high heat until they open. Drain, shell, and debeard them, discarding any that have not opened. Strain the cooking liquid through a sieve lined with a wet paper towel.

Halve the rock lobster tails lengthwise, cutting through the shells, and then cut each half into 3 or 4 pieces.

Sauté the garlic and *peperoncino* in the olive oil in a large (5 to 6 quart) heavy-bottomed pot. When the garlic is lightly golden, press the pieces briefly against the bottom of the pan and discard them, along with the *peperoncino*.

Add the lobster pieces and sauté 3 to 4 minutes, until they lose their translucency. Remove them to a plate. Add the mussel cooking liquid and boil briskly until it is reduced by half. Then stir in the tomato sauce, the parsley, and a sprinkling of salt and pepper. Stir all together and keep warm while cooking the pasta.

Bring 5 to 6 quarts of water to the boil with 1 tablespoon salt. Add the *spaghettini* and cook until about three-quarters done. Drain the pasta and add it to the sauce, along with the mussels and the lobster pieces. Simmer all together 2 minutes, then serve.

WINE SUGGESTION
An excellent white wine like Greco di Tufo matches well with this dish.

Tommaso's Capellini
[CAPELLINI ALLA TOMMASO]

We were taught this dish by one of the best of southern Italian cooks, Tom Verdillo, the owner-chef of Tommaso's in the southern Italian province of Brooklyn. It is simple and quick—cooking takes less than half an hour, plus whatever time you need to shuck clams—and yields a sauce at once delicate and rich with the taste of the sea. Take note: The sauce should not be a uniform-textured purée; there should be bits of tomato and olive and pieces of clam adrift in a fragrant, juicy, almost-broth. *Capellini* are very thin, long pasta, akin to *capelli d'angelo*. If neither of those is available, use the thinnest pasta you can find—nothing thicker than *spaghettini*.

---

24 small fresh clams, 2 inches in diameter
4 garlic cloves
16 Gaeta olives
3 cups canned plum tomatoes
3 tablespoons olive oil
2 *peperoncini rossi*

1 tablespoon chopped fresh basil
4 tablespoons chopped parsley
¼ teaspoon plus 1 tablespoon salt
Freshly ground black pepper
1 pound imported Italian *capellini*
Oregano

Scrub the clams. Shuck them over a plate, saving their liquid. Cut each clam into 2 to 3 pieces (more if you are working with larger clams). Strain the clam liquid through a sieve lined with a dampened paper towel.

Peel and lightly crush the garlic. Pit and halve the olives. Chop the tomatoes on a plate to catch the juices they give off.

Warm the olive oil and sauté the garlic and *peperoncino* lightly for 2 minutes. Add the olives, basil, and parsley. Stir together for a minute and add the clam juice. Raise heat and reduce the liquid by half. Discard the *peperoncino*.

Add the tomatoes and their juices, ¼ teaspoon salt, and pepper, and cook for 20 minutes over low heat, stirring occasionally. Set aside until pasta is nearly ready.

Bring 4 to 5 quarts water to a boil, add 1 tablespoon salt, and the *capellini*. Cook until *al dente*. As the pasta is nearing doneness, bring the sauce back to a simmer, add the clams, and cook for 1 minute, just to heat them through. Off heat, stir in a pinch of oregano.

Drain the pasta, place it in a warmed serving bowl, and toss it with the sauce.

WINE SUGGESTION
This superb dish matches well with an excellent white wine like Greco di Tufo.

Pasta with Fresh Sardines
[PASTA CON LE SARDE]

This Sicilian specialty may be the supreme achievement of Italian pasta-and-seafood cookery. It's also a dish that violates the general rule for seafood pasta by demanding a short, tubular pasta for best results. In Sicily it is made only with the greens of wild fennel, which are highly pungent and aromatic. To capture some of that perfume and flavor, we've added fennel seeds to the spicing; the result is not as overwhelming as the original dish, but it is certainly in the ballpark. Try this dish whenever you are able to get fresh sardines—they usually appear in the spring. Try it even if you can get only frozen sardines.

¾ pound fresh sardines (about 8)	1 *peperoncino rosso*
5 ounces fresh fennel leaves and thin stems	½ cup plus 2 teaspoons olive oil
	½ teaspoon fennel seeds
4 anchovy fillets	3 tablespoons pignoli
4 tablespoons golden raisins	⅛ teaspoon saffron threads
½ cup chopped onion	

---

1 tablespoon salt	½ cup fine fresh bread crumbs
1 pound imported Italian *ziti* or *penne*	

Clean and fillet the sardines. Rinse and drain the fennel greens. Chop the anchovy fillets. Soften the raisins in hot water in a small bowl.

Bring 4 to 5 quarts of water to the boil. Drop in the fennel and boil until tender, about 10 minutes. Drain, reserving the cooking water, and chop the fennel fine.

In a large sauté pan, cook the onion with the *peperoncino* in ½ cup of the olive oil until onion is soft. Add the fennel seeds and the chopped anchovy. Sauté, stirring, until the anchovy dissolves, about 5 minutes. Remove *peperoncino*. Add the raisins and pignoli.

Crush the saffron threads into ½ cup of the fennel cooking water. Pour it into the sauté pan. Stir and simmer gently for 5 minutes. Add the fresh sardines and the fennel greens. Cover and cook 3 to 4 minutes, depending on the size of the fish: They should be opaque and just beginning to break apart.

Bring the fennel cooking water back to a boil, add the salt, and drop in the pasta. Cook until *al dente*.

While the pasta is cooking, toast the bread crumbs in a small, heavy-bottomed pan until light brown. Add the remaining 2 teaspoons of olive oil and sauté, stirring, for 1 minute.

Drain the pasta, transfer it to a serving bowl, and ladle the sauce over it, stirring gently to spread it uniformly without further breaking up the fish. Drizzle the oil and bread crumbs over the top and serve at once. No cheese, but pepper—red or black—is pleasing.

WINE SUGGESTION

Without question, a full-bodied dry white wine, and lots of it. Best choices are Regaleali or Greco di Tufo.

Ziti with Prosciutto
[ZITI ALLA SAN GIOVANNI]

This excellent little sauce adds up to more than the sum of its parts. The *prosciutto* gives it a character and depth that distinguish it strikingly from more typical southern sauces. Finishing the pasta in the sauce also ensures that the flavor goes right into the pasta itself, similar to the effect one gets more conventionally in a baked pasta.

1 pound plum tomatoes	Salt
¼ pound *prosciutto*, in one piece	Freshly ground black pepper
4 large basil leaves	1 pound imported Italian *ziti*
2 garlic cloves	½ cup grated *parmigiano*
4 tablespoons olive oil	

Drop the tomatoes into boiling water for 10 seconds, then drain, peel, and seed them. Cut them into strips ½ inch wide by 2 inches long. Roughly chop the *prosciutto*, or cut it into matchsticks. Shred the basil leaves into julienne strips. Cut each garlic clove into 2 to 3 slices.

Sauté the garlic in the olive oil in a large pan over moderate heat. When the garlic is golden, press the pieces against the pan, then remove them. Add the *prosciutto*, stir briefly to coat it with the oil, then add the tomatoes. Salt and pepper lightly, and cook, covered, for 15 minutes.

Bring 4 to 5 quarts of water to a boil, add 1 tablespoon of salt, and then add the *ziti*. When the pasta is still slightly firm, drain it quickly; it should remain slightly moist. Then add the pasta to the sauce in the pan and toss to coat. Add the shredded basil and cheese. Over a medium-high flame, toss everything together for 2 minutes, then serve.

WINE SUGGESTION

A relatively simple red wine works well here. Lacryma Christi is a good choice.

Rigatoni with Ham Sauce
[RIGATONI ALLA SAN GIOVANELLO]

Here is a variant on the preceding *prosciutto*-tomato sauce. This one—equally quick and hearty—from Apulia gets a lot of mileage out of a quarter-pound of plain old boiled ham. It is excellent on *rigatoni* or similar broad tubular macaroni shapes. For a spicy accent, try adding a small *peperoncino* with the garlic (remove it before serving).

269
Primi

3 ounces lean boiled ham, in one ¼-inch-thick slice
1 garlic clove
¾ cup freshly grated *pecorino romano* cheese
1½ tablespoons minced fresh basil
4 tablespoons olive oil

2 cups drained canned plum tomatoes
Salt
Freshly ground black pepper
1 pound imported Italian *rigatoni*

Dice the ham into ¼-inch cubes. Chop the garlic fine. Mix the grated cheese with the minced basil. Chop the tomatoes on a plate, saving their juices.

Heat the olive oil in a large skillet. Add the garlic and ham and sauté over moderate heat for 3 to 5 minutes. Add the tomatoes, their juices, and a generous amount of freshly ground black pepper. Bring to a simmer and cook gently, uncovered, for 15 minutes, then taste for salt and pepper. (If the ham was quite salty, no salt may be needed.)

Bring 4 to 5 quarts of water to a boil, add 1 tablespoon of salt, then the pasta. Cook until *al dente*, then drain and place the pasta in a warmed serving bowl. Toss it with the sauce, then add the basil-cheese mixture and toss again. Serve immediately, passing more grated cheese at the table.

WINE SUGGESTION

A *relatively simple red wine works well here. Lacryma Christi is a good choice.*

Rigatoni with Ricotta and Sausage
[RIGATONI ALLA PASTORA]

Sauces can hardly be made more simply than this utterly basic peasant recipe from Basilicata. Nevertheless, the four ingredients combine to create a surprisingly sophisticated sauce. It takes no time at all to prepare, and can be started after the pasta water is put on to boil. The sausage must be *luganega* —other types are too fatty. Also important is a good, freshly grated *pecorino*. Finally, don't stint on the black pepper. The sauce loves it, and diners will probably add even more at table. Additional grated cheese passed at table is nice, too.

½ recipe parsley and cheese sausage (page 37), or 1 pound commercial *luganega*
1 tablespoon salt
1 pound imported Italian *rigatoni*

12 ounces *ricotta*
Freshly ground black pepper
½ cup freshly grated *pecorino romano* cheese

Peel the skin off the sausage. Crumble it into a pot, add 1 cup water, cover, and cook over moderate heat for 10 minutes.

Bring 4 to 5 quarts of water to a boil, add the salt, and then the *rigatoni*. Cook until *al dente*.

While the pasta is cooking, push the *ricotta* through a sieve into a large serving bowl. Mix in the sausage cooking liquid a little at a time, stirring to make a smooth cream. Then stir in the sausage bits and at least ½ teaspoon of black pepper.

Drain the cooked pasta (not too thoroughly), add it to the serving bowl, and toss well with the sauce. Then mix in the grated *pecorino* and serve at once —preferably in heated bowls.

WINE SUGGESTION
Uncomplicated red wine works best with this dish: Castel del Monte or Corvo are the first choices.

Neapolitan Cannelloni
[CANNELLONI ALLA NAPOLETANA]

There are dishes that, at first taste, cause diners to sigh, and, at last taste, cause them to pat their stomachs and smile inanely. This is one of them. It takes more time to make than boiled pastas do, so save it for a weekend if you must—but don't skip it, whatever you do. It can be prepared completely in advance, covered, and refrigerated until you're ready to bake it—in which case, add a few extra minutes of oven time.

½ recipe basic egg pasta (page 24)

½ pound *mozzarella*
2 ounces boiled ham
½ pound *ricotta*
¼ cup grated *parmigiano*

1 egg
¼ teaspoon salt
Freshly ground black pepper

---

1 tablespoon salt
½ recipe basic southern tomato sauce
(see page 31)

3 tablespoons olive oil
¼ cup grated *parmigiano*

Make up the pasta dough and set it aside to rest while you make the filling.

Cut the *mozzarella* into ½-inch dice. Chop the ham. Crumble the *ricotta* into a large bowl. Add the *mozzarella*, ham, *parmigiano*, egg, salt, and pepper. Mix well.

Roll the pasta to the next-to-last setting on the pasta machine, then cut sixteen 4-inch squares. Bring 4 to 5 quarts of water to a boil, add salt, and put in the pasta. Remove after about 1 minute, before the pasta is fully done. Plunge the pasta squares into a bowl of cold water to stop the cooking, then spread them on a clean dish towel until ready to use.

Preheat the oven to 375 degrees F. Bring the tomato sauce to a simmer. Oil a 12-inch square baking pan and spread a small amount of sauce over it.

Put one square of cooked pasta on a work surface. Spread a heaping tablespoon of the prepared filling in a strip along one end. Roll it up and place it in the pan. Continue with the other pieces, making two rows of 8 *cannelloni*.

Spoon a light coating of sauce over the *cannelloni*. Don't feel obliged to use it all: This dish should not be soupy. Sprinkle with the *parmigiano* and 1 or 2 tablespoons of olive oil. Put in the oven and bake 15 minutes. Remove and let rest several minutes before serving.

WINE SUGGESTION

This excellent dish will take red or white wine, as you choose. Regaleali for red and Lacryma Christi for white will do very well.

Baked Macaroni with Peppers
[MACCHERONI E PEPERONI AL FORNO]

This lush, filling, totally vegetarian dish comes from the region of Campania around Naples. It's based on a simple sauce of sweet peppers liberally seasoned with capers, olives, parsley, and oregano. Red and yellow peppers make the most attractive presentation, but green peppers will also do. The dish requires approximately 1 hour for preparation and a half hour for baking.

1½ pounds sweet red or yellow bell peppers
½ cup plus 2 tablespoons olive oil
2 garlic cloves, minced
½ cup fine dry bread crumbs
4 tablespoons capers, rinsed and drained (chopped if large)
18 Gaeta olives, pitted and quartered

⅓ cup chopped fresh parsley
Salt
Freshly ground black pepper
1 teaspoon oregano
Butter and bread crumbs for the baking dish
¾ pound imported Italian *penne*, *mezzani*, or other short, tubular pasta

Turn a gas stove burner to its highest flame. Set a pepper directly on the grate. As the skin blackens in the flame, turn the pepper with tongs until its entire surface is black. Then drop it in a brown paper bag, close the bag, and leave it while preparing the remaining peppers. When all are done, scrape off all the blackened skin of the peppers with a paring knife, working under a thin stream of running water. Cut the peppers open, remove all seeds and membrane, blot them dry with paper towels, and cut them into strips ½ inch wide by 2 inches long.

Heat ½ cup of olive oil in a skillet. Add the cut-up peppers, garlic, bread crumbs, capers, olives, parsley, and a generous amount of freshly ground black pepper. Mix everything well, bring to a simmer, cover, and cook over a very low flame for 10 minutes, stirring often to prevent sticking. Taste for salt and pepper. The sauce should be a bit oversalted at this point so it will adequately season the pasta. Add the oregano, then set aside until ready to use.

Preheat the oven to 425 degrees F. Generously butter a broad 2-quart baking dish and coat with bread crumbs.

Bring 4 to 5 quarts of water to a boil, add 1 tablespoon of salt, and then the pasta. Cook until about three-quarters done, then drain and place it in a large bowl. Toss the pasta with 2 tablespoons olive oil, then with half the peppers and their sauce. Place the pasta in the baking dish and spread the remaining peppers and sauce on top. Bake 25 to 30 minutes, uncovered.

A *well-chilled white wine makes the best accompaniment to this dish. Cirò would be fine, as would Castel del Monte.*

Baked Ziti

[ZITI AL FORNO]

This very widespread country preparation is somewhat unusual, for a southern recipe, in that the commonest versions of it all use *parmigiano* rather than *pecorino romano*. (You can quite successfully substitute *romano*, however, if that is your preference.) The beaten egg topping melts down into the pasta as it bakes and marries all the flavors in a very satisfying way.

---

4 ounces *prosciutto*
1 tablespoon olive oil
2 eggs
¼ cup grated *parmigiano*
Salt

Freshly ground black pepper
1 pound imported Italian *ziti*
¾ cup *ragù napoletana* (page 287)
  or basic southern tomato sauce
  (page 31)

Preheat the oven to 400 degrees F. Cut the *prosciutto* into tiny dice. Oil a large baking dish. Beat the eggs together in a small bowl with half the *parmigiano* and a little salt and pepper.

Bring 4 to 5 quarts of water to a boil, add 1 tablespoon of salt, and then the *ziti*. Cook until not quite *al dente*. Drain the pasta and place it in a large bowl. Toss it with the *ragù*, the *prosciutto*, and the remaining *parmigiano*.

Put the dressed pasta into the baking dish and spread it out evenly. Pour the egg-cheese mixture over the top. Sprinkle on freshly ground pepper and put the dish in the oven for 15 minutes.

WINE SUGGESTION

A *white with good body or a relatively uncomplicated red will both serve here. Lacryma Christi is a good choice for either; so is Corvo.*

SECONDI

Southern *secondi*, like all the rest of the southern cuisine, display a tremendous variety within a relatively narrow range. The variety comes from
the sauces and spicings and herb mixtures that give each dish a distinctive
fragrance and appeal. The narrow range lies in the main ingredients of the
dishes. The greatest diversity among main ingredients can be found in the
category of fish, where everything that swims or floats or creeps in or on or
under the waters of the Mediterranean has a fair chance of ending up on the
table. Fish is immensely popular, and it and poultry appear as *secondi* at least
as often as meat does, and probably more. The real narrowness occurs among
the meats, where many cuts and preparations that seem indispensable to Americans simply do not exist. Large cuts, for instance—roasts and hams and legs
and big steaks—are almost completely absent. This is not to say that in the
South one never roasts a lamb or grills a steak—but it is to say that such
cooking lies very far from the heart of this cuisine.

Stuffed Swordfish Rolls
[INVOLTINI DI PESCE SPADA]

In southern Italian hands, swordfish is a highly versatile substance. The rich,
dense flesh can be pounded as thin as veal *scaloppine*, rolled around any
number of tasty fillings, and braised, broiled, or baked, with or without a
sauce. The filling given here is a Saracen-style combination of anchovy, raisins,
and pignoli. It's a pretty dish and easy to make; it can be fully assembled in
advance and refrigerated until needed. Ideally, for this recipe you want swordfish steaks ¼ inch thick, each weighing about ¼ pound; but unless your fish
store will cut them right off the fish for you it's hard to find steaks that thin.
You can ask the fish man to halve thicker pieces, or you can do it yourself
with a sharp slicing knife. If you partially freeze the swordfish first, it will be
easier to cut.

4 swordfish steaks, ¼ inch thick
(about 1 pound)
2 teaspoons golden raisins
1 anchovy fillet
4 teaspoons chopped onion

4 tablespoons fine fresh bread crumbs
1 teaspoon pignoli
½ teaspoon lemon juice
Freshly ground black pepper
7 bay leaves

Lay the swordfish steaks on wax paper and pound them to a thickness of about ⅛ inch. Cut 2 3-inch squares from each piece, reserving the trimmings. Soften the raisins in a small bowl of hot water for 15 minutes, then drain them.

Chop together 2 tablespoons of the swordfish trimmings, the anchovy fillet, onion, bread crumbs, pignoli, raisins, lemon juice, and several grindings of pepper.

Put 1 tablespoon of this filling on each square of swordfish and roll them up. Line them up in a row with a bay leaf separating each two rolls and pin them together with 2 long skewers, run parallel through the row. Lay them on an oiled heatproof dish.

Preheat the broiler with the rack at its lowest setting. Broil the *involtini* 10 minutes, turning them once. Remove the skewers before serving.

WINE SUGGESTION
   An excellent white is called for to partner this dish. Greco di Tufo or Fiano di Avellino should be your first choices.

Baked Swordfish Steaks
[PESCE SPADA A SFINCIONE]

The preceding recipe illustrated southern ingenuity in working with swordfish. This one retains the basic fish-steak shape and bakes it with bread crumbs and a bright basil-tomato-anchovy topping. If your swordfish steaks are thicker or thinner than those called for, simply adjust the baking time.

—————————

⅓ cup minced onion
1 anchovy fillet
2 tablespoons olive oil
½ cup basic southern tomato sauce
   (page 31)
Salt
Freshly ground black pepper

4 swordfish steaks, ½ inch thick
   (about 1¾ pounds)
½ cup fresh bread crumbs
1 tablespoon fine dry bread crumbs
¼ teaspoon oregano
1 tablespoon chopped fresh basil

Bring a small pot of salted water to the boil. Drop in the minced onion. As soon as the water returns to a boil, drain the onion in a sieve. Cut the anchovy fillet into several small pieces.

Sauté the onion and anchovy in a pan with 1 tablespoon of the olive oil for 5 minutes, stirring to dissolve the anchovy pieces. Add the tomato sauce and a sprinkling of salt and pepper. Set aside until ready to use.

Preheat the oven to 350 degrees F. Rinse the swordfish steaks and shake excess water off them. Lightly coat them with the fresh bread crumbs and lay them in an oiled baking dish. Distribute the sauce over them. Top with the dry bread crumbs, oregano, basil, and remaining 1 tablespoon of olive oil. Bake 10 minutes, or until the swordfish flesh is opaque but still juicy.

WINE SUGGESTION
A *full-bodied white wine like Regaleali or Greco di Tufo will match deliciously with this dish.*

Neapolitan Salt Cod

[BACCALÀ ALLA NAPOLETANA]

In Naples, this dish is almost certain to appear on family tables as one of the courses of Christmas Eve dinner. It is a rich, lush dish, and needs only a simple green salad to accompany it—though in an American-style meal, it also welcomes the companionship of boiled new potatoes. Remember, the *baccalà* has to soak for 3 days before you use it.

1¼ to 1½ pounds dried salt cod	5 tablespoons olive oil
1 heaping tablespoon golden raisins	1 garlic clove, sliced
1 ounce Gaeta olives	1 *peperoncino rosso*, optional
1 heaping tablespoon pignoli	2 cups drained canned plum toma-
1 heaping tablespoon tiny capers	toes
Flour for dredging	Salt
	Freshly ground black pepper

Three days before serving:
Cover the *baccalà* generously with cold water and let it soak, changing the water at least twice a day.

On serving day:
Cut the *baccalà* into 2- to 3-inch chunks and dry them with paper towels. Soften the raisins in hot water for 15 minutes, then drain. Pit and halve the olives. Chop the pignoli (and the capers, if they are large).

Dredge the pieces of *baccalà* in the flour and fry them, a few at a time, in 3 tablespoons of the olive oil until nicely golden. Drain them on paper towels.

Put the remaining 2 tablespoons of olive oil in the bottom of a casserole and add the garlic and *peperoncino*. Cook gently over low heat. When the garlic is golden, discard it. Set a food mill fitted with the medium blade over the casserole and mill in the tomatoes. Add ½ teaspoon of salt and several grindings of pepper and cook gently, uncovered, for 10 minutes. Discard *peperoncino* if desired. Add the *baccalà*, the olives, capers, pignoli, and raisins. Cook, covered, for 30 minutes, stirring often to prevent sticking and adding a few tablespoons of water or the tomato liquid if necessary.

Taste for seasoning and serve.

WINE SUGGESTION

The appropriate regional wine to serve with baccalà alla napoletana *would be either Lacryma Christi—the dry, still white, of course—or Greco di Tufo.*

Mussels in Spicy Red Sauce
[ZUPPA DI COZZE]

The most important prerequisite for this delicious dish is access to fresh, clean mussels. Nothing can be done to overcome strong muddy ones.

4 pounds mussels

4 thick slices day-old country-style bread

2 cups drained canned plum tomatoes

2 garlic cloves

1 *peperoncino rosso*

3 tablespoons olive oil

½ teaspoon salt

2 tablespoons chopped parsley

Scrub and debeard the mussels very carefully. Dry and lightly toast the bread slices in an oven. Pass the tomatoes through a food mill or chop them fine. Peel and halve the garlic cloves.

In a large pot, sauté the garlic and the *peperoncino* in the olive oil until the garlic is lightly golden, then press it and discard. Either discard the pepper now, or leave it in until the end, depending on how spicy you want the sauce. Add the tomatoes and salt. Cook for 10 minutes over medium-low heat, stirring occasionally.

Lay the bread slices in the bottom of a large serving bowl and leave it in a warm place.

Add the mussels to the pot, stir to mix them with the tomatoes, cover, and cook about 4 minutes, until the mussels open. Discard any that do not open after another minute's cooking.

Stir in the parsley, transfer the mussels and all their liquid to the bread-lined serving bowl, and serve at once. Pass additional bread at the table.

Some cooks twist off the top shell of the mussels before serving them. It isn't necessary, though it does make things a bit easier for the diners.

WINE SUGGESTION
Choose a dry white wine like Cirò or Corvo or Castel del Monte.

Sicilian Fish Stew
[ZUPPA DI PESCE SIRACUSANA]

This recipe presents a technique for preparing the classic mixed-fish stew totally different from that of our northern recipe (page 106). Here the pieces of fish are laid on top of the vegetables, the broth poured on, and the entire dish is then baked. To get the most out of this you need some gelatinous fish in the mixture, such as sea robin, eel, dogfish, monkfish, blowfish tails. Whiting are a standard component of the recipe, though weakfish makes an admirable substitute for them; sole can be used instead of sea bass. The most traditional versions of this recipe do not use any shellfish, only finfish. If you are having your fish man trim and cut the fish for you, make sure he saves you the scraps, frames, heads, and tails for making the broth.

1 sea bass, about 1 pound	Salt
1 pound small whiting (2 to 3)	1 garlic clove
1 pound gelatinous fish (see note above)	1 cup drained canned plum tomatoes
2 celery stalks	Freshly ground black pepper
¾ cup coarsely chopped onion	5 tablespoons olive oil
2 bay leaves	½ cup dry white wine
2 tablespoons chopped parsley	8 slices day-old country bread, crusts removed

Clean the fish and cut them into serving-size pieces, saving the heads, tails, and bones. Put the fish trimmings in a pot with a quart of cold water, 1 celery stalk cut in several pieces, ¼ cup of the chopped onion, 1 bay leaf, 1 tablespoon chopped parsley, and ½ teaspoon of salt. Cover and boil for 30 minutes. Strain the liquid through a sieve lined with a damp paper towel, pressing down lightly on the solids. Boil the liquid down, if necessary, until there is 1 cup of fish broth.

Preheat the oven to 350 degrees F. Finely chop the remaining onion and celery together. Spread them on the bottom of an ovenproof casserole. Add the remaining parsley and bay leaf and the whole garlic clove. Coarsely chop the tomatoes and spread them over the vegetables.

Lay the pieces of fish on top of the vegetables and salt and pepper them generously. Pour on the olive oil, then the white wine, then the strained broth. Cover the casserole and bake it in the oven for 40 minutes.

While the fish is cooking, trim the crusts off the slices of bread and toast them lightly in the oven.

Put 2 slices of bread at the bottom of each diner's bowl and ladle the fish and broth over them. Serve at once.

WINE SUGGESTION
Any southern white wine.

Sautéed Chicken with Basil and Tomatoes
[POLLO ALL'ISCHITANA]

When we started collecting recipes, we were struck by the number of dishes that at first glance seemed "ordinary"—calling for almost the same ingredients and techniques—but that turned out to be very different from each other and quite extraordinarily good. This is one of them. A chicken with tomatoes, basil, garlic, wine, olive oil. Surely it will taste like a dozen other chickens in tomato sauce? Believe us, it doesn't. Better yet, don't believe us: Put it to the test. The recipe works equally well with rabbit or guinea hen. Simply adjust the cooking time to the tenderness of the animal.

1 chicken, about 3 pounds	Salt
1½ pounds ripe plum tomatoes	Freshly ground black pepper
¼ cup olive oil	⅔ cup dry white wine
2 garlic cloves, minced	2 tablespoons chopped fresh basil

Rinse the chicken and cut it into 20 to 24 small pieces, using knife and poultry shears. Carefully remove any loose fragments of bone. Pat the chicken pieces dry with paper towels. Drop the tomatoes into boiling water for 10 seconds, then drain, peel, seed, and coarsely chop them.

Warm the olive oil in a sauté pan; add the minced garlic and sauté over low heat until golden. Raise heat to medium, add the chicken pieces, and sauté, mixing frequently, until the chicken colors and firms—about 5 minutes.

Sprinkle with salt and pepper and pour on the wine. Toss everything once or twice, then let the wine absorb slowly (5 to 8 minutes). Add the tomatoes and basil; stir together and cook gently, partly covered, for 30 minutes, stirring from time to time. At the end, the sauce clinging to the chicken should be dense, not at all soupy or even very "saucy."

WINE SUGGESTION
A good full-bodied white wine, like Regaleali or Greco di Tufo, matches well with this chicken, but even better is a quality red wine like Aglianico del Vulture, or a non-riserva Taurasi.

Chicken with Capers
[POLLO CON CAPPERI]

Intriguingly complex on the palate, this dish is simplicity itself to make. The wine vinegar reduction gives depth to the mildness of the chicken, and the capers and parsley add zest. Total preparation time is just about 45 minutes.

1 chicken, about 3 pounds, cut into serving pieces	3 tablespoons olive oil
	Salt
3 tablespoons capers	Freshly ground black pepper
2 tablespoons chopped parsley	¼ cup red wine vinegar

Rinse the chicken pieces and dry them thoroughly with paper towels. Drain and rinse the capers. If they are not the tiniest nonpareil capers, chop them together with the parsley.

Warm the olive oil in a large pan and brown the chicken pieces, salting and peppering lightly. Raise heat and pour on the vinegar. Cook until it evaporates, stirring and scraping up any browned bits from the bottom of the pan.

When vinegar is completely gone, add ¼ cup water and the parsley and capers. Cover and cook over low heat, turning the chicken pieces occasionally, for 30 minutes.

Rabbit in Sweet-Sour Sauce
[CONIGLIO IN AGRODOLCE]

The list of ingredients may lead you to think that this is a strongly spicy dish, but in fact it turns out very restrained and elegant, a fine dish for an important dinner. The *agrodolce* technique and seasonings are widely employed in the South on a variety of foods, sometimes even greens like escarole or rape. This recipe can be adapted to chicken (shorten the cooking time) or to guinea hen (lengthen it a bit). For rabbit, the total cooking time is about 1 hour and 10 minutes, plus marinating time.

———————◆———————

FOR THE MARINADE

1 cup dry red wine	1 bay leaf
1 cup thinly sliced onion	3 peppercorns

———————◆———————

1 rabbit, 2 to 2½ pounds, cut into serving pieces	Freshly ground black pepper
½ cup chopped onion	1½ teaspoons sugar
3 tablespoons lard	1 tablespoon wine vinegar
Flour for dredging	1½ tablespoons pignoli
Salt	1½ tablespoons golden raisins

Bring marinade ingredients to a boil. Boil 1 minute, then let cool. Rinse and pat dry the rabbit pieces, lay them out in a nonaluminum dish, and when the marinade is cool, pour it over them and let sit several hours.

Soften the chopped onion in the lard and sauté 5 minutes. Dry the rabbit pieces, flour them, and put them in the pan. Salt and pepper them lightly and brown them on all sides. Strain the marinade and add half of it to the pan. Cover and cook 10 minutes, stirring once or twice, then add the rest of the marinade. Continue cooking until rabbit is tender, 40 to 50 minutes in all, adding a few spoonfuls of hot water if the sauce seems to be drying out.

Remove the rabbit and keep it warm. Degrease and boil down the sauce, if necessary, until it is thick enough to coat.

In a small pan, dissolve the sugar in the vinegar over low heat. Add the pignoli and raisins and bring to a simmer. Return the rabbit pieces to the pan, stir to coat them with the sauce, and pour the sugar-vinegar mixture over them. Stir again and simmer very gently for 2 minutes. The sauce should not be runny or abundant, just a little more than a dense coating over the pieces of rabbit. Serve at once.

WINE SUGGESTION
This rabbit preparation goes splendidly with a dry red wine like Aglianico del Vulture. If that is not available, try Regaleali or a top-flight Lacryma Christi.

Palermo-Style Breaded Veal Chops
[COSTOLETTE DI VITELLO ALLA PALERMITANA]

This dish should remind you of *costolette alla milanese* (page 114). Within their broad similarities, the differences highlight the distinctive styles of northern and southern cooking. As with the Milanese version, top-quality veal is essential to capturing the real magic of this recipe. You need thin-cut rib chops—no more than ½ to ¾ inch thick. Since American rib veal chops are about twice that thick, you need to ask the butcher to do the following: Knock off the bottom bone, leaving only the curving rib bone; trim all the possible fat off the meat, exposing an inch or two of the rib bone above the eye of the chop; butterfly the meat back to the rib, then split the rib lengthwise to give two thin rib chops; pound the meat flat as if for *scaloppine*.

---

4 rib veal chops, ½ to ¾ inch thick
4 teaspoons red wine vinegar
2 eggs
4 tablespoons chopped parsley
1 garlic clove

½ to ⅔ cup freshly grated
  pecorino romano
1½ cups fine dry bread crumbs
Salt
Freshly ground black pepper
5 tablespoons olive oil

Pound the veal chops to flatten them. Sprinkle each with 1 teaspoon of the vinegar and let them sit 45 minutes to 1 hour.

Beat the eggs and parsley together in a broad shallow bowl. Put the garlic clove through a press into the egg mixture. Combine the grated cheese and the bread crumbs on a plate.

Pat the chops dry. Salt and pepper them lightly. Dip them in the egg mixture, then in the crumb mixture, pressing to make the crumbs adhere. Sauté the chops in the olive oil, allowing a maximum of 10 minutes to a side. Serve at once.

Veal Marsala

[SCALOPPINE ALLA MARSALA]

A classic dish, simple, quick, and elegant. Get the best quality, palest veal you can lay your hands on, and forget about all the mediocre-restaurant versions of this dish you've ever eaten. The real thing is much different, and much better.

———————————◆———————————

4 veal scallops, 3 to 4 ounces each	1½ tablespoons olive oil
2 teaspoons softened butter	½ cup dry Marsala
2 teaspoons flour	2 lemons, quartered

Pound the veal scallops flat between pieces of wax paper. Rub the butter and flour together to form a smooth paste.

Heat the olive oil in a large sauté pan almost to the smoking point. Put in the veal scallops, two at a time if necessary so as not to crowd them. Sauté them over medium-high heat, about 1 minute on a side. Remove to a serving plate and keep warm.

Turn heat high, pour in the Marsala, and boil it briskly, stirring and scraping up browned bits from the bottom of the pan. When it is reduced by half, stir in the butter-flour paste. Lower heat and simmer, stirring, for 2 minutes. If the sauce gets too thick, add a tablespoon or two of water.

Pour the sauce over the scallops and serve, garnishing the plate with lemon quarters.

WINE SUGGESTION
Same suggestions as for preceding recipe.

Veal Scallops Stuffed with Artichokes

[INVOLTINI CON CARCIOFI]

The assertiveness of the artichokes blends very nicely in this recipe with the delicacy of the veal. You'll need 30 to 45 minutes to prepare and precook the artichokes and 30 to 45 minutes for the final assembly and cooking.

4 small artichokes (½ pound)
½ lemon
2 ounces *prosciutto*
5 tablespoons butter
8 small thin veal scallops (1 pound)

4 tablespoons olive oil
Flour for dredging
4 tablespoons chopped onion
½ cup dry white wine
Salt

Trim the artichokes:

Holding an artichoke with the top facing you, snap off the outermost few layers of leaves at the base. Continue until you reach the soft, pale green or yellow leaves. Slice off about the top half of the artichoke cone. With a vegetable peeler, pare away all the green exterior of the artichoke bottom, leaving white flesh. Rub the cut parts all over with a piece of lemon, to prevent darkening.

Bring a pot of water to the boil and squeeze the lemon into it. Drop in the artichokes and boil 15 minutes, or until tender. Drain them upside down on paper towels until cool, then quarter them. Cut out the chokes if they are well developed.

Mince the *prosciutto* and work it into 3 tablespoons of the butter to make a paste.

Pound the veal scallops to flatten them again. Smear a quarter of the butter-*prosciutto* paste on each; place 2 pieces of artichoke along one edge and roll the veal around it. Tie the *involtini* with kitchen string.

In a sauté pan heat the remaining 2 tablespoons butter with the olive oil. Flour the veal rolls and add them to the pan along with the chopped onion. Brown the veal on all sides over medium heat. Add the wine, ½ cup water, and a sprinkling of salt. Turn heat to very low and cook, covered, for about 30 minutes, turning occasionally, until the veal is very tender. Serve at once.

WINE SUGGESTION

A *relatively uncomplicated white wine would be best here*; Corvo or Re-galeali are both good choices.

Veal Scallops with Prosciutto and Mozzarella

[SALTIMBOCCA ALLA NAPOLETANA]

The famous (and original) Roman version of this dish uses only veal, *prosciutto*, and fresh sage. This Neapolitan recipe gives your palate more to consider, without losing any of the vividness of the Roman version. About 20 minutes' preparation time, 10 minutes' final cooking.

½ pound ripe plum tomatoes
¼ pound *mozzarella*
1 garlic clove
2 tablespoons olive oil
2 teaspoons chopped fresh basil
½ teaspoon oregano

Salt
Freshly ground black pepper
1 pound veal scallops
3 tablespoons butter
¼ pound thinly sliced *prosciutto*

Drop the tomatoes into boiling water for 10 seconds, then drain, peel, seed, and coarsely chop them. Slice the *mozzarella* thin.

Slice the garlic into 3 or 4 pieces. Sauté it in the olive oil in a small pan until golden, then press and discard. Add the tomatoes, basil, oregano, and a sprinkling of salt and pepper. Simmer 10 minutes over moderate heat, then set aside.

Preheat the oven to 375 degrees F. In an ovenproof sauté pan large enough for the veal to fit in a single layer, sauté the scallops in the butter, for 1 to 2 minutes on each side.

Off heat, salt and pepper the veal lightly, lay slices of *prosciutto* over them, and the *mozzarella* over that. Spread a thin veil of tomato sauce over all. Put the dish in the oven for 5 to 10 minutes, until the cheese melts and the veal is heated through.

WINE SUGGESTION

A light red wine—Lacryma Christi, Cirò, Castel del Monte—works very well with this dish, though a full-flavored white such as Greco di Tufo will also taste fine.

Stuffed Veal Roll

[POLPETTONE ALLA SICILIANA]

Polpettone literally means a big meatball, but that's not what this very pretty, very tasty dish actually is. Small, stuffed rolls of meat are popular all over Italy, but nowhere so much as in the South. This recipe makes the granddaddy of them all, a family-sized roll of veal wrapped around a rich and typically southern filling.

3 slices day-old country-style bread, about 1 ounce each
2 eggs
1 slice *prosciutto* (about 2 ounces)
1 slice *provolone* (about 2 ounces)
1 garlic clove
¼ pound ground beef
4 tablespoons grated *pecorino romano*
1 tablespoon chopped parsley

Salt
Freshly ground black pepper
1 to 1¼ pounds veal sirloin or top round in a single piece, opened out and pounded flat (at least 9 by 12 inches)
2½ tablespoons olive oil
½ cup dry red wine
1 tablespoon tomato paste

Remove the crusts from the bread. Soak it in cold water for 5 minutes, then drain, squeeze, and shred it. Hard-boil 1 of the eggs. Cut the *prosciutto* and *provolone* into small dice. Halve the garlic clove.

In a mixing bowl, combine the ground beef, the bread, grated *pecorino*, parsley, the raw egg, ⅛ teaspoon salt, and a few grindings of pepper.

Lay out the slice of veal on a work surface and pound it again to flatten it. Salt and pepper it lightly. Spread the ground meat mixture over it in an even layer. Slice the hard-boiled egg thin and lay the slices over the meat mixture. Strew the cubes of *prosciutto* and *provolone* evenly over all. Roll the piece of veal like a jelly roll and tie it securely with kitchen twine.

In a casserole, warm the olive oil with the garlic over medium heat. When the garlic is lightly golden, press the pieces lightly and discard them. Add the veal and brown it on all sides. Raise heat to medium-high, add the red wine, and reduce it by two-thirds. Dissolve the tomato paste in ½ cup of water and add it to the casserole. Cover and cook 1½ hours, or until the veal is tender.

Slice and serve hot.

WINE SUGGESTION
Choose a good red wine for this dish: Il Falcone or Rosso del Conte, Aglianico Riserva or Taurasi.

Beef in Ragù

[CARNE AL RAGÙ]

This robust dish is distantly related to *stracotto* (page 203). It is probably also the unintentional and blameless parent of all those overcooked tomato sauces that Italo-American greasy spoons turn out by the gallon. Made only with tomato paste and an unusually large amount of meat for the region, this seems to be a southern winter recipe, designed to simmer gently on the back of the stove all day long, incidentally warming and perfuming the kitchen and finally yielding both a richly flavored sauce for a *primo* and a tender, moist meat for *secondo*.

Southern *ragù*, as you will see, is very different from northern. Rather than being composed of many tiny pieces of meat, this sauce takes its intensity from a single large piece—which after having contributed enough flavor to the sauce, is then eaten as a dish in its own right. The recipe works best with inexpensive cuts of beef that reward long cooking: Bottom round is the very noblest cut you should use, and you certainly can substitute chuck—but start with a slightly larger piece, because it will shrink more. The dish is also sometimes made with pork—usually in that case a piece with a bone in it for extra flavor (shoulder is good)—and the whole cooking time is reduced.

1½ ounces *prosciutto*
2 ounces *pancetta*
1 tablespoon chopped parsley
2 to 2½ pounds bottom round, in one piece
Freshly ground black pepper
5 ounces onion

1 garlic clove
1½ ounces lard
Salt
⅔ cup dry red wine
1 can (6 ounces) tomato paste

Chop the *prosciutto*, half the *pancetta*, and the parsley in a food processor. Cut one or two pockets in the meat, so it opens like the leaves of a book. Generously pepper the inner sides of the meat and spread the *prosciutto* mixture in it. Tie the meat with string.

Chop the rest of the *pancetta*, the onion, and the garlic together, or pulse them in the food processor.

Melt the lard in a heavy-bottomed pot. Add the *pancetta*-onion mix and sauté gently to render the *pancetta* somewhat, about 2 minutes. Add the meat, salt and pepper it, cover, and let cook very gently, turning occasionally, for 10 minutes. Uncover, pour on the wine, continue cooking until it evaporates, still on a low flame.

Raise the heat and start adding tomato paste, 1 to 2 tablespoons at a time.

Stir each portion in and let it darken for 1 to 2 minutes before adding more. When all the tomato paste has been incorporated in the sauce, add ¾ cup of water (one tomato-paste canful). Stir all together well, cover the pan, lower heat to the minimum, and let simmer very gently for 2 to 2½ hours. Check from time to time, turning the meat and adding a bit more water if necessary.

When the meat is very tender, remove it and continue cooking the sauce very gently for at least 5 hours in all, adding water as necessary if it gets too thick.

Defat the sauce, if necessary. Taste for salt and pepper. Return the meat to the sauce to reheat for the final 30 minutes of cooking. Serve the sauce over 1 pound of pasta (*spaghetti, fusilli, penne, ziti, rigatoni*) as a *primo*, reserving just enough to lightly dress the beef.

WINE SUGGESTION

A good but simple red wine is best here: Lacryma Christi, Regaleali, even, if you're feeling expansive, a non-riserva Aglianico.

Stuffed Beef Roll

[BRACIOLONE ALLA NAPOLETANA]

Another family-size, rolled and stuffed meat—beef this time. Flank steak lends itself well to this sort of cooking, but this recipe can also be made with round steak, either cut or pounded thin. The important point is that the meat wrapping shouldn't be too thick. The rest of the preparation is simplicity itself: The only thing you have to watch out for is that the sauce doesn't reduce too much.

━━━━━━━━━◆━━━━━━━━━

1 butterflied flank steak (1½ pounds)

FOR THE STUFFING

3 ounces *prosciutto*	2 ounces grated *pecorino romano*
2 garlic cloves	½ cup bread crumbs
2 tablespoons chopped parsley	2 eggs
2 ounces golden raisins	Salt
1 ounce pignoli	Freshly ground black pepper

━━━━━━━━━◆━━━━━━━━━

1 carrot	3 tablespoons olive oil
1 celery stalk	¾ cup white wine
½ cup sliced onion	1 tablespoon tomato paste

Pound the flank steak to flatten it thoroughly. Chop or grind the *prosciutto*, garlic, and parsley together in a meat grinder. Mix all the stuffing ingredients together. Lay out the flank steak, salt and pepper it lightly, and spread it with the stuffing. Roll and tie it with string.

Chop the carrot, celery, and onion together. Dissolve the tomato paste in ½ cup of warm water.

Soften the vegetables for 10 minutes in the olive oil in a large casserole. Add the *braciolone* and brown it well on all sides. Pour on the white wine and let it reduce by half over medium-high heat, scraping up any browned bits from the bottom of the pan. Then add the dissolved tomato paste, cover, and cook very slowly for 1 hour, or until the meat is tender when pierced with a fork.

Either serve the *braciolone* whole, carving and passing the sauce at table, or slice, arrange on a platter, and mask with the sauce.

WINE SUGGESTION

This braciolone *calls for a good red wine: Salice Salentino, Il Falcone, Rosso del Conte, Aglianico del Vulture, Taurasi—any of these will match splendidly with it.*

Stuffed Pork Chops

[COSTOLETTE DI MAIALE RIPIENE]

Americans aren't the only people to love stuffed pork chops. This Sicilian recipe offers homey flavor and a very easy preparation, about 45 minutes from start to finish.

4 loin pork chops, 1½ inches thick	4 teaspoons freshly grated *pecorino romano*
1 egg	
¼ cup chopped onion	Freshly grated nutmeg
4 tablespoons olive oil	Salt
3 tablespoons fine dry bread crumbs	Freshly ground black pepper
1 tablespoon chopped parsley	Flour for dredging
	2 tablespoons butter

Cut a pocket in each pork chop, going right to the bone. (You could have the butcher do this when you buy the chops.) Separate the egg.

Sauté the onion in 2 tablespoons of the olive oil for 5 minutes, or until soft but not colored. Add the bread crumbs and parsley. Stir once and turn off heat.

In a small bowl, mix the egg yolk with the cheese, a grinding of nutmeg, and a sprinkle of salt and pepper. Stir in the onion mixture. If the mixture looks dry, add some or all of the egg white.

Fill the cavities in the pork chops with this mixture and sew them closed, using a darning needle and thread. Dredge the chops in flour.

Warm the butter with the remaining 2 tablespoons of olive oil in a large sauté pan. Add the chops, salt and pepper them lightly, and sauté over moderate heat for 10 to 15 minutes to each side. Remove the thread before serving.

WINE SUGGESTION
Either a full-bodied white like Regaleali or a soft, medium-bodied red— Regaleali, Castel del Monte, Lacryma Christi—will work equally well with these pork chops.

Stuffed Pork Rolls

[BRACIOLE ALLA NAPOLETANA]

A very satisfying dish, and very easy to make. The whole process takes about 45 minutes. Beef fillets—round is a good cut—can be substituted for pork; they are a bit drier and not as sweet as pork, but the dish is still excellent.

2 tablespoons golden raisins	Freshly ground black pepper
¼ pound *prosciutto*	1 garlic clove
2 tablespoons pignoli	3 tablespoons olive oil
8 thin pork cutlets (about 1½ pounds)	2 teaspoons tomato paste
Salt	

Soften the raisins in hot water for 10 minutes, then drain and chop them together with the *prosciutto* and pignoli.

Pound the pork fillets to flatten them. Lightly salt and pepper them and spread the raisin mixture on them. Roll them up and secure each roll with a toothpick or string.

Halve the garlic clove. Brown it lightly in the olive oil in a large sauté pan, then press the pieces and discard them. Next, brown the *braciole* on all sides.

Dissolve the tomato paste in 1 cup of hot water and add it to the pan. Cover and cook at the lowest possible flame for about 30 minutes, turning the *braciole* every 10 minutes. Remove toothpicks or string, arrange the rolls on a serving plate, and pour the pan juices over them.

WINE SUGGESTION
  Choose either a full-bodied white like Regaleali or a soft, medium-bodied red such as Regaleali, Castel del Monte, or Lacryma Christi.

Vegetables Baked with Tomato and Cheeses
[VERDURE PIZZAIOLA]

This meatless country recipe makes a complete meal by itself. It can also, if need be, serve as a *contorno* with simple roast or grilled meats. This is not an elegant dish, but we have never seen anyone less than enthusiastic about it. Precise quantities are not crucial, so if you're a lover of potato or pepper or whatever, by all means add some more of your favorites to the mix. The dish requires a bit less than 1 hour of preparation and 1 hour of baking.

2 large potatoes	2 tablespoons minced fresh basil
2 small onions	2 teaspoons fresh oregano leaves
2 carrots	Salt
1 small eggplant	Freshly ground black pepper
3 small zucchini	1 pound *mozzarella*
2 green peppers	½ cup olive oil
¼ pound green beans	1 cup fine dry bread crumbs
2 large ripe tomatoes	1 cup freshly grated *parmigiano*

Peel and cut into ¼-inch slices the potatoes, onions, carrots, and eggplant. Drop the potato, carrot, and eggplant slices into boiling salted water and blanch 5 minutes, then drain.

Scrub the zucchini and slice them, unpeeled, into ¼ inch rounds. Wash and halve the green peppers, remove their seeds, and flatten the halves by slitting the ends. Wash and snap the green beans and cut each one in two pieces.

Drop the tomatoes into boiling water for 10 seconds, then drain, peel, and finely chop them. Put them in a small bowl and stir in the basil and oregano. Season with salt and pepper.

Chop the *mozzarella* or grate it coarsely. Preheat the oven to 375 degrees F.

(continued)

Film a large casserole with olive oil and lay in the potato slices. Put a few tablespoons of the tomato mixture on them, then sprinklings of bread crumbs, *mozzarella*, *parmigiano*, salt, and pepper; finally drizzle with olive oil. Continue with succeeding layers of carrot, onion, pepper, zucchini, eggplant, and green beans, adding the tomato, cheeses, and seasonings between each layer. The topmost coat should be a somewhat heavier dressing of the tomato, cheeses, and seasonings.

Bake uncovered for 1 hour. Serve hot, warm, or at room temperature.

WINE SUGGESTION
The robust flavor of this dish demands a good red wine. Regaleali, non-riserva Aglianico, or non-riserva Taurasi would all be fine choices.

Eggplant Baked with Mozzarella
[MELANZANE CON LA MOZZARELLA]

This is one of the many southern variations on the theme of eggplant and cheese. It can be served hot, warm, or at room temperature, and it makes an excellent *antipasto* as well. It takes 30 minutes to drain the eggplants and 30 to 40 minutes to cook them.

3 pounds eggplant	1 cup basic southern tomato sauce
Salt	(page 31)
1 pound *mozzarella*	1½ cups olive oil
2 eggs	5 to 6 tablespoons freshly grated
Freshly ground black pepper	*parmigiano*

Peel the eggplants and cut them into ½-inch-thick rounds. Salt them generously and let them sit on edge in a colander for 30 minutes. Cut the *mozzarella* into half as many slices as there are eggplant rounds. Beat the eggs together with a little salt and pepper and ½ cup of the tomato sauce.

When the 30 minutes are almost up, heat ½ inch of olive oil to 350 degrees F in a small, heavy-bottomed sauté pan. Dry the eggplant rounds with paper towels, pressing them firmly to get out as much liquid as possible. Fry them a few at a time until golden brown, and remove them to paper towels to drain.

Preheat the oven to 400 degrees F. Oil a baking dish just large enough to hold half the eggplant rounds. Lay them out in it. Cover each round with a

slice of *mozzarella* and top with the remaining half of the eggplant rounds.
Briefly beat the egg and tomato sauce mixture to recombine it and pour it over the eggplant. Top with the remaining tomato sauce and sprinkle on the grated cheese. Bake 15 minutes. Let cool briefly before serving.

WINE SUGGESTION
You can follow your own preference for color here. Simple whites like Cirò and Castel del Monte and Corvo taste fine with this dish, and so do simple reds of the same denominations.

CONTORNI

In many southern meals, especially during the summer and fall, the *contorni* steal the show from the *secondi*. Southern Italians love the bright, vivid flavor of fresh vegetables, and they consume them with enthusiasm, whether simply or elaborately cooked, whether prepared by themselves or in combination. It's really only a slight exaggeration to say that southern Italian dining habits are halfway to vegetarianism. Southern vegetables are treated with respect, with tact, and with style, as we hope the following recipes will show.

A good many of these *contorni* can be served at room temperature as *antipasto* dishes, just as many vegetable *antipasti*, in the South, may also appear at table as *contorni*. Beyond that, several of both are also eaten as light *secondi*. All in all, these are some of the most versatile preparations in the whole Italian repertoire.

———◆———

Baked Artichokes

[CARCIOFI ARROSTI]

This exquisitely simple preparation brings out all the rich fleshiness of artichokes and dresses them up with a delicate aroma of garlic. Boiling artichokes dissipates their flavor; baking concentrates it—and it also reduces substantially their antipathy to wine. This dish makes an excellent *antipasto*. About 1 hour cooking time, plus the time needed to trim the artichokes.

———◆———

4 large globe artichokes	2 teaspoons chopped parsley
4 garlic cloves	8 tablespoons olive oil

Preheat the oven to 400 degrees F. Rinse and drain the artichokes. Remove dry leaves from around the base of each one and trim the bases so they will stand straight. Cut the sharp tips off the ends of the leaves. Work your fingers into the heart of the artichoke and loosen the leaves all around, to open the flower somewhat.

Set the artichokes in a deep baking dish (one that can be covered). Peel and lightly crush the garlic cloves and put one into the center of each artichoke, along with ½ teaspoon of parsley and 1 tablespoon of olive oil. Drizzle the remaining oil over the outsides of the artichokes, or rub it over them with your hands.

Cover the dish and bake 45 to 60 minutes, until the artichokes are tender at the base, checking once or twice and basting with the oil and pan juices. Remove the artichokes to serving dishes, drizzle with the pan juices, and serve hot, warm, or at room temperature.

WINE SUGGESTION

A simple white wine will taste best with baked artichokes; Castel del Monte is a good choice, or Corvo.

Asparagus in Tomato Sauce
[ASPARAGI ALLA PUGLIESE]

This pleasant preparation is usually best appreciated at the height of asparagus season, when you've had enough simply prepared asparagus to want a change. It's a good way to use asparagus that have been sitting in your refrigerator longer than you intended: It freshens and enlivens them quite remarkably.

———◆———

1½ pounds thin asparagus (maximum ½-inch diameter at base)
4 tablespoons olive oil
2 tablespoons minced onion

1 tablespoon minced parsley
1 cup drained canned plum tomatoes, chopped
Salt

Wash the asparagus and snap off the hard parts at the base of the stalks. Bring a large pot of lightly salted water to a boil, add the asparagus, and cook for 10 minutes, until asparagus are not quite tender. Drain and spray them with cold water.

Warm 2 tablespoons of the olive oil in a sauté pan, add the onion and parsley, and sauté over moderate heat for 3 minutes. Add the tomatoes and ¼ teaspoon of salt. Cook 15 minutes.

In another pan, heat the remaining 2 tablespoons of olive oil. Add the drained asparagus and turn them gently in the oil for 2 minutes. Add the tomato sauce, mix well, and cook 2 to 3 minutes longer. Serve at once.

WINE SUGGESTION

Follow the suggestions for your secondo.

Al Cirillo's Beans

[FAGIOLI AL CIRILLO]

This recipe derives from an old friend and one of the best cooks we know, Professor A. R. Cirillo of Northwestern University. He in turn learned it from his mother, who learned it from hers, and so on, probably (with the exception of the tomatoes) back to the time when Naples was founded, if not before that.

2 pounds fresh cranberry beans
½ pound plum tomatoes
1 cup chopped onion
3 garlic cloves, minced
½ cup olive oil

Broth, optional (page 45)
½ teaspoon salt
Freshly ground black pepper
2 to 3 tablespoons chopped parsley

Shell and rinse the beans. Drop the tomatoes into boiling water for 10 seconds, then drain, peel, seed, and roughly chop them.

Sauté the onion and garlic in the olive oil for 3 minutes. Add the beans. Cook, stirring, for 3 minutes, then add the tomatoes and ½ cup water or broth. Cover and simmer, stirring often, for 30 to 45 minutes, or until the beans are tender. Add a little broth or water, if necessary, to prevent the beans from drying out. Just before serving, taste for seasoning, add salt and pepper to taste, and stir in the chopped parsley.

WINE SUGGESTION
Follow the suggestions for your secondo.

Broccoli in White Wine

[BROCCOLI AL VINO BIANCO]

This is a down-home way of treating broccoli that remarkably sharpens its flavor. About 10 minutes' preparation time, 30 minutes' maximum cooking time.

3 pounds broccoli
¾ cup olive oil
1½ tablespoons minced garlic

Salt
Freshly ground black pepper
¾ cup dry white wine

Put the broccoli heads on a cutting board and cut off the stems just where they begin to branch. Separate the upper halves into florets and wash them carefully. Trim the dry base off the lower halves and peel the stalks, going deep enough to remove all the tough parts. Cut the peeled stems into 2- to 3-inch lengths and add them to the florets.

Heat the olive oil in a large pot. When it is very hot, turn off heat, stir in the minced garlic, then add the broccoli and toss it vigorously to coat all the pieces with oil. Salt and pepper generously.

Put the pot back onto high heat. As soon as the oil begins to sizzle again, add the white wine, stir everything once, and cover the pot. Lower heat to medium and braise, stirring from time to time, about 20 minutes, until broccoli is tender but still crunchy. Transfer the broccoli to a heated serving dish and pour on any liquid remaining in the pot.

WINE SUGGESTION
Follow the suggestions for your secondo.

Carrots in Marsala

[CAROTE IN MARSALA]

Another simple, classic preparation: The interplay of the vegetable sweetness of the carrots and the wine-richness of the Marsala is very, very pleasing. A very gentle flame is the only trick here, to "sweat out" the carrots' own juices so that their flavor is never diluted by water.

1½ pounds carrots	Salt
¼ pound butter	¼ cup dry Marsala

Peel the carrots and slice them very thin—e.g., using the 2-millimeter blade on a food processor.

Melt the butter in a heavy-bottomed pan. Add the carrots and toss to coat them with the butter. Cover and cook over low heat for 30 to 40 minutes, or until the carrots are tender and their own liquid has been absorbed.

Uncover the pan and turn heat to medium. Lightly salt the carrots and add the Marsala. Cook, stirring, for 1 to 2 minutes, until the Marsala is completely reduced. Serve at once.

WINE SUGGESTION
Follow the suggestions for your secondo.

Deep-Fried Eggplant
[MELANZANE FRITTE]

Deep-fried eggplant is easy to make and quite delicious. Any leftovers can be sprinkled lightly with good vinegar and a mincing of fresh herbs (mint or thyme are excellent), covered overnight with plastic-wrap, and served next day as an *antipasto* or cold side dish.

———◆———

4 small eggplants (about ¾ pound)   Oil for deep-frying
Salt

Peel the eggplants and slice them into ½-inch rounds. Salt them heavily and stand them in a colander in the sink to drain for 1 hour. Then dry them with paper towels, pressing them firmly to remove their remaining liquid.

Heat frying oil to 375 degrees F. Fry the eggplant slices, a few at a time, for about 2 minutes, until deep golden on both sides. Drain on paper towels.

WINE SUGGESTION
Follow the suggestions for your secondo. *If you are serving these eggplants as an* antipasto, *accompany them with a well-chilled white wine such as Lacryma Christi or Castel del Monte.*

Potato Salad with Hot-Pepper Oil
[PATATE AL DIAVOLICCHIO]

The South's beloved hot red pepper, *il diavolillo*, has the starring role in this fine hot-weather dish, which is especially good with the season's first, freshly dug, new potatoes. The boiled, sliced potatoes are dressed only with salt and olive oil in which a *peperoncino rosso* has been seethed. The result is not a fiery hotness but a mellow warmth that enriches the potatoes' own flavor. Very nice with simply grilled or broiled meats.

———◆———

1½ pounds small boiling potatoes   ⅓ cup olive oil
Salt   1 *peperoncino rosso*

Boil the potatoes whole in their jackets in salted water until just tender. Let them cool briefly, then peel and cut them into ⅓-inch slices. Lay them out in a broad serving dish, sprinkle them generously with salt, and let them cool completely.

Just before serving, heat the olive oil in a small pan. When it is just short of smoking, add the *peperoncino*, and as soon as the pepper darkens, pour the hot oil over the potatoes and serve at once. Discard the *peperoncino*.

WINE SUGGESTION
Follow the suggestions for your secondo.

Boiled Potatoes with Herb Dressing
[INSALATA DI PATATE]

Parsley, mint, a touch of garlic, and *peperoncino rosso* combine to make a vibrant dressing for boiled potatoes, served either hot or cool. As with the preceding recipe, this dish is at its best with the season's first, freshly dug potatoes, but the herb dressing will liven up a potato of any age. The dish also works well as the base for a summer lunch or picnic dish; add to it canned Italian tuna and/or hard-boiled eggs, with fresh tomatoes to accompany and good bread on the side.

———————◆———————

1½ pounds small boiling potatoes
1 tablespoon chopped parsley
1 tablespoon chopped mint
1 garlic clove

1 *peperoncino rosso*
3 tablespoons olive oil
½ teaspoon salt

Boil the potatoes in their jackets in lightly salted water until done. While they are cooking, purée all the remaining ingredients in a mortar, food processor, or blender.

As soon as the potatoes are tender, drain, peel, and cut them into ⅓-inch slices. Toss them gently but thoroughly with the dressing. Serve at once or cooled to room temperature.

WINE SUGGESTION
Follow the suggestions for your secondo.

Baked, Sliced Potatoes and Tomatoes

[PATATE IN TEGAME]

A Calabrese summer potato dish, best made when tomatoes are bursting-ripe and most flavorful. Americans rarely think of combining potatoes with tomatoes; this dish should therefore provide food for thought as well as for the palate. It needs about 1 hour from start to finish.

———————————◆———————————

1½ pounds potatoes	2 tablespoons grated *pecorino*
2 garlic cloves	*romano*
¾ pound large ripe tomatoes	4 to 5 tablespoons olive oil
Salt	

Preheat the oven to 350 degrees F. Peel the potatoes and cut them into ½-inch slices. Sliver the garlic cloves. Drop the tomatoes into boiling water for 10 seconds, then drain, peel, and slice them thick.

Oil a large baking dish. Spread the potato slices in it in a single layer. Salt them lightly. Top with the tomato slices and salt them lightly as well. Strew the garlic slivers over the tomatoes, sprinkle on the *pecorino*, and drizzle on the olive oil.

Bake 45 minutes, checking every so often and adding a little hot water if the dish appears to be drying out. Let cool 10 minutes before serving.

WINE SUGGESTION
Follow the suggestions for your secondo.

Baked Peppers

[PEPERONI AL FORNO]

Italian frying peppers are the thin-fleshed, long-bodied (in proportion to their width) variety that are sometimes, because of their appearance, mistaken for chili peppers or banana peppers. Rest assured: Frying peppers are not hot but sweet, deliciously so. They are usually harvested and sold when light green, but there is absolutely nothing wrong with the flavor of red ones, should they be available. This simple roasting yields a delicious *contorno* or a pleasing *antipasto*, as you choose. A little charring of the skin does no harm: Some people think it enriches the taste.

———————————◆———————————

8 to 12 firm, glossy, light green	Salt	301
Italian-style frying peppers	Freshly ground black pepper	*Contorni*
¼ cup olive oil		

Preheat the oven to 375 degrees F. Wash and dry the peppers. Oil a gratin dish. Using your hands, rub olive oil over all the surfaces of the peppers. Arrange them in the dish and sprinkle lightly with salt and pepper.

Bake 15 to 20 minutes, until they soften and wrinkle; turn them once if they darken too fast. Serve hot, warm, or at room temperature.

WINE SUGGESTION

To accompany these peppers as antipasto, *either a light white or red will do: Cirò, Castel del Monte, Corvo. When they are served as* contorno, *follow the suggestions for your* secondo.

Pepper Stew

[PEPERONATA]

This is another classic pepper preparation, found all through southern Italy. Because you don't want to overpower the taste of the peppers, the best onions to use for this dish are the small fresh white ones that look like giant scallions; their heads are about 2 inches in diameter, with fresh green stems attached. Unfortunately, their season is fairly short, so if you can't find them, use large, sweet Bermuda onions.

1½ pounds bell peppers, preferably	½ cup olive oil
mixed red, yellow, and green	1 bay leaf
1¼ pounds fresh ripe tomatoes	Salt
½ pound onions (see note above)	Freshly ground black pepper
2 garlic cloves	

Wash the peppers, quarter them, and remove the seeds and membrane. Wash and quarter the tomatoes. If you are using fresh white onions, wash and trim them like scallions, cut off roots and stems, and quarter them lengthwise, leaving a bit of the hard base on each to hold the pieces together. If you are using larger onions, cut them into pieces about 2 inches in diameter. Slice the garlic cloves lengthwise into several pieces each.

In a pan large enough to hold all the ingredients, warm the olive oil and add the onion, garlic, and bay leaf. Sauté gently for 5 minutes. Add the peppers, season them with salt and pepper, and cook over medium heat 10 minutes, turning them often. Add the tomatoes and continue cooking, uncovered, adjusting heat to maintain a simmer and stirring often, until the peppers are fully tender—about 15 minutes.

WINE SUGGESTION
Follow the suggestions for your secondo.

Sautéed Zucchini
[ZUCCHINI IN PADELLA]

This is the way zucchini is prepared in southern homes most of the time. It is the simplest and often the tastiest of the scores of Italian zucchini preparations.

6 small zucchini (1½ pounds)	2 tablespoons chopped parsley
3 garlic cloves	Salt
4 tablespoons olive oil	Freshly ground black pepper
1 *peperoncino rosso*	

Scrub the zucchini, dry them, and slice them ¼ inch thin or thinner. Slice the garlic thin.

Warm the olive oil in a sauté pan, add the garlic and the *peperoncino,* and sauté over medium heat until the garlic is lightly golden. You may discard the *peperoncino* at this point if you wish. Raise heat somewhat and add the zucchini, turning them several times to coat them with the oil. Sauté, regulating heat and turning often, for 15 to 20 minutes, or until the zucchini are all wilted and some have begun to brown. Stir in the parsley, lightly salt and pepper, toss everything together, and serve.

WINE SUGGESTION
Follow the suggestions for your secondo.

Cianfotta

Every southern province has its own spelling and pronunciation of *cianfotta* (*ciambotta* in Calabria, *ciammotta* in Basilicata, and so on) and its own recipe for the dish. The basic premise, however, remains the same: Take a mixture of vegetables at their seasonal best, cook them briefly together, and enjoy the result. Dishes like this, accompanied by a lot of sturdy country bread, are often served as a light meatless lunch or supper. You can easily perform all the necessary peeling and slicing during the hour the eggplants are draining. The actual cooking takes not quite 45 minutes.

¾ pound eggplant	5 to 6 large basil leaves
Salt	Few sprigs of parsley
1 pound bell peppers	1 garlic clove
1 large potato (⅓ to ½ pound)	3 tablespoons olive oil
½ pound onions	Freshly ground black pepper
¼ to ⅓ pound tomatoes	

Wash and trim the eggplant. Cut it into ½-inch slices. Salt them well, stand them in a colander, and let them drain for an hour. Then dry them with paper towels, pressing to remove as much liquid as possible.

Peel and dice the potato. Wash and core the peppers and cut them into 1-inch squares. Slice the onions. Drop the tomatoes into boiling water for 10 seconds, then drain, peel, seed, and roughly chop them. Chop the basil and parsley together.

Soften the onion with the garlic in the olive oil in a broad sauté pan. Add the eggplant, peppers, potatoes, tomatoes, ½ teaspoon salt, and several grindings of pepper. Cook, covered, at low heat, stirring occasionally, for 30 minutes.

Uncover the pan, raise the heat to medium-high, and stir until remaining pan liquid evaporates. Stir in the parsley and basil, and transfer the vegetables to a serving dish.

Allow to cool partially before serving. The dish is also good at room temperature.

WINE SUGGESTION

If served as a secondo, *accompany* cianfotta *with a light red wine such as Castel del Monte or Corvo. If it is a* contorno, *follow the suggestions for your* secondo.

DOLCI

Desserts in the South differ from those of the rest of Italy only in the variety of the fruits that are offered. Figs are much more common, dates frequent, and in Sicily even such exotica as prickly pears make an appearance. In the abundance of the growing season, fruits are often dried, to reappear months afterward, briefly freshened and plumped in—or long and lavishly steeped in—wine or spirits. We can accomplish much the same here in the United States, working with good-quality dried fruits (those sold in bulk in fancy-food stores, not those found on supermarket shelves in hermetically sealed boxes). Steamed for five minutes and then covered with red wine to marinate for a few hours (or all day), dried fruits become a very presentable family dessert. Almost all dried fruits, especially figs and peaches, take well to the red-wine treatment. Several other combinations are particularly pleasing.

- Prunes in dry Marsala
- Apricots in maraschino
- Peaches in red Italian vermouth
- Pears in white Italian vermouth—probably the best combination of them all

As elsewhere, sweet wines—Marsala and Passito—are just as often substituted for dessert as drunk with it.

———————◆———————

Strawberries in Orange Juice
[FRAGOLE ALL'ARANCIA]

This is Sicily's favorite way of serving strawberries, as compared to *al limone* (with sugar and lemon juice) or *con panna* (with whipped cream) that are the alternatives offered most everywhere else in Italy in strawberry season. Fine as those are, this orange-juice treatment is quite intriguing. In Sicily they use blood oranges, but even our Florida juicers give an unexpected sweet tang to the berries. Look for the small, plump, very dark red variety of strawberry, which seems to have a more intense flavor than the larger, paler kind. And, of course, eliminate the sugar if both the berries and the orange juice are very sweet in themselves.

¼ cup freshly squeezed orange juice   1 pint ripe strawberries
   (juice of 1 small or ½ large orange)
1 teaspoon granulated sugar

Put the orange juice into a bowl and dissolve the sugar in it.

Hull and briefly rinse the strawberries. Halve or even quarter them if they are very large, and add them to the bowl with the orange juice. Mix thoroughly and chill at least 30 minutes before serving.

Zabaglione
[ZABAIONE]

Zabaione is surely southern Italy's—maybe all Italy's—most famous dessert, and with good reason. The smoothness and lightness of the wine-and-egg-yolk foam are marvelously delicate grace notes on which to end a meal. While Marsala is the traditional wine to use in *zabaione*, the dish can be prepared with any good sweet wine, such as a Passito or—to be completely extra-territorial—a Vin Santo or even a California late-harvest wine. If you happen to be pandering to an utterly decadent sweet tooth, you can nestle a ball of ice cream in the bottom of each goblet before pouring in the foamy custard. *Zabaione* takes only 10 to 15 minutes to make, from separating the eggs to serving.

3 egg yolks   ⅓ cup dry Marsala
3 tablespoons granulated sugar

Put the egg yolks and sugar in the top of a double boiler. With a wire whisk or hand-held electric mixer, beat until they become a pale cream.

Set the mixture over boiling water. Add the Marsala and continue beating until the cream foams, swells, and mounts into a smooth custardy mound— about 3 minutes.

Scoop the *zabaione* into 4 large goblets and serve at once, possibly with a crisp nut cookie alongside.

WINE SUGGESTION

Serve whatever wine you use in making the zabaione.

Coffee Custard

[COVIGLIE AL CAFFE]

A gentle, coffee-flavored custard, one of the most soothing desserts you'll find anywhere. It should be made well in advance and allowed to firm for several hours in the refrigerator. *Piccoli napoletani* (page 308) are the traditional accompaniment to *coviglie al caffe*.

---

1 cup milk
1 piece of vanilla bean, about
  2 inches long
⅓ cup granulated sugar
2 teaspoons instant *espresso*
  coffee granules

2 egg yolks
1 tablespoon flour
1 cup heavy cream
12 to 16 whole Italian-roast coffee
  beans

Put ¾ cup of the milk, the vanilla bean, and the sugar in the top of a double boiler. Over direct heat, bring the milk to a simmer, stirring to dissolve the sugar. When the milk is simmering, stir in the instant espresso, turn off heat, and set aside.

In a large bowl, beat the egg yolks with a wire whisk until just blended. Gradually beat in first the flour, then 3 tablespoons of cold milk. When the mixture is smooth, gently beat in the hot, flavored milk, a little at a time, trying to avoid a build-up of foam. Discard the vanilla bean.

Pour the mixture back into the top of the double boiler and set it over boiling water. Cook 2 to 3 minutes, stirring constantly, until the custard thickens. Remove from heat and let cool completely, stirring occasionally to dissolve any skin that forms on top.

Whip ½ cup of the cream and delicately fold it into the cooled custard. Divide the mixture among 4 attractive dessert dishes and chill it for at least 3 hours.

When ready to serve, whip the remaining ½ cup cream and mound it over the custard. Garnish the tops with a few whole coffee beans.

WINE SUGGESTION
A sweet or dry Marsala Superiore or a small glass of Passito would go very nicely, particularly with the piccoli napoletani.

Chocolate Pudding

[SANGUINACCIO]

Sanguinaccio is a traditional southern dessert, always served on great occasions like Carnevale. Everyone who tastes it loves it. But such is the world we live in, that half the people who find out what goes into it never willingly eat it again. True *sanguinaccio* is made with pig's blood, which it converts into the world's richest, most luscious chocolate pudding. But we aren't going to ask that of you. This recipe is for *sanguinaccio senza sangue*, without the blood. Even the most squeamish ought to enjoy everything about it but its name. About a half hour for cooking, plus time for the pudding to chill thoroughly.

———————◆———————

1½ ounces candied citron and orange peel	1½ tablespoons flour
1 tablespoon butter	1 tablespoon cornstarch
1½ ounces unsweetened cocoa	2 cups milk
1 cup granulated sugar	1 teaspoon vanilla extract
	¼ teaspoon ground cinnamon

Finely chop the citron and orange peel. Melt the butter.

Mix the cocoa, sugar, flour, and cornstarch thoroughly in a large bowl. Gradually add the milk, stirring carefully to avoid lumps. Stir in ½ teaspoon of the vanilla, the cinnamon, and the melted butter.

Strain the mixture into a heavy-bottomed pan and cook over low heat, stirring, until it comes to a boil. Off heat, stir in the chopped candied fruits and the remaining ½ teaspoon vanilla. Transfer to a large serving bowl and chill thoroughly before serving.

Mount Vesuvius

[MONTE VESUVIO]

This dessert was the whimsy of a Neapolitan restaurateur. It is the cousin, and the reverse, of *Monte Bianco*. The latter shows a dark base with white snow (cream, that is) atop, while *Monte Vesuvio* shows a white base of sweetened fresh *ricotta* and a dark top of chestnut "lava." The imagery is a bit strained, but consuming this serendipitous mixture of *ricotta* and chestnut is no strain at all. Except for the time needed to chill the sweetened *ricotta*, this recipe is almost quicker to make than to read.

(continued)

| 1 pound *ricotta* (2 cups) | 1 tablespoon granulated sugar |
| 2 tablespoons sweet Marsala | 1 jar (12 ounces) marrons glacés |

Beat the *ricotta* until smooth and light. Beat in the Marsala and sugar. Refrigerate until serving time.

Drain the chestnuts, reserving their syrup. Grate 4 to 6 chestnuts into fluffy shreds (the coarse blade of a rotary grater works well).

Form the *ricotta* into conical mounds on 4 dessert plates. Top with the shredded chestnut. Drizzle a teaspoon of the chestnut syrup over the top of each mound and another teaspoon (or more, if desired) in a pool around the base of each.

Neapolitan Almond Cookies

[PICCOLI NAPOLETANI]

These "little Neapolitans" love *coviglie al caffe* (page 306) almost as much as their human namesakes do. This recipe makes about 4 dozen, and they keep well for a long time in a tightly covered tin.

6 ounces chilled butter	1 cup granulated sugar
8 ounces blanched almonds	1 whole egg plus 1 yolk
1 cup flour	¼ teaspoon vanilla extract

Cut the butter into 12 to 16 pieces. Grate the almonds into light fluffy particles (a small rotary grater works well).

Stir the almonds, flour, and sugar together in a large bowl. Cut the butter into the mixture, as in making pastry, to obtain an oatmeal texture.

Beat together the whole egg, the extra yolk, and the vanilla. Stir them into the dry ingredients, mixing only until the dough holds together. If necessary, add a few drops of water to bring the mass together. Gather the dough into a ball, wrap it in wax paper, and refrigerate it for 1 hour.

Preheat the oven to 375 degrees F. Butter and flour 2 large baking sheets. Divide the dough into several pieces. Roll them out on a floured surface to a thickness of ⅜ inch. Cut rounds with a 2-inch cookie cutter and delicately— because the dough is very tender—transfer them to the baking sheets. With a 1-inch cutter, cut "doughnut holes" in the circles. Remove the inside circles of dough, knead them together with remaining scraps of dough, then roll and cut more cookies.

Bake each sheet of cookies for 6 to 7 minutes, or until lightly browned. Watch them carefully because they burn easily. As soon as the cookies are done, remove them from the baking sheet and cool them on a spread-out dish towel.

WINE SUGGESTION
Marsala, sweet or dry.

Cinnamon-Anise Biscuits
[BISCOTTI DI SAN FRANCESCO]

These austere-looking plain brown cookies were probably named for the simple brown habits of the Franciscan friars, but there's nothing austere about their cinnamon-anise spiciness. Make them up in quantity and keep them handy in a tin for as long as they last. These quantities will yield 2 to 2½ dozen.

1¾ cups flour	5 tablespoons vegetable shortening
6 tablespoons granulated sugar	6 to 7 tablespoons water
1 package dry yeast	4 teaspoons aniseed, crushed
⅛ teaspoon ground cinnamon	

Butter 2 baking sheets. Stir together in a bowl the flour, sugar, yeast, and cinnamon. Cut in the shortening and work as for pastry, to obtain an oatmeal texture.

Gradually mix in the water, until a smooth dough forms. Knead 5 minutes. Add the crushed aniseed and knead 5 minutes longer.

Pull off scant tablespoonfuls of the dough. Roll them between your hands or on a work surface into cylinders about 3 inches long and ½ inch in diameter. (The texture of the dough will be very much like modeling clay, and it can be worked just as easily.) Lay them on the baking sheets 2 inches apart.

When all the *biscotti* are formed, cover the baking sheets with a clean dish towel and leave them to rise in a warm place until double in bulk, about 3 hours.

Preheat the oven to 300 degrees F. Put in the baking sheets and bake 25 to 35 minutes, until the *biscotti* are lightly browned. Cool them on a rack, then put them in a tin for 24 hours before eating. They keep well.

Sweet Biscuit Rings

[TARALLI DOLCI]

The dough for these simple cookies is just as malleable as the previous recipe's; in fact, the method of handling starts out very similarly. It doesn't stay that way, however. The *taralli*, which look like baby bagels, get treated like bagels—a quick boiling before their baking. The rum transmutes into a subtle fragrance for the savory little rings.

1⅓ cups flour	3 tablespoons rum
3½ tablespoons granulated sugar	1 teaspoon lemon juice
¼ teaspoon salt	4 tablespoons water
2 tablespoons vegetable shortening	

Preheat the oven to 350 degrees F. Mix the flour, sugar, and salt together. Cut in the shortening as if making pastry. Mix the rum, lemon juice, and water together in a cup. Stir them into the dry ingredients and knead thoroughly to form a firm, elastic dough.

Divide the dough into 20 nuggets. Take one and roll it, first between your palms and then on a very lightly floured board, into a cylinder about 5 inches long and as big around as your little finger. (You should be able to work the dough like modeling clay.) Bend it into a ring and press it closed. Form the remaining *taralli* in the same way.

Bring a large pot of water to the boil. A few at a time, drop the *taralli* into the boiling water and cook them for 2 minutes. Drain them briefly on paper towels, then arrange them on a greased baking sheet.

Bake for 1 hour. Cool on a rack. These will keep well for a long time in a covered tin.

Pastiera Napoletana

This elaborate and exhilarating pastry used to be prepared with pride every Easter in every Neapolitan home. Being a very time-consuming preparation, it tends to be bought more often than made these days, even in its ancestral *paese*. But as a bow to tradition and a safeguard against the passing of yet one more endangered species, here is the whole, authentic recipe. Quantities given are enough for an 11-inch round pastry. Anything smaller would be unworthy of Easter!

The two characteristic ingredients of *pastiera* are orange-flower (or rose) water, and *grano*, which is a type of soft white wheat kernel that is beginning to be available in this country in Italian specialty stores and sometimes even in health-food stores. In a pinch, you can substitute a light orange liqueur, like Triple Sec, for the orange-flower water, but without *grano* you cannot make a *pastiera*.

FOR THE PREPARATION OF THE *GRANO*

½ pound *grano*
2 cups milk
Peel of ½ lemon

1 piece of cinnamon bark, about
   1 inch long
1 tablespoon granulated sugar
⅛ teaspoon salt

FOR THE PASTRY CRUST

2 cups flour
¾ cups granulated sugar

5 ounces vegetable shortening
3 egg yolks

FOR THE PASTRY FILLING

3 ounces mixed candied citron and
   orange peel
4 whole eggs plus 2 extra whites
1 pound *ricotta*

1 cup granulated sugar
⅛ teaspoon cinnamon
2 tablespoons orange-flower water or
   Triple Sec
Grated peel of ½ lemon

Prepare the grano:

Soak the *grano* in water to cover for 8 days, changing the water every day.

Drain it and weigh out 9 ounces into a heavy-bottomed pot. Cover the *grano* with cold water, bring to a boil, and boil 15 minutes. Bring the milk to a boil in another pot.

Drain the *grano* after 15 minutes, return it to its pot, and pour on the boiling milk. Add the lemon peel, cinnamon, sugar, and salt. Cover and cook at a slow boil until all the milk has been absorbed—about 2 hours. Spread the *grano* out on a plate to cool. Discard the lemon peel and cinnamon.

Make the pastry:

Blend the flour and sugar together. Cut in the shortening, mixing to the consistency of coarse meal. Beat the egg yolks together in a bowl and stir them gradually into the flour mixture, mixing only long enough to gather it into a dough. Add cold water by teaspoonfuls, if necessary, to incorporate all the dry ingredients. Wrap the ball of dough in wax paper and refrigerate it at least 1 hour.

(continued)

Finish the pastiera:

Preheat the oven to 375 degrees F. Chop the candied citron and lemon peel until fine. Separate the eggs. In a large bowl, mix together the egg yolks, candied fruits, and all the remaining filling ingredients together with the prepared *grano*.

Roll the pastry between wax paper to a thickness of ⅛ inch. Line an 11-inch round baking dish with it, cutting off excess and gathering it back up into a dough.

Whip the egg whites into soft peaks and fold them into the *grano* mixture. Transfer the mixture to the prepared dish and smooth the surface. Roll out the remaining dough, cut it into ½-inch strips, and delicately lay a lattice across the top of the filling.

Bake 1½ hours, until the top is a rich golden brown and a skewer or toothpick inserted between the lattice strips comes out clean. Let the *pastiera* sit 24 hours before serving.

WINE SUGGESTION:
The intense sweetness of a Passito makes a perfect match with pastiera.

Ricotta Cake

[TORTA CON LA RICOTTA]

Despite the fact that there's cheese in it, this qualifies as a cake rather than a cheesecake. It makes a pleasing, moist cake and a light, elegant dessert.

———————◆———————

4 eggs	1 cup flour
¾ cups granulated sugar	1 teaspoon baking powder
½ pound *ricotta*	4 tablespoons pignoli
Grated rind of ½ lemon	

Preheat the oven to 350 degrees F. Bring the eggs to room temperature and separate them. Butter and flour a 9-inch pie dish.

Beat the egg yolks together with the sugar until the mixture is pale yellow and creamy. Push the *ricotta* through a sieve into the egg-mixture. Add the grated lemon rind and stir all together well. Sift the flour and baking powder into the *ricotta* mixture, a little at a time, stirring to mix thoroughly.

Whip the egg whites until firm but not dry. Stir a quarter of them into the *ricotta* mixture, along with 1 tablespoon of the pignoli. Then gently fold in the remaining egg whites.

Transfer the mixture to the prepared pie dish, smooth the surface, and strew the remaining pignoli over the top. Bake 30 minutes, or until top is golden. Serve warm or cold.

WINE SUGGESTION

A glass of Marsala Superiore, dry or sweet according to your preference, will taste very welcome alongside this cake.

APPENDIX

ON WINE-FOOD PAIRINGS, WINE TASTING, AND WINE CELLARS

Throughout this book, we've given you suggestions for combining dishes and wines of the same region. Most of these have been traditional pairings, juxtaposing foods and wines that have evolved together over the centuries. That long symbiosis makes them natural partners, and it works to give you some very satisfactory dining. But traditional doesn't mean compulsory, and the fact that those combinations work well doesn't mean that others won't provide equal pleasure. There is no reason in the world why you shouldn't feel free to cross regional or international borders in matching foods and wines.

This is easiest to do at the level of relatively simple, everyday wines. You need have no qualms whatever about drinking, let us say, a northern Soave either with a dish from the Center, where we've suggested a Frascati, or with a recipe from the South, where we've called for a white Cirò. Similarly, the Frascati or Cirò can stand in equally well for the Soave or for each other. This same flexibility holds true for simple reds. A young Chianti can be interchanged with a Barbera, just as a Castel del Monte can substitute for a Montepulciano d'Abruzzo or a Dolcetto or young Merlot, and vice versa. You could even try a young California Zinfandel instead of any of these wines. (The grape has Italian grandparents, after all.) In each case, you won't get exactly the same food-and-wine synergy you would with the regionally authentic pairing, but you will still get a very pleasing interplay—and it is entirely possible that your palate will prefer the less traditional combination.

At the level of grander wines and more complex dishes, you have to exercise more care and greater discrimination in making changes in the traditional pairings. True, there are some dishes—the guinea hen with cabbage and mushrooms, for instance—with which a Taurasi or a Brunello could replace a Barolo. But there are also others—*la finanziera* springs to mind—where, as satisfying as either Taurasi or Brunello might be, a Barolo or Barbaresco would give you still more. By the same token, a Barolo or Barbaresco might taste fine alongside a stuffed beef roll but unpleasantly tannic and harsh with a stuffed veal roll. With complex wines and complex dishes, the palatal chemistry gets a lot more finicky and precise.

So how do you find out about these things if you don't already know them? The awful truth, dear reader, is that there is no way to learn but to eat and drink—and remember. And if you can't remember (what *was* that lovely white wine you had last week?), take notes. Write down the names of wines, their producers, the foods you had with them, and your impressions. It takes two minutes, but once you've done it you've got the information forever.

You can arm yourself in advance with some knowledge of the sorts of wines that you prefer, or the sorts that will be compatible with a dinner you want to serve, by doing a little comparative wine tasting. This is definitely not a hardship. The process is not difficult and the occasion need not be solemn. All you need are the wines about which you feel some curiosity (as few as two), clean glasses, a white tablecloth and good light (to enable you to see the wines' color clearly), and a pad and pencil. A receptacle to spit in is not a bad idea, especially if you have ambitions of tasting a lot of wines, and a corkscrew is, of course, a necessity. But that's all. With that little, you're equipped to taste wines like a professional.

Professional tasting technique is equally easy:

- Pour one or two ounces of each wine into the glasses.
- Pick up a glass by the stem and hold it so the light falls directly on and through the wine. Look at it. You're looking for brilliance and clarity. Whether it's white, red, or rosé, the wine should be clean, bright, and clear. Muddiness or cloudiness are bad signs, as is brownness in dry whites or young reds. Jot down on your pad what you see.
- Swirl the wine gently in the glass (a slight wrist motion should do it) to release its aroma, and smell it, breathing in deeply. Try to put a name to what you smell—fruits, flowers, vegetables, road tar, tobacco, whatever. Write down what you discern.
- Now take a sip of the wine. Roll it all over your tongue. Let it touch all the taste receptors in your mouth, and try to verbalize what you're tasting. Is it fruit, or bread, or nuts? Whatever you taste, write it down.
- Pay attention to the wine's finish, the flavor that persists in your mouth after you swallow or spit out your wine. The better the wine, the more

persistent, pleasing, and/or interesting its finish should be. Write that down too.

• Add your overall impression of the wine, and then go through the same procedure—it takes more time to describe than to do—for your other wine(s).

If you've never done anything like this before, the first thing that's going to strike you is how placing two wines side by side enables you to taste more perceptively than you ever thought you could. Just by the contrasts, you're made aware of details and flavors that you otherwise wouldn't notice at all or wouldn't pay attention to. The second thing you'll be struck by is how comparative tasting guides you to verbalize taste sensations and differences that you didn't think you could ever articulate. Just having a pole of comparison enables you, at very least, to say that #1 is drier or sweeter, sharper or smoother, lighter or heavier, than wine #2. From there it's an easy step to decide that you'd rather drink wine #1 with a delicately breaded veal chop and wine #2 with a hearty oxtail stew. And don't forget to write that decision down, too, for future use.

Comparative tasting is the very best possible way to teach yourself about wine. You can do it alone, or with your spouse, or with friends. As you grow more confident, you can organize your tastings around the wines of a vintage (half a dozen 1986 whites, for instance) or a region (different Chianti zones, or Sicilian white wines) or a varietal (different Dolcettos or Pinot biancos of the same vintage). Or you can try what is called a vertical tasting—a tasting of the same wine in successive vintages—to learn how a particular wine changes with age. Vertical tastings can tell you a lot about when it's best to drink some wines, notably big, full-bodied reds, like Barolo or Amarone or Brunello, or such complex whites as Pomino and Gavi and Fiano.

Once you've reached that stage of expertise—and probably a lot sooner—you're going to want to have an available supply of the wines you're discovering you like. You'll no longer be satisfied with the hit-or-miss wine selection method (dashing out on the day of a dinner and, if you're lucky, finding the wine you want, and if you're not, making do with whatever your retailer has in stock). Being a canny shopper, you will have noticed that as fine wines get older, their prices rise in the wine shops. And you will have noticed, too, that most wine shops give nice discounts—10 or 15 percent is normal—on purchases of full cases of any wines. All this will naturally suggest to you the usefulness of establishing a wine cellar: you'll save money on wines you drink often and on wines you mature yourself, and you'll enjoy the ease and pleasure of having readily available the wines you want, when you want them.

There are lots of myths about the care of fine wine, and one of the most exaggerated is the "cobwebbed cellar cut out of the living rock" notion. A wine cellar need not literally be a cellar. A relatively cool space, out of direct sunlight, where the temperature does not vary suddenly or dramatically over the course of the year, and where the wines will be free from vibrations—any such space can become a perfectly usable wine cellar.

An *ideal* cellar would be completely dark, at a constant temperature of about 50 degrees, and with a comfortable humidity. But that is an ideal; it becomes a necessity only if you want to lay down wine for your grandchildren to enjoy. Under those conditions, great red wines and complex whites mature very, very slowly. Brunello from a great vintage under circumstances like those will live a century, Barolo fifty years. But the trade-off is that neither will be in prime condition until it's twenty-five or thirty years old.

Heat is the major element in maturing wines. Keep them in a warmer place and they mature faster, are readier to drink sooner, and of course will fade sooner. Keep them in a very warm place and the cycle is so accelerated that the wine can be ruined. White wines are particularly susceptible to such destruction; they turn brown, oxidize, and die very quickly when stored in real heat. Red wines don't kill quite so quickly, but heat dramatically affects their taste and shortens their life spans.

For most people, the goal of cellaring, beyond simply keeping a supply of wine on hand, is to obtain affordable access to mature wines to drink within their lifetimes. This means that less-than-ideal cellaring conditions may very well be perfectly adequate. A corner of the basement, away from the oil burner and water heater and the washing machine and drier, or a solidly built interior closet away from heat risers, hot water pipes, and elevator shafts, can serve perfectly well to keep wines for drinking next week and wines for drinking twenty years hence.

Once you've got the space reserved, then you need to choose the wines to put in it. A well-balanced cellar of Italian wines should hold a selection usable for three broad purposes: (1) wines for aperitif and everyday drinking—light whites and simple, fruity reds; (2) wines for better-than-average dinners—fuller-bodied, complex whites, and medium- to full-bodied reds of some aging ability; and (3) wines for exceptional or important dinners (a few very fine white wines and the great, long-aging reds).

Below is a representative selection of Italian wines for a well-rounded small cellar. All three categories of wine in the following model come to a total of sixteen cases, that is, 196 bottles of wine, which is by no means an extravagant amount. It will certainly be a large expense if you go out and try to buy all the wines at once, but that's not really the way to do it. Sampling and shopping is half the fun of assembling a cellar. As far as the cost is concerned, you'll appreciate your savings when you start drinking at ten years old some of those wines you bought at two years old; the price difference can be enormous.

APERITIF AND EVERYDAY-DRINKING WINES:

Sparkling	6 bottles dry spumante (Prosecco or Cartizze)
White	12 bottles Pinot grigio and/or Soave and/or Verdicchio; 12 bottles Lacryma Christi and/or Chardonnay
Red	24 bottles Dolcetto, Chianti, Cabernet, Montepulciano d'Abruzzo, and/or Cirò

These wines will be constantly changing, because these are the wines you will be consuming with the greatest frequency. All should be young, the reds ideally two to three years old, the whites one to two.

BETTER-THAN-AVERAGE-DINNER WINES:

Sparkling	6 bottles champagne-method Brut Spumante (Martini & Rossi's Riserva Montelera, Banfi Brut)
White	24 bottles Tocai (Livio Felluga), Sauvignon (Gradnik, Borgo Conventi), Pinot bianco, Torre di Giano, Greco di Tufo
Red	12 bottles Nebbiolo (Ceretto, Vietti, Prunotto) or Gattinara or Sassella; 12 bottles Chianti Riserva (Badia a Coltibuono, Monte Vertine, Villa Selvapiana), or Rubesco; 12 bottles Taurasi or Aglianico del Vulture Riserva (d'Angelo) or Rosso del Conte

This group of wines serves well for company dinners and family feasts. The whites drink best at about three years of age but most are not harmed either by being drunk sooner or held a year longer. The reds should probably be drunk at about five years of age, but in most vintages will hold well for a few years beyond that.

IMPORTANT-DINNER WINES:

Sparkling	12 bottles Ca' del Bosco Brut Crèmant or Ferrari Brut Gran Riserva
White	24 bottles Vintage Tunina (Jermann), La Scolca Gavi, Pomino Il Benefizio (Frescobaldi), Fiano di Avellino (Mastroberardino)
Red	12 bottles Barolo Riserva or Barbaresco Riserva from Ceretto, Di Gresy, Gaja, Prunotto, Vietti; 12 bottles Amarone and Brunello Riserva (Barbi, Banfi, Altesino); 12 bottles Carmignano Riserva (Capezzana) or Taurasi Riserva (Mastroberardino)

These are the wines for your pull-out-all-the-stops dinners. The whites can all be drunk as soon as bottled, but all will also gain depth and complexity with two to three years of bottle age. The reds should in most vintages be drunk starting when they are about ten years old. Many of them will not peak until some years after that, and may very well hold at a high plateau of quality for a decade still beyond that point.

If your taste buds and your collector's instincts carry you past this stage, there is still a lot of Italian wine for you to explore: the Bordeaux-like blends from Venegazzù and Ca' del Bosco, the Chardonnay and Cabernet of Angelo Gaja, Sassicaia and Antinori's Tignanello, the great, rare dessert wines like Picolit, plus experimental wines from all over the peninsula as well as many more traditional wines than there has been space to talk about here. For more detailed information about Italian wine, read Burton Anderson's magisterial *Vino* (Atlantic-Little, Brown) or his booklet, *Wines of Italy* (written for the Italian Trade Commission and available free by writing to the Italian Wine Center, 499 Park Avenue, New York, NY 10022), or Victor Hazan's *Italian Wine* (Knopf), or Nicolas Belfrage's *Life Beyond Lambrusco* (Sidgwick & Jackson, London).

Cent' anni!

INDEX